The International Library of Sociology

WORK AND LEISURE

Founded by KARL MANNHEIM

The International Library of Sociology

THE SOCIOLOGY OF WORK AND ORGANIZATION
In 18 Volumes

I	Apprenticeship	*Liepmann*
II	Industrial Disputes	*Eldridge*
III	Industrial Injuries Insurance	*Young*
IV	The Journey to Work	*Liepmann*
V	The Lorry Driver	*Hollowell*
VI	Military Organization and Society	*Andrzejewski*
VII	Mobility in the Labour Market	*Jeffreys*
VIII	Organization and Bureaucracy	*Mouzelis*
IX	Planned Organizational Change	*Jones*
X	Private Corporations and their Control - Part One	*Levy*
XI	Private Corporations and their Control - Part Two	*Levy*
XII	The Qualifying Associations	*Millerson*
XIII	Recruitment to Skilled Trades	*Williams*
XIV	Retail Trade Associations	*Levy*
XV	The Shops of Britain	*Levy*
XVI	Technological Growth and Social Change	*Hetzler*
XVII	Work and Leisure	*Anderson*
XVIII	Workers, Unions and the State	*Wootton*

WORK AND LEISURE

by
NELS ANDERSON

LONDON AND NEW YORK

First published in 1961 by
Routledge

Reprinted 1998, 2000 by
Routledge
2 Park Square, Milton Park, Abingdon, Oxon, OX14 4RN
Simultaneously published in the USA and Canada by Routledge
711 Third Avenue, New York, NY 10017
Transferred to Digital Printing 2007

Routledge is an imprint of the Taylor & Francis Group

First issued in paperback 2013

© 1961 Nels Anderson

All rights reserved. No part of this book may be reprinted or reproduced or utilized in any form or by any electronic, mechanical, or other means, now known or hereafter invented, including photocopying and recording, or in any information storage or retrieval system, without permission in writing from the publishers.

The publishers have made every effort to contact authors/copyright holders of the works reprinted in *The International Library of Sociology.* This has not been possible in every case, however, and we would welcome correspondence from those individuals/companies we have been unable to trace.

British Library Cataloguing in Publication Data
A CIP catalogue record for this book
is available from the British Library

Work and Leisure
ISBN 978-0-415-17694-1 (hbk)
ISBN 978-0-415-86363-6 (pbk)

Publisher's Note
The publisher has gone to great lengths to ensure the quality of this reprint but points out that some imperfections in the original may be apparent

To my Teacher
ERNEST W. BURGESS
University of Chicago
who taught the first Class
in the Sociology of Play
and to
JOFFRE DUMAZEDIER
who through his Research
in France stimulated a wider
European Programme of Research
into Work and Leisure

CONTENTS

PREFACE   *page* xi

1. WESTERN SOCIETY FACES LEISURE   1

    Leisure's Ambiguous Position—Our Industrial Culture — Globality of Urbanism — Security and Accumulation—Mobility and Integration—Temporal Implications—Mass Organization—Individualism and Authority—Social Class in Western Society—Summary

2. THE WORK-LEISURE DICHOTOMY   25

    By the Sweat of the Brow—The Motives for Work — Work Competition and Leisure — Looking Closer at Leisure—The Functions of Leisure—Leisure and Non-work Obligations—Where Recreation Comes in—Play and Amusement—Idleness and Unemployment—Summary

3. SOME DIMENSIONS OF TIME   50

    The Time-investment Cult—The New Time Awareness—The Coming of Clocks—Time, Work and Tempo—Money Values and Time—Time, Money and Leisure—Work and Leisure in Lockstep—Habitual Time-use Patterns—Tradition and Time-use Patterns—Of Man's Total Time—Summary

Contents

4. THE PROVOKING GIFT OF LEISURE 75

 Leisure, the Uninvited — Leisure Must be Earned—The Do-something Complex—Protest Against Passivity—Culture and Mediocrity—'Spectatoritis' or Participation—On Viewing with Alarm—Ambiguities of Leisure—New Thinking about Leisure—Summary

5. SOME PERTINENT ASPECTS OF LEISURE 98

 Leisure as Consumer Spending—Involvements in Leisure Spending—Time Given to Leisure—Leisure for Wives and Mothers—Holidays and Vacations—The Conventional Vacation—Leisure Planning and Preferences—Commercial Amusement—Leisure and the Sexes—Alcohol and Leisure—Reading, High and Low—Summary

6. YOUTH AND THE LIFE CYCLE 130

 When Play is Tolerated—Play and Social Discipline—The Educational Function—Education for Work and Leisure—The Distant Goals—Work Comes to the Rescue—Work as the Young Find it—Are New Work Values Needed?—Where the Fun Comes in—Adaptation and Conformity—Summary

7. ACTIVE YEARS OF THE LIFE CYCLE 156

 Family in the Life Cycle—Social Class and Occupation—Pursuits of Status and Happiness—Social Mobility and Display—Using Leisure at Home—Fashion and Zestful Living—Domestic Accumulations—The Seeming Unimportance of Things—Non-typical Families and Households—When Wives also Work—Spending and Saving—Summary

Contents

8. WITH TIME ON THEIR HANDS   182

    A Man and His Worth—What Retirement Means—Old-age Status and Security—Retirement and Loneliness—From Loneliness to Loneliness—With Wheels to Ride on—The Old and their Housing—Old Age in Germany—Age and Life Enjoyment—Summary

9. HOW MEN MANAGE THEIR BEHAVIOUR   205

    Conformity and Sociality—The Ordering Influence of Work—Culture and the Work Place—The Disciplines of Leisure—Conformity and the Social Game—Keeping the Hands Busy—Unrest, Leisure and Idleness—Small-group Vitality—Formal Associations and Groups—Associations for the Common Good—Public Service in Work and Leisure—What goes on the Record—Summary

10. TIME-USE TRENDS AND PROSPECTS   232

    What the Future may Hold—Speaking of Automation—On Knowing What to Fear—Uses of Atomic Energy—Of Man's Work and Security—Wider Citizenship Perspectives—A Rationale of Existence—Yet, People are Living Longer—Leisure Choices and Pressures—Mixing Leisure and Culture—Leisure and Obligated Time—Summary

    INDEX   259

PREFACE

WRITERS about work rarely have much to say about leisure. This has already been said in one of the chapters which follow, but I think it bears repeating. It also bears repeating that writers about leisure give very little attention to work. Another neglect, it seems to me, concerns the kind of society we live in today; the meaning of work and leisure in this society. The way of life is that of people, most people including countrymen, set in the midst of an industrial urban environment largely of man's own making. Much of this way of life is new, almost unrelated to precedent, and not only new but changing.

That writers on work look in one direction and writers on leisure look in another should not surprise us. Rather, it emphasizes how work and leisure under industrial urbanism have been separated. But this separateness appears to be a passing thing. We must remember that research in both work and leisure is new, most of the literature has appeared during the past three decades, and the most penetrating materials have appeared during the past decade. In fact, some of the most promising studies are only now under way.

What we can hardly escape recognizing, once we examine work and leisure in relation to each other is that we are dealing with uses of time, and different dimensions of time. Because time has been used efficiently in work we get leisure. We sell time so that time not sold may be used as we like. We find that production and consumption are opposite uses of time and in both kinds of activity time may be measured in money values. But time as an abstraction becomes the measure of such other abstractions as space, distance and motion, so pertinent to technological and scientific development incident to more

Preface

efficient production. Industrial urban man has moved out of the sphere of natural time into that of mechanical time, dominated and paced by the clock in both work and play.

Yet the clock-paced man remains a life-cycle creature. He tries to extend his life expectancy but the life cycle stands and it becomes the central problem of his existence. If he lives the full estimated cycle, a little more than half of his life will be given to productive work, nearly a fourth of his years will be used in growing up and in preparing for a career. At the conclusion a fifth to a fourth of his years will be occupied with trying to hold on a little longer in the labour market or trying to live outside of it. But the entire cycle is lived in situations of clock-time values and of social values themselves responsive to the time-paced tempo of the mode.

The course of the cycle is no longer a series of easy transitions from one phase to another. In each phase of his life the individual finds his economic worth changes both as producer and consumer. His roles change and in matters of leisure he is a different customer for the leisure industries. Because of this obvious importance of life-cycle changes I endeavored to examine it in relation to work and leisure; hence the chapters on youth, the middle years and old age.

In the course of preparing this book the materials seem to point to certain conclusions. Although I have hesitated to venture into conclusions, I have at least implied a number of theses, and four of these seem especially pertinent. Each of these opens a special field of study.

1. *Non-work Obligations.* Definitions of leisure often include categories of activities, but many off-the-job activities turn out to be nothing like paid work nor yet like leisure. One works in the garden, helps around the house, does favours for the neighbours, works for the trade union, the political party, the church, the community centre and so on. These are often called non-work obligations and they often yield leisure-like satisfactions. The more the individual is integrated into family life, organized group life and community life the more of his free time is likely to be given to such activities, and often the less interest he has in leisure. There is good reason to believe that as people become more identified with non-work activity the less need they have for leisure and the more their leisure is linked with these activities.

2. *Family and Home Leisure Centredness.* Contrary to fears

Preface

about family disintegration, studies of leisure indicate that most family members spend half or more of their leisure-activity time at home where they can be reached by telephone and where they have world contact by radio and television. This is in addition to time at home spent on non-work obligations. It seems that even this so-called one-generation family is very much concentrated on living, and for each family member the home is the accumulation of leisure-use things, and of prestige things essential to social living, a phase of leisure.

3. *Declining Worker Interest in the Job.* It is generally recognized that most workers who sell their time seem to have little interest in the job or in the enterprise. This is often regretted and experts have designed various methods for reviving worker interest. Some of the experts, including industrial sociologists, are asking what the worker has to gain and how would industry benefit by drumming up a 'company consciousness', that being what management is paid for. As far as I know, there is no evidence that this worker attitude is detrimental to his efficiency; productivity increases and worker efficiency does not decline. The worker sells his time and skill, a business transaction; the transaction complete, at quitting time he puts work out of mind. He is no longer the slave of a routine job, but has worked out a sensible relationship with it. He is not bored with his job; he has come to terms with it. He will strike to hold his job and he will give an honest day's work. He can take pride in his work, but still he leaves thinking about it at the plant.

4. *Passivity and the Cultural Level.* Here it is necessary to take issue with a great many intellectuals who complain that the great mass of people are helpless when faced with leisure. They settle into meaningless dull routine, floating with the tide, lacking a zest for life, surrounded by opportunity but developing no special interests. This adds to the conclusion that the level of culture is doomed to decline. Actually the level of culture (however measured) is not declining. We need but step back in imagination to 1850 or even 1900. The answer is a long-perspective look at things.

This final thesis is not sheer optimism. I would add that while we are looking at the changes in the lowest level of culture we examine some of the present trends in uses of leisure. I find it hard to share the view that the mass of people is incapable

Preface

of using leisure, that they stand helpless before a great emptiness. This is arguing that a people who continue to be experimental in their work cannot be experimental in their leisure.

Little has been said about the pathologies of leisure, particularly in that direction where leisure activity extends into areas of vice and crime. For this omission I offer the explanation that to enter the twilight zones of leisure would call for much more space than this small treatise could yield. Moreover, in this special field of research there already exists an abundance of good literature. Our subject lies in the other direction; not where leisure meets vice and crime, but where leisure meets work.

Nor has much been said about *the* leisure problem, wrapping the entire subject into a single package. Without quarreling with the use of that term by some students of leisure, it is hard for me to see leisure in one dimension; rather, a cluster of problems is involved. But I can accept grouping under such an expression as 'the work-leisure dilemma'. Of the many leisure problems, some are acute, some chronic and others hardly identifiable. Each changes with time and from place to place. Each is a changing problem, and the relations between them change. Moreover, all may change with changing work conditions.

To speak of *the* leisure problem has often been a neat approach to arriving at definite conclusions about what should be done about it. Many researches have ended on that note. There is no one answer. If some one solution is found for some particular leisure problem, it rarely remains the right answer for long. New answers must be found, ever and again. This should not be discouraging. We do not object to making new approaches again and again in the field of economics. Happily this area of life is fluid. Happily in this area life never ceases to bubble and spring forth in all sorts of unexpected ways.

In preparing this book I received help from many people, much of it out of their written works. Where I have borrowed thought I have given full credit and now I express thanks. However, much help came out of conversations, mostly with friends also interested in this subject. I am also grateful to them, some of whom will see themselves here and there in these pages.

NELS ANDERSON

1
WESTERN SOCIETY FACES LEISURE

LEISURE is best understood against the background of work. It was begotten of work and is rooted in work, but the two have parted company. Man has always lived by work and with it, yet only modern man, because he has worked so well, also has leisure and his task is learning to use it. In this chapter we shall consider how modern man, the worker, through the force of labour has created a kind of society that is rich in things, conveniences and what has always been rare, free time. Let us look at that society.

In the next chapter we will define leisure more in detail. For the moment we think of it as the time a man (or woman) is free from work, when his work makes few or no demands on him. We will think of work as the purposeful effort a man expends to earn his livelihood. Or we may think in more direct terms of work as time given to a job, for which one is paid.

LEISURE'S AMBIGUOUS POSITION

As Domenach observed, work and leisure in our society reflect and supplement each other. He sees Western man working that he might have leisure, and enjoying leisure as a diversion from work.[1] While this is true, it is equally true that traditionally Western man works to get ahead. In the ideology of his work we find no intent to create leisure. Rather, leisure turns out to be an unprepared-for by-product of work.

[1] Jean-Marie Domenach, "Loisir et travail," *Esprit*, 87 année, No. 274, juin 1959, pp. 1103–1110.

Although leisure reflects and supplements work, it is also used as a release from work. Some are of the view that unless a man has worked he cannot really enjoy leisure. They hold that while a man is working to earn a wage or salary, he also 'earns' leisure. It is only work, they assert, that can put one in a frame of mind to enjoy leisure.

Leisure, that elusive anomaly about which books are written, comes on the scene, not in a region where life is lived easily, but in Western society where life is strenuous. No trait of Western man is more evident than his determination to load himself with work, to find in work the main values of life and to use his gains to extend his work into wider areas. His main interest in science and technology is to use them in advancing his work, so to get more gain out of the labour expended. With each gain he widens the scope of his activity.

Not only has Western man forced work upon himself and learned to like it, he tries with missionary earnestness to stimulate others in accepting his strenuous way of life. Those who do not respond with energy are regarded as backward. Because of this global encompassing urge, Toynbee speaks of ours as a 'world-wide Westernizing Society'.[1] All industrialized and urbanized Western countries are identified with these missionary objectives, but the term 'westernizing', extending our way of life, applies especially to the United States.

It is precisely in this hard-working society that leisure comes out in the open and confronts its creators with baffling problems. Here more than elsewhere man tries to build more efficient factories, to create more effective cities, to improve his networks of communication and transportation; all so he can work to greater advantage. Inadvertently, he also gives himself more leisure, and this leisure in different ways gets between him and his work.

Working, building, and then rebuilding the structural side of our civilization, man also changes the social milieu. More people who must become urban oriented, also adopt the radically new urban way of life. As the organization of life becomes complex, the tempo of life quickens, which again is disturbing. More than ever people find themselves mixed into urban agglomerations, becoming part of 'life en masse'. And all the while this society with its level of culture achieved

[1] Arnold J. Toynbee, *A Study of History*, London, 1955, Vol. IX, p. 561.

Western Society Faces Leisure

through organized and strenuous work finds itself confronted with leisure.

Leisure was always present in our work-conscious society but earlier it was the privilege of a small upper class. Now this unplanned-for gift comes to the many who, as some believe, lack the background for making use of it. However, as we look about we find they are learning, but in the meanwhile the position of leisure in our society is ambiguous.

OUR INDUSTRIAL CULTURE

When we speak of Western man as a machine-user, this applies also to the Western farmer. We chronically think of making things with machines. If we own things made entirely by hand labour they are apt to be heirlooms. We organize machines into networks, called factories and factories are formed into networks called industries; steel, rubber, textiles, automobiles, farm machinery and so on. The cynic says we do it as work to make money, but in the process man is served. The more efficient he is with machines the better he is served.

While creating these mechanized networks, Western industrialized man adds to the natural environment a man-made environment, which is nearer to him most of the time. The effectiveness of this man-made environment, which man himself manipulates, is seen in his ability to produce more with less labour. That is, he can produce for himself more goods and services and yet give himself more free time.

Meadows reminds us that industrial society is more than machines and factories, it is the whole complex of technics and techniques and even more. Thus industrialism includes the mechanisms, the labour force with its skills and the social organization which is adapted to this milieu.[1] Such a society must possess such traits, among others, as these:

1. Man no longer lives in cherished isolation, as in the old-time village, but must live in contact with large agglomerates, co-ordinating his interests and efforts to the wider group. This is a new form of collective living. The city man is extremely collective in both work and play.
2. The mass production needed to keep industry vigorous demands mass consumption; that is, behaviour and taste

[1] Paul Meadows, "Cultural Theory and Industrial Analysis," *Annals of the American Academy of Political and Social Science*, No. 274, March 1951, p. 14.

uniformities over wide areas. Millions sleep on the same sort of mattresses, own the same kind of radio sets and listen to the same programmes, read the same newspaper, wear the same kind of shoes, etc. Yet with all the conformity and uniformity one can achieve variety.

3. In the mechanized man-made environment one must be acquainted with the use and potentialities of hundreds of mechanisms and be alert to them every waking hour. Being alert and informed is to co-operate in their proper use, whether the mechanism be an automobile, a street traffic control, a building elevator, a vending machine, a juke box or gadgets in the home.[1]

Modern man has created such a civilization that he can neither work nor play without being producer nor consumer in one industrial process or another. He can do no other than to accept standards and uniformities, and he is being educated every day so to do. In his study of village life among the Equadorean Indians, Salz tried to foresee the problems of industry establishing itself in such a culture and the problems the people would have in adapting to industry. He recognized that the change would be quite disturbing for they would have to learn urban ways as well as industrial ways. Very little of their semi-primitive culture could be transferred.[2]

Equadorean village life is one sort of collective living, industrial life is quite another and involves a different situational discipline. Only as man is disciplined to machines are the machines able to respond effectively to his discipline. For man to live to advantage in this industrial environment of his own making, and which he continually re-makes, he must be competent in at least three different respects; ways of adjustment.

1. Modern man must keep on learning; skills, habits and manners of yesterday may not suffice for today. As he must learn new work ways, so he must learn new play ways. Falling behind the procession is a mark of ageing. He must know the latest gadgets as he must also know about the latest songs.

[1] On this subject see Louis Wirth and Edward Shils, "Urban Living Conditions," *Urban Planning and Land Policies*, Vol. II, Washington, National Resources Committee, 1939, p. 164.
[2] Beate R. Salz, "The Human Element in Industrialization," *Economic Development and Cultural Change*, Vol. IV, No. 1, Part 2, October 1955, p. 5.

2. He must be able to adjust to increasingly complex situations, since innovation tends to move from the simple to the complex. We see the complexity trend in the automobile; how it introduces variety in the work spheres, how it changes the use of leisure, how it affects public services, how it introduces innovations in family and individual life (courting practices, for example). Similarly we can see this complexity trend with the introduction of mechanisms in offices and in the household.
3. With the greater integration and development of the industrial order its area of contact and influence widens. People must learn to think in wider terms. Where the grandfathers were amazed that words could be telegraphed from San Francisco to New York in the 1860's the grandsons are not impressed at all to hear voices radioed from the South Pole. We think casually both about global communication networks as well as of global transportation networks. Different industries; oil, automobiles, metals and many more are linked in global markets. Basketball has become a world game and, like boating and other sports, is uniformly so. As one becomes associated with the thinking that matches this global trend his mental reach must widen.

GLOBALITY OF URBANISM

Meadows emphasizes that learning to live in the industrial environment calls for more than mechanical skills and knowledge. It 'entails a community organization which requires living quarters and which demands behaviour patterns and controls for the human beings responsible for business and industrial functions: urbanism".[1] Urbanism, as Wirth put it in his classic article of that title, is a way of life.[2]

A way of life is a cluster of behaviour patterns (political, economic, social) to which a people conforms; values and beliefs they hold regarding these ways of behaviour, and the social inheritance from earlier generations. But a way of life also acquires its unique character from the material and social

[1] Paul Meadows, "The Industrial Way of Life," *The Technological Review*, Vol. 48, No. 5, March 1946.
[2] Louis Wirth, "Urbanism as a Way of Life," *American Journal of Sociology*, Vol. 41, No. 1, July 1938, pp. 1–23.

milieu in which a people lives, the things they use and the things in the environment to which they must become adapted. Industrialism is a major part of that way of life we call urbanism.

Industrialism may be found in areas far from cities, mining developments, for example, but the head office of the mining company will more than likely be in a great city and the ores produced will find their way into urban controlled markets. Urbanism itself existed long before the rise of powered industry, but it was a simpler type of urbanism. We can point to modern cities in which no industry is found, but these have status only as they are linked with other cities that are industrialized.

Insofar as work and leisure are concerned, and these embrace a good part of the whole of life, urbanism today is unique in several ways. This thought is illustrated somewhat in such characteristics as the following:

1. *Urbanism is Highly Non-traditional.* Anciently, in the Middle Ages or today, towns and cities have always been places of work, trade and authority. They have also been play centres where the leisure arts developed and changed. Whatever the work activity, its history as a part of urban life can be followed back into time, as seen in the handicrafts. Whatever the leisure activity, its development reaches far back, which can be seen in the stage, music, dancing, the sports and so on. We can also trace the evolution of the structures people have used either for work or for play.

Yet we must conclude that modern urbanism has moved so far, even from its recent past, that the evolutionary links are only lightly evident, and often they seem to be deliberately disregarded. Much of factory work is quite unrelated to the old handwork crafts. The old skills seem as far removed as the fireplace in the old-fashioned kitchen is from the modern kitchen. Consider man's all-purpose use of the streets in the modern horseless city, how far removed it is from the uses of streets in the past.

We can find links with the past in the many types of leisure today, but leisure is now enjoyed under such different circumstances. The role of the individual in family life is not the same, and the role of the family in community life has changed. The relation of the individual and that of the family to both work and leisure have acquired new meanings. It all adds up to the observation that urbanism was probably never more free than today from the guiding hand of tradition.

2. *Modern urbanism is highly sophisticated.* One may say with truth that urbanism has always been more sophisticated than ruralism. But earlier forms of urban sophistication were limited to a small part of the population. That circle has been widening to include most of the population. Some will remind us, and correctly, that much of this sophistication, like learning the latest radio jokes, is mere shallow smartness at a low cultural level. Even when admitting that there are levels of sophistication, we must say there is more of it today and, as always, its creative centre is the urban community.

Sophistication finds expression in the various pursuits of fashion; in dress, manners, speech, reading and even in things one strives to possess. The pursuit is more of an interest today because we are more an urbanized people than ever before. We have more leisure than ever before, and it is in leisure that sophistication shows itself, especially in the competitive social phases of leisure.

3. *Modern urbanism is highly dynamic and outreaching.* Again we must say that this is not new. Cities came into being only because they were places advantageously situated that were dynamic and outreaching in their influence. Perhaps as they gained power they oppressed and exploited lesser places, thus gaining more power and wealth. As Turner postulates, cities grew not only because they were dynamic, but because they were able to garner the surpluses of other places.[1] For their sustenance cities had to give something in return. They had to be creative and have continued so. Because they were creative they have attracted creative people, and because they have always been places of work they have attracted more and more people in search of work.

As cities have grown, and they have grown exceedingly during the past century, they became increasingly dynamic and outreaching. They have passed out of the stage of being exploiters of their hinterlands and must now be markets for the hinterlands. On the other side, the hinterlands are the markets for the goods and services produced in urban places.

[1] Ralph Turner, *The Great Cultural Tradition*, New York, 1941, Vol. II, pp. 1250 to about 1290.

In this struggle for new and wider markets urbanism has become global.

Urbanism as a phenomenon of growth is one thing, but urbanism being dynamic, creative and imaginative that it might expand more is something else, for out of this creativeness urbanism continually changes within itself. It remains a way of life ever different, ever sharper and more resourceful than the non-urban. To survive, this way of life must radiate itself outward, extending with a type of missionary energy to all places that are less urban.

4. *Anonymity and Interdependence under Urbanism.* Many complain about the anonymous nature of urban life. They see in its evident coldness a decline of sociability and the human touch, assumed to be essential for community living. One does not know his neighbour and may not wish to. With a manner of unconcern, one moves unnoticed through the crowd as if the people around him were as so many trees in the forest. The individual is seen as isolated and ignored, and we hear that this is contrary to the nature of man. In the urban agglomerate one can have contact without acquaintance and, while the crowd may isolate him, he may also for reasons of his own isolate himself. This is the reason for complaint, anonymity is alleged to be conducive to temptation.

We must recognize anonymity as a natural development, a social and psychological necessity for mass living. A man cannot know all his neighbours nor the many in his work place, and he would not wish to know the mixture of people who join in the same leisure activities. He must be selective in his contacts, and fortunately in the urban milieu it is possible to be selective. His personal contacts necessarily are utilitarian in terms of social, economic, fraternal or other interests. To extend his contacts beyond the necessary would call for more energy and time than he can spare. Outside the essential contacts lies anonymity and, what is more important, privacy. The urbanized individual is not isolated in moving through the crowd; he is merely going from contact to contact. Others in the crowd are doing the same. A few may be isolated or stranded, as they might be in the village.

The main counteracting factor to this anonymity is the impersonal interdependence of all the units in this agglomerate. Each has his own network of contacts and each network of contacts intertwines with others, the entire agglomerate is a veritable criss-cross of networks. There are systems of networks with which individuals are linked in relationships of interdependence through which all are sustained. We are made aware of these linkages even if a minor relationship system fails, as when the supply of bottles is stopped by a strike, or when for the same reason newspapers are not printed for a few days. Even the least intellectual people in the urban agglomerate know about this interdependence which provides the underlying order to the heterogeneity of urbanism. Dubin observed:

> But underpinning this heterogeneity and diversity is a fundamental human interdependence that flows from the far-flung division of labour. The real experiencing of this interdependence and the sensing of it comes from the daily job. On the job the urbanite learns more directly and acutely than anywhere else how dependent he is upon those about him. There may follow from this the unity of interdependent action that is such an imperative feature of industrial work.[1]

Those who worry about urban anonymity are more concerned about leisure than work relationships. Interdependence relationships in work are stabilizing in their operation because of the usual firmness and regularity of work. But the same stabilizing influences are not so evident in leisure, and here anonymity is thought to go hand in hand with temptation. As we shall see in later chapters, this is less true than feared, for there are interdependent relationships of other kinds, equally compelling in their influence.

SECURITY AND ACCUMULATION

Modern society, especially in the West, has for its habitat a type of community which is industrial in a new sense and urban in a new way, but it still faces the old problem of making its living and being secure.

Except to have seed for the next year and food for the winter, the farmer is traditionally not a saver, but the industrial urban community would not be here were it not for saving and accumulation. It is not only the accumulation of the wealth

[1] Robert Dubin, "Industrial Workers' Worlds," *Social Problems*, Vol. 3, No. 3," January 1956, pp. 131-142. On urbanism, see Nels Anderson, *The Urban Community, a World Perspective*, 1959, pp. 1-3, 36-39, 57-59.

out of which industry grew; in the cities knowledge is accumulated and put into libraries, art is accumulated and put into museums and experience is accumulated to find expression in the skills of the artisan, in the science of the laboratory and in the techniques of the work place. All of this is a by-product of the efforts of urbanites collectively to make themselves secure against want, a problem that the man living with the resources does not have.

Thus the communities built by Western man, the worker, becoming centres of wealth, have become centres of power. Much of the wealth is now corporately owned or publicly owned. And while much is individually owned, curiously enough, urbanites as individuals have generally been insecure. The urban way of life has never permitted any great number of individuals to achieve life-long security. Yet this very insecurity has finally given rise to many schemes of collective security in which saving takes corporate form or public form through government insurance. Or government assumes leadership for full employment, and now that agriculture becomes somewhat subordinate to industrial urbanism, government must assume leadership for price stability for rural production.[1]

This accumulative society was made possible by effective work, but only by effective collective integration can it be secure for the individual. Security means continuity of employment, opportunity to enjoy leisure and riddance of fear against want. If these goals have not been realized in full in the modern society, at least the trends toward them may be seen.

MOBILITY AND INTEGRATION

The vigour of our industrial urban order might very well fall to zero if people no longer moved from house to house or from place to place and if movement from one kind of work to another were to cease. With an end to the in-moving of outsiders, the cities would stagnate; physical mobility would decline. Professional mobility would pass if there would be no moving from one occupation to another. Every child would stay in the social class of his father and there would be no social mobility. That would be returning to the state of things in

[1] Alessandro Pizzorno, 'Accumulation, loisirs et rapports de class', *Esprit*, No. 274, *juin* 1959, pp. 1013-1014.

Western Society Faces Leisure

primitive times. At this point we cite a small study done by Lundberg who questioned students about the meaning of the proverb, 'A rolling stone gathers no moss'. He found that about 60 per cent of these young Americans understood the old warning not as an admonition to 'stay put', rather it meant, 'if you don't keep rolling along the moss will grow on you' (our paraphrasing). This reversal of meaning means a reversal of attitude toward mobility itself. Once a bad thing, it is now a virtue.[1]

Through the readiness of people to move, cities have grown and continue to expand, industry was stimulated to greater development, and people in the competitive urban life were driven to greater creativeness. Because people dared to cross the seas the new-found lands were occupied, and because they were challeneged by the land frontiers the frontiers of civilization were pushed forward. The land frontiers occupied and the cities built, the restless mobility-hungry spirit found other means of expression. The farmer on holiday goes in his automobile to the city and the city dweller on holiday drives to the country. Owen mentions that between 1948 and 1958 American automobile ownership increased from 30 to 67 million, and on a holiday most of these are in motion.[2]

This urge to be mobile in free time increases as people get more leisure, and with more leisure more money to spend. Now after the fashion of Americans, millions of Europeans spend their vacation in neighbouring countries. Vacation trade is big business. In 1957 nearly a million Americans went to foreign places as tourists, and of these 351,000 visited Europe for an average of 40 days each at an average cost of $20 per day.[3] Such tourist-vacation mobility is leisure oriented. People do not change their work or place of residence.

Work-oriented mobility has been the great dynamic in the evolution of Western society. Leisure-oriented mobility brings strangers to the city but they look around, spend their money and go home. Work-oriented mobility brings strangers who

---

[1] This information was received from Professor George A. Lundberg, University of Washington, in a letter.
[2] Wilfred Owen, 'Automotive Transport in the United States', *Annals of the American Academy of Political and Social Science*, Vol. 320, November 1958, pp. 1–8.
[3] 'Americans go Abroad', *The Economist*, Vol. 188, No. 5998, 9 August, 1958, p. 450. A British view of the money value to Europe of the allegedly free-spending American tourist.

want homes and a place in the labour market. They stimulate competition and change. Such mobility over the past century has fed a continuous stream of strangers into towns and cities, people of many origins. These then have moved from town to city or city to city. They have had to adapt socially and economically. They may be a disturbing element, but they do become assimilated. The different sorts of people must learn to work together, and they learn to play together.

People not only have been moving from place to place and job to job, they have moved upward or downward into different occupations. Such mobility entails change to higher or lower income, which in turn calls for changes in one's way of living, especially in his social and leisure-time contacts. Each type of mobility necessitates adaptation if one is to be integrated into the social milieu and feel himself integrated.

TEMPORAL IMPLICATIONS

Much is said of speed in modern society, and of tempo, precision, duration and other concepts of little concern to preindustrial people. Space and distance have acquired new meanings. Working and living in ever-widening circles, modern man is forced to conceptualize ever-widening spatial as well as temporal areas. He is obliged to be more precisely time-conscious. The implications of time will be considered more in the third chapter. He must *be places* at appointed times and spatially, moreover, he must conceive of persons and things as being *at places* widely dispersed.

The temporal implications of modern life as they concern work and leisure can be illustrated in the case of a young couple, Frank and Mary who live in a small city of about 10,000. Frank is a bank clerk and Mary a secretary in a starch factory. His work place is at the town centre, hers at the north edge of town two miles from the town centre. Her home is about three miles to the west of the town centre and five miles from the factory. She travels by bus to the town centre and from there takes another bus to her work place. Frank lives with his parents on a garden farm four miles south of the town centre. He goes to and from work in his own automobile.

Frank and Mary met two years earlier when they were commercial students at the central high school. Frank had

Western Society Faces Leisure

been a basketball and football star, a factor in getting his job in the bank. When Mary found a position as secretary she decided not to enter college, but Frank feels the need of a college degree and is taking evening courses. He is saving money so he can be a full-time college student later. During their acquaintance most of the members of Mary's circle of friends have met most of the friends in Frank's circle. The pair frequently meet these mutual friends in one another's homes, at dances or at locales in different parts of town.

On the course of a week Frank and Mary meet four or five times, usually by telephone appointment. Sometimes after work Mary goes by bus to the town centre doing shopping or meeting girl friends until Frank's work is finished. He drives her home and usually lingers a while, perhaps staying for dinner. Then he must drive the seven miles to his home, but this is time taken from his study. Mary has other duties too. She is a leader in a girls' club and must be two evenings a week at the neighbourhood house. More than that, she has work at home to do. She must see her friends. She must visit the beauty parlour, go shopping and do other things more than she has time for.

As for Frank, in addition to his studies, he also has work at home, and must take care of his car. He must meet occasionally with his comrades in sport. With all this he must find time for his meetings with Mary. With him as with her each day is a race against time.

Life in this small city is far less complex than in the metropolis, thirty miles away, but for this couple the struggle to use time to the greatest advantage would not be less if they lived in the metropolis. And this observation would apply to other couples of their acquaintance. It is not merely a matter of Frank matching his round of appointments each day to keep his date with Mary, or of Mary to keep an appointment with him; each must also meet other people other places at other times. They must be continuously time-conscious. This is an imperative of living in mass society where individuals, as Cohen saw, must learn the art of living with the minimum of friction.[1]

Adjustment to such a milieu of accelerated movement in time and space calls for increasing facility in work where not only the time of labour, but the time of machines has a money

[1] Morris R. Cohen, *American Thought a Critical Sketch*, 1954, pp. 62-63.

measurement and that same measurement figure is going here and there keeping to a schedule. To the adjusted person such acceleration is satisfying and is normally justified, as Mumford remarks, 'in terms of pecuniary rewards.'[1] As in work, this tempo carries over to leisure activities in which, as with Frank and Mary, one is pacing himself from breakfast to bedtime by the ticking of the clock. Here is something that Mary's grandmother, who lives with the family, cannot understand. She complains about 'this everlasting hurry. Things were not that way when I was a girl.'

These temporal implications of modern life, calling as they do for precise time schedules, were not so conspicuously present when the grandparents were young. Their appointments were not so widely scattered and the number of their contacts were much fewer, nor was there such a variety of conflicting demands on their time. Besides themselves being in a situation making demands on their time, all their friends are in the same situation. The diverse demands usually mean diverse interests.

However able one may be, the number of interests to which one can give attention is limited, because time and energy are limited. Yet one must work that one might live; work and living make different demands on his time. What *living* is may be very much of a private definition. If living means merely to have fun and be with friends, as it does to many, then one's day is likely to be frustrated with the demands of work and other obligations on one's time. One may from time to time, if not continuously, feel frustrated and yearn for occasional escape to a desert oasis or a South Sea island. Escape is necessary and wholesome, if one knows what one would escape from, but 'escape from it all' is equally frustrating. A selective escaping would mean to find a balanced orientation to those demands on time which are most pertinent to those interests and areas of activity most pertinent to the individual.

In these temporal phenomena of the modern society we have a situation which is unique to our time, a man must learn to live in the midst of movement and change. He must be able to co-ordinate his day to day living, to use time, and to be selective in his interests and activities. That may require much more self-guidance than many people have. In consequence, there tends to be for many a retreat into a state of passivity,

[2] Lewis Mumford, *Technics and Civilization*, 1934, p. 198.

Western Society Faces Leisure

perhaps a very natural psychological defence mechanism, often called the cult of passivity.

The cult of passivity and so-called relaxation is one of the most dangerous developments of our time. Essentially, it too may represent a camouflage pattern, the double wish not to see the dangers and challenges of life, and not to be seen. We cannot escape all the tensions that surround us; they are part of life, and we have to learn to cope with them adequately and to use our leisure time for more creative and gratifying activities.[1]

MASS ORGANIZATIONS

Except as natural conditions did not permit, man has always lived in compact groups. Even the ancient cities were made up of clusters of small groups, each with its primary unity, and all oriented to a common central area. Those cities were not urban in the present sense, and did not need to be. Western urbanism cuts across familialism and most forms of localism and finds expression in a new type of community life which tends toward impersonal anonymous relationships. Western urbanism gives rise to mass society, great agglomerations of people.

Mass society means mass organization, mass administration, mass production, mass distribution and consumption, mass transportation and even mass leisure. But it also means global uniformities and standardizations, as well as new forms of human association. Our understanding of work and leisure must take account of this new phenomenon, mass living.

As to mass administration, here we see how the government or the management of vast agglomerations must be something different from any previous control system. It operates, not by folk rules but under law. Government becomes a neutral, impersonal, but systematic and professional mechanism for order, else society *en masse* could not function. The movement of people and goods must be reasonably free, and the entire aggregate of individuals and their groups must be able to work or play with the minimum of friction. To feel the pervasiveness of mass administration one needs but to study the work of the police in a modern city, how this service facilitates order in all

[1] Joost A. M. Meerloo, *The Rape of the Mind*, 1956, p. 172.

phases of life and how it stands in a supporting role to all other public services from the factory inspector, to the health officer, to the teacher to the life guard on the bathing beach. And this service links with corresponding public services far into the hinterland.

It is because of mass production that these impersonal aggregates of people came to be, and without it they could not subsist. Through mass production Western man has achieved leisure, and he will realize more leisure only as mass production is improved. Mass production is possible only as there is mass consumption of goods and services. This calls for effective, wide-reaching distribution networks, which carry goods and services outward, but also goods and services back. This means that modern agglomerate living calls for uniformities and standardization in consumption over ever-extending areas.[1] On the work side mass production is possible only if there is an ever-sensitive division of labour, not alone the occupational distinctions between workers, but also a division of labour between communities, and this we see all around.

Western society could not function by mass administration alone, there is need also of mass associations of the people. Without such private aggregates, mass production and distribution would flounder in disorder. Mass organization of people with special interests makes possible collective thinking and collective behaviour over wide areas (also made possible by mass media of communication). These aspects of modern society are new. People have learned to create associations for living *en masse*. Actually, the mass divides into many large interest groups, each of which is preoccupied with some phase of the aggregate life, although often in competition with other large associations. Thus the individual is identified with the mass through the trade union, the commerce association, the Rotary Club, the medical association; if a lawyer through the bar association. Some of his interests may be represented by the political party, others by the veterans association, others by his sport club and so on.

[1] Pipping remarked how increasingly services for leisure are handled on a mass basis, necessary to reduce cost, and this makes for increasing uniformity in behaviour and taste. 'Holiday journeys, week-end trips, restaurants and movies, race and sport matches are all similar throughout the country and, to a certain extent, in different countries also.' Hugo E. Pipping, *Standard of Living, the Concept and its Place in Economics*, Copenhagen, 1953, p. 159.

Western Society Faces Leisure

Some complain that such association is too anonymous and impersonal and does not provide the intimate satisfactions of old-fashioned community life.[1] They do not recognize that old-fashioned community life cannot function in the mass society, and other ways of living have evolved. The old way breaks down, much as did the old-fashioned three-generation family. But all the essential primary intimacies are present and can be experienced in the new mass society.

In particular, these intimacies are found in the leisure phases of modern living. Here again we find mass production and mass association which are needed in mass leisure as mass leisure is needed in the mass society. Examples are commercialized sport, movies, television, radio and the comic-book industry. Wider and faster roads are needed so the work-connected traffic can move freely, but mass transportation may be more evident on holidays than on work days, as Owen reminds us.

As increasing productivity provides the average American family with more income and more leisure time, there will be still further opportunities for week-end and vacation trips and other leisure-time travel. It is this growing component of the transport total, rather than the week-day commuter traffic, that may become the factor deciding the kind of transportation system that metropolitan regions will need in the years ahead.[2]

Western man tends to be much more facile and resourceful in his leisure than in other forms of consumption, and more imaginative than in his work. In his leisure he has more choices and greater freedom. He can escape in his free time the regimenting elements some find in their work, as well as certain uniforming pressures which certainly exist in some types of leisure activity.

Western mass society is often described as contractual, being outside the realm of the spoken word alone, and of agreements trusted to memory. The spoken word retains its importance for informal contacts, but in formal relationships the written word has taken its place. Agreements between strangers or even

---

[1] To Brownell mass society is a 'fictitious solidarity of more or less massive groups'. One is obliged to join hands with strangers and contacts are ever transient or anonymous. Baker Brownell, *The Human Community*, New York, 1950, p. 20.

[2] Wilfred Owen, *Cities in the Motow Age*, New York, 1959, pp. 81–82.

between friends, or persons far apart, find their way into contracts enforced by law. Records become highly essential and are kept on file. A man can find his school record, his work record, his record as a club member or as a trade unionist, and he can find a record for every contact he ever had with public bodies. The story of his life from birth certificate to death certificate can be found on paper. Thus ours is a contractual, record-keeping society, otherwise the individual would be lost in the agglomerate. For the citizen the record may be basic to his feelings of security; in it he finds the political equality of citizenship, as Marshall uses the term.[1]

INDIVIDUALISM AND AUTHORITY

In many ways our modern society belongs to the individual. It is the individual, not the family, who joins the production process, and the wage is paid to him. In large measure, the individual chooses his occupation, his friends and his fun. His citizenship is an individual matter and his family is not responsible for him (once he attains adulthood) to the community. The emergence of the individual was one of the first essentials to the rise of industrial urban society. Said Santayana, the order of the old society is cumbrous and dull and 'immerses man in instrumentalities, weighs him down with atrophied organs, and by subjecting him eternally to fruitless sacrifices renders him stupid and superstitious, and ready to be himself tyrannical when an opportunity comes.' For such reasons he declared that 'individualism is therefore the only ideal possible'.[2] Evolution in society was possible only as the individual could shake off somewhat the fetters of traditional control, enabling inventiveness and creativity in the face of competition.

Americans are widely recognized as individualists, and often the term is a negative appraisal. They have done much to spread this idea through extolling their self-made heroes. For Americans, individualism was the crowning imperative virtue of the frontier. That frontier, where success in the end often forgave the means of achieving it, has passed into history. Americans are now individualists in another sense, for the

[1] T. H. Marshall, *Citizenship and Social Class*, 1950, p. 33.
[2] George Santayana, *Atoms of Thoughts*, Anthology edited by Ira D. Cardiff, New York, 1950, p. 29.

spirit of the frontier has carried over to the vigorous industrial urban society now developing. Commager speaks of American frontier individualism as having been born of dissent, and having such an origin it was also expressive of tolerance for nonconformity.

Individualism, too, required nonconformity and paid dividends: the American was always taking a short cut to freedom, a short cut to fortune, a short cut to learning, and a short cut to heaven. A society which had not had time to nourish its own traditions invited nonconformity. Indeed, had the American wished to be a traditionalist, he would have found it difficult to determine what tradition he should honour. . . .[1]

We find a type of individualism in all cultures. In the words of Flugel, 'The important difference between primitive and civilized society lies in the greater individualization of the latter, the individual mind takes over functions that were formerly exercised by the group.' The assertion of the individual may be, and often is, a break with group authority, 'he goes it alone.' Again Flugel, 'This process is not without its dangers, difficulties and disadvantages, exhibited more especially in the less easy group cohesion on the one hand, and the greater liability to individual mental conflict (and consequent neurosis) on the other.'[2]

The individualism of Western society, for all its dissent element, was also ideologically permitted. Puritanism transferred to man's conscience much of the authority which in other ideologies had been institutionalized. Western man was left largely to supervise himself, and on the frontier he did that, his nonconformity being more against traditionalism than institutional authority, which was present but not sternly imposed by outside forces. The individual was on his own but he still had to live with his conscience, still had to do good works and somehow finally get himself into heaven. Here may be one good reason why among Americans, more than in the rest of the world combined, private wealth has found its way into trusts and foundations for service.

Individualism is present in Western society to whatever

[1] Henry Steele Commager, *The American Mind*, New Haven, 1950, pp. 20–21.
[2] J. C. Flugel, *Men, Morals and Society*, 1948, pp. 252–253.

degree permitted by social tradition and required by the technological and economic organization of the man-made environment. It may not be rampant frontier individualism, overplayed by the movies, yet it is freer in the new countries where, using Riesman's term, behaviour is less 'tradition-directed'.[1] In our society individualism has meaning only as it functions within the framework of essential disciplines and authority. Moreover, the more disciplined one is the more freedom one finds for individual expression in that frame of reference. In these terms Americans rate well, especially are they disciplined individuals in their work.

But leisure is largely released from the latitude and discipline of work into permissive time uses which allow for greater individual choice of activity. The freedoms are greater and the disciplines imposed are fewer and less precise; at any rate they are different, as will be seen in the next chapter. The controls over leisure behaviour differ from those over work, which is understandable. The phenomena of control will be examined more fully in Chapter 9.

SOCIAL CLASS IN WESTERN SOCIETY

The society of Western man, the worker, is fragmented into many social classes, which is nothing new; every society has its social gradations and status distinctions. In non-industrial societies class may be hereditary and the lines between classes are strictly drawn. In Western society classes can be distinguished but only in general terms, while the lines between waver and change and, as never before, there is movement up or down between classes, and it tends to increase.

Social class, wrote Marshall, 'permeates the whole community, so that its application yields a single scheme of location which, in theory, assigns a place to every component part of the whole.'[2] Although social class is an unequal division of the community, people cling to it and in their day to day associations contribute to its maintenance. This may be evidence that the class system serves the function of social order, as did the caste system, but with less than caste rigidity.

As many studies have shown, people recognize themselves

[1] David Riesman, with Nathan Glazier and Reuel Denney, *The Lonely Crowd*, New York, 1953, p. 329.
[2] T. H. Marshall, op. cit., p. 94.

Western Society Faces Leisure

as belonging to classes, but, as Mayntz found, people differ very widely when asked to name the classes. If asked to name their own class they often contradict their own definitions of class. Mayntz found a tendency for lower class people to grade themselves upward and for upper-class people to rate themselves downward. Yet all admit the class system and in work or leisure behave toward it.[1]

Clément and Xydias, in their study of a small French city, reported that 76 per cent of the men and 70 per cent of the women rated themselves as proletariat (workers), but 22 per cent of the men and 29 per cent of the women rated themselveas middle-class. They found that the basis of judging class was income by 66 per cent of the proletariat, but for the middles class 63 per cent based their judgments on occupation and family, while 82 per cent of the upper-class mentioned family and education.[2]

However much they complain, people accept social class and contribute to its continuance even while complaining. We say it is a useful device for social order and frequently we hear that it is necessary for social progress, or has served that purpose. Bell argued a generation ago:

> Because few are born with the ability to discover for themselves that world of thought and feeling whence comes our choicest pleasures; because the abilities of these rot and run to seed in the open; because to be civilized, society must be permeated and, what is more, continually nourished by the unconscious influence of this civilizing elite; a leisured class is indispensable. The majority must be told that the world of thought and feeling exists; must be shown, lying just behind the drab world of practical utility, a world of emotional significance.[3]

Bell also pointed to the dullards in the leisure class and he thought that membership through birth had cluttered the traditional leisure class with too much dead wood, hence a new method of selection to membership was needed. The new method, apparently emerging, is the process by which the

---

[1] Renate Mayntz, *Soziale Schichtiung und soziale Wandel in einen Industriegemeinde* Stuttgart, 1958, pp. 103, 119.
[2] Pierre Clément et Nelly Xydias, *Vienne sur le Rhone*, Paris, 1955, Ch. II.
[3] Clive Bell, *Civilization*.

21

Western Society Faces Leisure

various elites are being chosen. Leadership becomes less the inherited function of a class and more a competitive relationship between the elites (political, social, economic, intellectual), which include the high and well-born who qualify as well as the climbers-up. This change has been taking place since Veblen held the American leisure class of the 1890's up to ridicule.[1]

The class concept, then, has now become a device for putting people into different social categories on the basis of wealth, or occupation, or education, or family, or some combination of these. It is a classification system used in various ways by different people, and it is ever changing. For example, modern industry, especially in the United States, uses less and less unskilled labour. That social class is vanishing, but the skilled and semi-skilled occupations expand. The upper middle-class spills over into the lower upper-class. In the world of practical affairs, however, social class as such becomes less important and the elites more important. This is new, much as industrial urbanism is new.

SUMMARY

Reminding ourselves that work and leisure supplement each other is to say nothing new, but the increasing separation of leisure and work with leisure standing out to be seen is new. The two are rarely engaged in at the same time. Work and leisure have different meanings and each is different from what it was in pre-industrial society. Largely the difference is due to the complexity of industrialism on the one hand, and the dynamics of urbanism on the other. Our thinking about work and leisure must change accordingly.

It is no accident that leisure, as we know it, emerged in Western society where men have always been and still are dedicated to work. They created leisure without intending to and now must find ways of living easily with it. In this chapter we have tried briefly to consider some of the salient aspects of this Western civilization, as an approach to understanding the meaning of work and leisure today. Admittedly, Western society has its roots in the past, but now it surrounds itself with a civilization that has very few precedents.

[1] Thorstein Veblen, *The Theory of the Leisure Class*.

Western Society Faces Leisure

Industrialism also is not new, but there is a new industrialism that impels a division of labour in the factory only to unite all work in the plant into a unified production process, and it redefines and organizes work outside the factory as well. An industry, with its many plants and special units widely dispersed, becomes an integrated network. Industries and networks are linked with other industries and networks into a competing and co-operating global whole. All sorts of work everywhere come under this single dominating influence to which man must co-ordinate his uses of time. These phenomena are new.

Equally new is the urbanism of today. While cities have long existed, they were never so oriented to industrialism on a global scale, and never more detached from the mandates of tradition. Neither the farmer nor the primitive, coming under this outreaching influence, can resist it, but they also become urbanized to some degree. The urban way of life has always been more sophisticated than the rural, but sophistication becomes much less the privilege of the privileged. Anonymity in cities is nothing new, but it becomes more a necessity if people are to live effectively in the great agglomerations. They find ways of impersonally sharing work and resources. A multitude of interdependencies develop inter-relating all units in the mass. However interdependent, they still have a wider range of choices in their uses of time.

Cities have always accumulated wealth, rendering services for goods, else they could not have originated and could not survive. Increasing in size and wishing to live better, they have had to find new sources of supply and invent new services to give in return. They have had to be creative and become more so. They make leather into shoes but they sell style with the shoes. They sell clothing but also spread fashion in dress. Now that leisure is here, they sell entertainment for food, iron ore and so on. They extend their influence in organizing work and production over all. This is new.

Because industrial urbanism is competitive, it must also be facile and free-moving. Mobility is characteristically urban, moving from place to place, job to job and even from class to class. Capital must be equally mobile, going anywhere it can be most productive. Mobility, like urbanism itself, becomes global to a degree never before imagined.

Also, because the urban way of life is competitive, it becomes more precisely time-oriented; not to the cycles of nature as the farmer is, but to the clock. Work is measured in time units as time is measured in money units. In the course of selling work time, leisure as time not paid for is acquired. But the use of leisure also becomes a time-related activity. The clock is the mechanism dominating all others, pacing also the movement of man, and is limited only by man's ability to endure. Thus the tempo of both work and leisure is left to human control. This also is new.

Society *en masse* can be managed only by mass administration. It can be articulate only through mass organizations. Work must become mass production which is possible only through mass distribution and consumption. Yet we speak of modern man as more individualistic than his ancestors. He is less under personal and traditional controls than were his ancestors, but he is subject to impersonal and secondary controls they did not know. He must co-ordinate himself with his mechanisms, the better to control them. Within this framework he has wider possibilities for individual expression than was possible for his ancestors. His situation is one in which he is stimulated by his better standard of living and his greater amount of free time to develop a lust for living. In this, even more than in work, he has opportunity for individual expression. Yet he tends to be socially integrated into groups and classes and in these connections he finds his goals and interests.

These are only some of the unique characteristics of the Western civilization which place time for work or leisure in an equally unique perspective. Our thinking about work and leisure must be guided in large measure by these realities.

2

THE WORK-LEISURE DICHOTOMY

EVERYONE is assumed to think of work as activity by which man provides himself with a livelihood, and that holds even if some learn to live without working. It is also assumed that work is activity to some productive purpose. But people may differ about what leisure is and what it is for. Often what people say about leisure, and sometimes about work as well, is coloured by what they think leisure and work should be. The object of this chapter is to examine some of these views about work and leisure, but we will also try to understand better how work and leisure are related.

BY THE SWEAT OF THE BROW

Whatever our behaviour on a job, most of us have learned to regard work with respect. To some degree we are dedicated to the Western ideology of work as it is defined in the Protestant Ethic. Describing what work meant under German Protestantism, Vontobel wrote, 'Work is any conscious, purposeful activity which with satisfaction serves the material and spiritual needs of the individual and the community. Work links man to man in the common affairs and puts men in contact with nature in efforts to earn their livelihood.' She continues with observations about the place of work in Christian ideology, for man's life and salvation depend on his work and good works.[1]

A similar ideology of work was brought by the Puritans from England to America where it became deeply implanted in the

[1] Klara Vontobel, *Das Arbeitsethos des deutschen Protestantismus*, Bern, 1946, p. 1.

social values of many who in other respects were anything but Puritans. Under German Protestantism, as noted by Vontobel, work puts men in contact with nature, but that was pre-industrial Protestantism. Industrial work detaches man from nature, but still he continues to regard work with respect, and while he may not like the work he does this does not prevent him from having high respect for work as such.

Under the industrial order most of those who work do it for hire. They have jobs and, whether they like the jobs or not, they accept the work as such. It is, as Soule puts the thought, the serious business of life. 'Work is regarded as praiseworthy because it is often not enjoyable, but contributes something others are willing to pay for.'[1] It is activity for which one sells his time. Even if the work has a captivating interest for him, he is still selling time to an employer who will sell the product. Modern work, stripped of all transcendental values, except for the fortunate few who have work with which they can become personally identified, has assumed a quasi-commodity character. In the contract society it acquires exchange value. Again quoting Soule: 'People sell time primarily so that they may acquire enough money income to buy products sold by others. What one does in sold time is "the job". Time sold is commonly thought of as work. Time not sold, "one's own time", "free time", is thought of as leisure, no matter what one does with it.'[2]

By this thinking, which is not unrealistic, work becomes impersonal much as 'labour' is to the economist or industrial engineer. Dumazedier answers that work is still a unique type of human experience. 'It puts man in rapport with materials, with tools and also with other men. Through work he acquires social status.'[3] And yet Dumazedier's Frenchman, like Soule's American, counts the hours and minutes at his job and demands extra pay for overtime, all he can get. While we cannot deny these material conceptions of work, it is possible to over-emphasize them, as we shall note later.

There are the fortunate ones mentioned above who can get interested in their work and who often forget to count the time.

[1] George Soule, *Time for Living*, New York, 1955, p. 124.
[2] George Soule, 'The Economics of Leisure', *Annals of the American Academy of Political and Social Science*, Vol. 313, September 1957, p. 16.
[3] Joffre Dumazedier with G. Friedmann and E. Morin, 'Les loisirs dans la vie quotidienne', *Encyclopedie Francaise*, T. XIV. 56.6.

The Work-Leisure Dichotomy

One is the farmer who owns his own land and another is the self-employed man. Still another is the professional worker who is occupied with creative things; the engineer, the architect, the artist. There are many kinds of workers who may be caught up in their work, but percentagewise they are a small part of all who work.

One very important thing that should be said about work in our industrial society is that less and less it can be described as toil or drudgery. Heavy-lifting, burden-bearing, strain-imposing types of work tend to go out of use. One reason for this trend is that workers turn away from these jobs. Perhaps a more important reason is that much of this type of work proves to be inefficient. Employers find ways of doing it by mechanical means. Still a great amount of work that is dull, heavy or strenuous remains, and much of that is done by women or children. Women in such employment are those who do cleaning at night in office buildings, or the 'day work' women who go from one household to another. It is hardly necessary to do more than mention domestic service, much of which is menial labour, and women have been turning from it in large numbers whenever they can find factory jobs. As will be noted more fully in Chapter 6, much of the work given to youth on entering the labour market is of the dull kind.

THE MOTIVES FOR WORK

Santayana named three motives for work; want, ambition and love of occupation. Want, the first of these and the most ancient, he thought, has about disappeared.[1] On that point Santayana was correct if he was thinking of Western society only. Want is very much an incentive in other world regions.

The noblest of work motivations is love of occupation, but unfortunately, as already mentioned, very few in the industrial society are favoured with work in which they can lose themselves in their tasks. Of such Durant wrote:

> Hence they need not search for compensation in other directions; they do not require soporifics from the world of amusement. When they have recourse to it, it is not because they experience an uncontrollable urge. Moreover, and this

[1] George Santayana, *Atoms of Thoughts,* Anthology edited by Ira Cardiff, New York, Philosophical Library, 1950, p. 34.

point is of supreme importance, they will tend to bring to such aspects of their lives the same attitudes and qualities of mind as are required and developed by their work.[1]

Almost every type of work holds some appeal for the worker, even the much maligned factory jobs. Actually such jobs may have more occupation appeal than do some types which are seldom mentioned by the critics, most of whom write books about factory work but neglect the many other kinds. It's so much easier to study workers in the big plants. Actually the job in big industry is not always as routine as pictured, rather it is definite. Each job has its niche in the work discipline of the plant, and for that very reason it yields a degree of occupation appeal. These jobs are part of a productive process. Each job, as Jaques describes it, has its prescribed and discretionary elements.

The prescribed elements constitute the boundary around the job. They set limits to what the person on the job may do. They state what he may not do. They also state the things he must do—the regulations, the policies, the methods, the routines, to which he must conform. Within these limits the person must use discretion. He must use his own judgment. He must choose what he thinks is the best course when faced with alternative possibilities.[2]

This is not the lust for work described above by Durant, but there is a measure of work appeal sufficient to keep the job from being dull. The 'love of occupation' motivation may be present on the job, even though the worker puts it out of mind when he checks out at the end of the shift. This type of job interest is found especially on ships where every man has his job and every job is precisely and traditionally defined. They move on and off duty with a clocked precision and they do the rounds of their work almost without supervision, and it's only the amateur seaman who does not take pride in it, but even he under the social pressure of the crew soon acquires the same attitude.

In his study of the workers in a meat packing plant, Blum

---

[1] H. W. Durant, *The Problem of Leisure*, London, George Routledge and Sons, 1938, p. 250.
[2] Elliott Jaques, *Measurement of Responsibility, a Study of Work Payment*, 1956, p. 87.

found that the jobs were not regarded as dull even though workers were prompt to get away from them at quitting time. He found, too, that while they seemed to put work out of mind when they got away from the plant, they did not in the main hold negative attitudes towards it.[1] These packing house workers were merely realistic; with non-work matters to think about and with the security of the job not in question, it would be mere wasted thought to have their minds on it when occupied with something more immediate.

Our thesis that 'love of occupation' is found to the necessary degree in most work would be challenged by many who see little to capture the interest of ordinary workers on most industrial jobs. Lafitte, for example, studied workers in several types of Australian industries. These did not include persons at the planning, specialist or supervisory level. He concluded that the worker is self-centred in his interests, or he is family-centred, 'but he is never work-centred'. He reasons that this must be expected among those excluded from creative work which is the monopoly of the upper echelons. Creativity is not expected of others; in fact: 'Most workers of any grade have no such scope, and factory workers certainly have no scope at all for creative activity; they do what is prescribed exactly by the task itself, and can do nothing less (unless they are prepared to be dismissed) nor more. For the factory worker, work can only be the means of earning a living.'[2]

The views of Lafitte are quite opposite to those of Jaques regarding the factory job yielding occupational satisfactions.

Ambition was another motive for work named by Santayana; one works to get ahead and there are many devices one can use. This is the most respected of motivations in Western society, and a treasured element in the Puritan ideology of work. A man may take training courses; he applies himself diligently to any task given; he cultivates the virtues that lead to advancement. He may take a low level job and hold on patiently if he is convinced that promotion lies ahead.

Some enterprises have incentive and promotion plans based largely on seniority, which ensure advancement and non-discrimination. Most seniority plans must assume that many will fall by the way on the long road from office boy to manager,

[1] Fred H. Blum, *Toward a Democratic Work Process*, New York, 1953, pp. 98, 104.
[2] Paul Lafitte, *Social Structure and Personality in a Factory*, 1958, p. 180.

from file clerk to secretary in the front office, from common worker to plant superintendent. Thus if one holds on, promotion is bound to come. Seniority is perhaps the most ancient and democratic of promotion systems, a perfect system in a situation of little change, for it discourages most of the snide and ruthless practices attending competition in the work place. Where strictly adhered to, as on the American railroads, there goes with it the assumption of long-term job security; the worker can foresee his job status five, ten or more years ahead. He can plan his non-work life accordingly.

On the other side, a well-rooted seniority system may discourage the more energetic ambitious workers who cannot wait on a lock-step system of promotion. Such restless ones move to other jobs which, in the long run, is an advantage to those who remain with the enterprise.

For reasons of ambition a worker may leave one job to find a better one, or leave one occupation to train himself for another. These may be calculated moves, or they may be random pursuits as of the prospector following one lead and then another hoping sometime, somewhere to strike gold. We hardly need dwell on the familiar American way to climb the ladder, that of the youth who foregoes part of his leisure, giving the time to study that he might advance.

Shopping for job experience is not American only. During the summer of 1959 the German press reported on the worries of teachers and parents because many teenagers were flocking to the labour market. There was full employment and jobs were easy to find. Teachers argued that the summer vacation should be used for play and rest. Middle-class parents were embarrassed that their daughters were taking jobs. The girls answered, 'We will be laughed at if we don't work.' For some the work was necessary, but for many it was a teenage craze. Even among those who would normally not work, the argument was given that this was a good way to gain work experience. But these, like many others who work, were also bent on using their earnings to buy leisure necessities; motor scooters, cameras, recording sets, canoes or camping equipment.[1]

More about ambition as a work motive in the next section. We might ask before going into that if most workers really give much thought to reasons for working. If asked they would in

[1] 'Der grosse Run zum Ferienjob', *Frankfurter Neue Presse*, 11 July 1959, p. 2.

The Work-Leisure Dichotomy

many cases give the answer commonly heard, 'It's a habit.' They work because others do, and one is expected to work. Since one must work in any event, then one should try by all means to advance himself and to get as much pay for it as possible. This sort of thinking does not imply at all that the worker is any less effective on the job. Nor does it mean that he works without some occupational pride. He can be fully competent and responsible and still put the job out of his thoughts when the day is done.

WORK COMPETITION AND LEISURE

In times of unemployment when people face need there may be sharp competition for the number of jobs available. Workers compete for jobs and any job will be in demand. Under full employment jobs compete for workers, and those that are heavy, dirty, noisy or dangerous are passed by, unless the pay is good. Strenuous want-motivated competition may be absent, but under full employment competition assumes other forms. Workers now need not cling to their jobs for without great risk they can cut loose and search for other work. This may be expressive of the ambition motive mentioned by Santayana. Under full employment, a man has less fear of dismissal, a fact which may be confidence-inspiring in his efforts to advance.

Describing the Polynesians as workers, Beaglehole said that one detects in their personalities no 'obsessive-compulsive perfectionist drives' so common to Westerners. He notes that Westerners generally condemn as laziness the 'happy-go-lucky casualness' of the Polynesians. They linger in their work and do not compete for that would be bad manners, but they are very apt to compete vigorously in leisure activities.[1] Westerners, on the other hand, not only compete in their work but they may use their leisure contacts to gain economic advantage.

This type of economic competition in which leisure activity must perform duty to advance a man in his job is more characteristic of upper level than of lower level occupations. At these levels a man may use his leisure to get more schooling, but he manages to let his superiors on the job know it. He may join the same gymnasium and perhaps 'by accident' find himself playing volleyball with the boss. Or he may try to meet the

[1] Ernest Beaglehole, *Social Change in the South Pacific*, 1957, p. 156.

right people that he may be invited to attend the *right* social occasions. But 'activities undertaken for ulterior motives such as advancement in the economic scale' are not true leisure, so claims Fitzgerald, and many recreationists would agree with him that leisure must be an end in itself.[1]

But if one were to refrain from using leisure for practical ends much of the spice would go out of it. The movies would be hard pressed for themes if the young man could no longer use leisure activity to win the lady, and not infrequently the lady in the movie is the daughter of the manager. Or it is the lady who plays her way into the heart of the manager's son. The audience might go home depressed if the hero who had worked his way through college came out of the story married to a hodcarrier's daughter.

There are many linkages between leisure and work, the use of leisure to get ahead in one's work is only one way of exploiting leisure. A man may exploit his work to advance himself in his leisure. Either type of exploitation may serve the Puritan success ideology. Or a man may also make work of his leisure activity. This is what the boy does who plays baseball assiduously to improve his game that one day he may have a high-paid spot in a major league team. It is this linkage between work and play that necessitates stern rules in sport for keeping professionalism out of the amateur ranks.

Inevitably industrialism has, and must, separate leisure time from work time, but it is not the same kind of separation for all who work. It is hardly a separation at all for a limited few, a partial separation for others (also a minority), and a fairly complete separation for the many. This thought has been expressed also, and better, by Wilensky, who, as a result of his studies in Detroit, concludes that 'we are heading toward an organization of work in which a small group of executives, merchants, professional experts and politicians labour hard and long to control and service the masses.' These elites will mix their work and leisure, as most of them do at present.

The masses below the elites will include the social levels from the upper-middle down, eighty per cent or more of the total. In each of these lower levels will be two kinds of people (mostly in the lower-middle and the upper-lower) with respect to status striving. One group will be aspiring to achieve upward

[2] Gerald B. Fitzgerald, *Community Organization for Recreation*, 1948, p. 31.

The Work-Leisure Dichotomy

social mobility, the other not being socially mobile, each group fading into the other. Each of these below-the-elite groups may be active in the pursuit of status but, since there is not room at the top for all, the great majority would find status in 'prestigeful patterns of leisure'. Those whose work least touches their personalities, are not left in the 'outer darkness'. They have free time and some or much purchasing power above necessity needs. They 'will continue to retreat from work and withdraw further into family and neighbourhood localism'.[1]

LOOKING CLOSER AT LEISURE

In the previous pages we defined leisure as time when one is free from the demands of work. We agreed with Soule that leisure is time not paid for, one's own time. We used the concept in the sense of Lundberg, leisure being 'the time we are free from the more obvious and formal duties which a paid job or other obligatory occupation imposes upon us.'[2] The concept has other ramifications. For example, Vontobel identifies leisure with qualities of refinement, holding it to be unique because it is often associated with spiritual or artistic values and, for those to whom leisure has such meanings, it also implies a tolerance for fantasy. Moreover, she associates leisure with aristocratic refinement, quiet dignity and graciousness.[3] This is the meaning of leisure she found in her study of Protestantism. It concerns attitude and behaviour in the use of leisure.

Leisure, as against work, is normally assumed to be task-free. However one may use leisure, the compulsions associated with work are absent. It is assumed that one at leisure is free to

---

[1] Harold L. Wilensky, 'Work Careers and Social Integration', *Inter-Social Science Journal*, Vol. XII, No. 4, October 1960 (Quotations are from Wilensky's manuscript sent to the writer before coming into print.) Greenberg sees this separation of work and non-work time as a result of industry's technical integration. Machines are paced one to another and all are paced to a single process in different production arrangements. There can be no slackening or acceleration of pace or diversion of attention along the line. The worker as a person belongs here only in a limited functional role. As a worker he may be efficient, which gives only partial satisfaction to his wole person. The rest of him finds satisfaction outside the work place. Clement Greenberg, 'Work and Leisure under Industrialism', *Commentary*, Vol. 16, No. 1, July, 1953, pp. 57–61.

[2] George A. Lundberg, Mirra Komarovsky and Mary A. McInerny, *Leisure; a Suburban Study*, New York, 1943, p. 2.

[3] Klara Vontobel, *op. cit.*, pp. 83–84.

choose his activities or to change them, and he need not be concerned about goals. One's leisure activity need not be firm or precise, regular or measured, in the sense that work must be. Modern work is pointless if it cannot be measured and predicted. Predictability in leisure activity would be balked by individual variability and volition. Ten persons performing the same kind of work will turn out comparable products. But the same ten may turn to different types of activity in their leisure. Their leisure interests may change from day to day, and their performances will not be comparable. Spontaneous activity and individual variation are expected in leisure behaviour.

Leisure, then, seems to afford more freedom of choice in activities, and people differ widely in their choices. Thus choices may be different as between the sexes or according to age groups. Differences may be seen as between persons of different educational level. But cutting across all these differences are those associated with social class. At one time certain leisure pastimes were the monoply of the high and well-born and were considered to be more cultured than the pastimes of the poor; attitudes which still survive.

Today the class lines are less strictly drawn; all classes attend the same ball games, the same prize fights, the same night clubs, even the same opera. All listen to the radio and view the same television programmes. All attend dances or go to the horse races. The difference is in money outlay; how much is spent for the fishing outfit, the automobile, the television set, the seat at the opera or the table at the night club. Mrs. Jones-Smith may spend more on a house party than Mrs. Jones. Here we come to the point, what of the satisfactions derived at the two parties?

Besides cost differences, general time-use patterns and attitudes toward leisure from one class to another, we may ask if there is any comparability in the satisfactions derived. Havinghurst has been conducting a study of the leisure interests of middle-aged persons in Kansas City. One objective was to determine what meanings different pastimes have, the satisfactions they yield according to social level. Among the answers were:

> ... a welcome change from work ... (certain activities) give one a chance to be with friends, they provide sheer enjoy-

The Work-Leisure Dichotomy

ment, they require mild physical activity, and they fit in well with the expectations held by other people. In other words, most of the working-class people who enjoy fishing do so for the same reasons as most of the upper-middle-class people who enjoy golf or sailing.[1]

Havinghurst observed that people of different classes may get similar satisfactions from the same type of activity, but may realize similar satisfactions from different activities. For comparison with the Kansas City study, a companion project was undertaken by Donald and Havinghurst in New Zealand. They found that different types of leisure activity had about the same meanings there as in Kansas City; meanings such as these: 'Just for the pleasure of it,' 'Welcome change from work,' 'Gives new experience,' 'Contact with friends,' 'Chance to achieve something,' 'Makes time pass,' 'Chance to be creative,' 'Helps financially,' among other satisfactions. They conclude that the values derived from an activity tend to be individually determined and are little affected by sex, age or social status. To summarize:

1. Different kinds of leisure activities have different patterns of value or meaning.
2. However, there is enough variability of meanings of a given kind of leisure activity so that a particular set of meanings can be found in various choices of leisure activities.
3. From the variety of choices open to him, a person can generally find the meanings he wants from his leisure.
4. The differences in the meanings or values people find in their leisure seem to depend more upon their personalities than upon their age, sex, or social class characteristics.[2]

Thus, while different people may derive similar satisfactions out of the same type of leisure activity and similar satisfactions out of different leisure activities, they may also derive different satisfactions out of similar types of leisure activity. Apparently

[1] Robert J. Havinghurst, 'Leisure Activities of the Middle-aged', *American Journal of Sociology*, Vol. 63, No. 2, September 1957, p. 152.

[2] Marjorie N. Donald and Robert J. Havinghurst, 'The Meanings of Leisure', *Social Forces*, Vol. 37, No. 4, May 1959, pp. 357, 360.

individuals may differ as much as the meanings derived as in the choices of leisure activities.

THE FUNCTIONS OF LEISURE

Dumazedier defines leisure in terms of what it does and he arrives at a definition the basis of which are three functions: relaxation, diversion and the development of personality, and their claims on the individual's time tend to be in that order. When leisure is preceded by work and fatigue then relaxation must have priority. Not so many decades ago when industrial operatives worked a 12-hour shift all of such leisure they could find had to be given to relaxation. Leisure for diversion and the development of the personality under such a work schedule hardly existed. Only when the individual is fatigue-free can he turn to diversion types of leisure or to self-improvement.

Diverting activities are normally the same that may be called amusements, and these are various, as Dumazedier found. Diversion may be any matter of the moment that amuses or pleases; something planned, or incidently experienced. Work unconnected with the job, performed during free time may be a diversion. Normally diversion is thought of as leisure activity not serving any practical purpose, although it may even do that. Leisure time used in the development of personality (if that can be done by taking thought) may also be diverting, as reading or study or engaging in the arts. And now Dumazedier's definition, *'Leisure is activity to which the individual may freely devote himself outside the needs and obligations of his occupation, his family and society, for his relaxation, diversion and personal development.'*[1] These three functions; *délassement*, *divertissement* and *développement*, are not always distinguishable. All three may be present in a single activity, as when a secretary, who is also an amateur artist, uses a leisure hour to sketch the outline of a landscape.

Development of the personality, or personal development, is a wider concept than 'self-improvement', as many use that term, and is not so loaded with moral compulsion. In the process of personal development the individual acquires self-discipline and poise, understanding, perhaps social orientation[2] It means more than merely using leisure to get ahead. As the

[1] Joffre Dumazedier with Friedmann and Morin, op. cit., T.XIV.54.5.
[2] Joffre Dumazedier, '*Realites du loisir ed ideologies*', *Esprit*, 27 annee, No. 274, *juin* 1959, p. 875.

The Work-Leisure Dichotomy

function of personal development is realized in one's life it means that he is developing into a more companionable human being in his social relations, a good sport in the highest sense of the word when he plays a game, and the sort of person another enjoys working with. It means developing those qualities of citizenship which identify one as a good neighbour, friend, family member, and without presuming to be the symbol of the good and right. It can also include work and study during leisure to advance oneself through education and training.

Huizinga, the Dutch scholar, in his philosophical study of play, observed its importance in the development of personality. His interest was not in the wider concept of leisure as we meet it today, but in play as seen in sport, in games and in fantasy activity, in the area where leisure behaviour most intimately involves the personality. He saw play as affording the individual opportunity for testing and rating himself against others in various play contacts, and as stimulation for enlarging certain capacities. He recognized that different kinds of play serve different individual needs, meaning that play serves different functions for the adult as well as the child. For either play is an invitation for the individual to display his talents and capacities that he may gain favourable recognition. One may win prizes and these for him become social symbols, which means that play experience can also be enjoyed in retrospect. Huizinga's definition of play is functional:

> Let us now enumerate what appear to be the characteristics of play. It is activity carried on within certain limits of time, space, and meaning, within a defined situation, according to freely-accepted rules, outside the sphere of the materially useful and necessary. The mood of play is relieving, either spiritually or simply festive, according to whether the play is ceremonial or merely enjoyable. Play will be accompanied by feelings of elation and eagerness and leads to pleasure and relaxation.[1]

We can accept the observation that play is 'outside the sphere of the materially useful and necessary' easier than we can accept the same observation in a definition of leisure. Whether we speak of play or of leisure, neither lies wholly

[1] Johan Huizinga, *Homo Ludens*.

outside the sphere of the materially useful and necessary. While Huizinga mentions the time and space elements in play, he was not thinking of the work-leisure-time complex in which leisure competes with work and non-work obligations for space on the clock. Although he did not relate play with work, he did relate it to the wider interests of life, and art.

We must recognize leisure as activity which is related to non-leisure activity, and as time-using activity which functions in relation to other forms of activity. 'Leisure represents time,' wrote Fitzgerald, 'time is opportunity. Leisure represents freedom; freedom allows for choice; and choice is opportunity.' He adds that choice is variously guided by education and the social values that influence the individual.[1]

There are those who do not regard an activity during free time as leisure if it does not serve what they feel to be a useful and moral purpose. Thus if one goes to a ball game, that is not objectionable, but if he spends the afternoon at the horse races that would not be called leisure. While in some countries gambling is a right, many would not call it leisure, and others would exclude dancing. These attitudes change with time, and they may not be the same from place to place. Usually they differ as between town and country. These taboo aspects of leisure, which will be considered further in Chapter 4, show how the social milieu helps determine how leisure should function; how people think it should be used or not used. Such views about what leisure is, or is not, are also met among professional recreationalists. Some would say that lying in the shade may be a pastime, but it serves no leisure function. Leisure to them means doing something. It is activity, and some would add, approved activity.

Re-reading Dumazedier's definition of leisure, quoted above, we note that he distinguishes between leisure time and time given to obligations. Leisure functions are wedged in between one's occupation and his other obligations. It is proper, as we have done, to speak of all non-work time as leisure. Turning from the wider look to a more precise one, we find that part of this free time is used for duty and obligations in which work and leisure are often mixed. We will now consider these non-work obligations.

[1] Gerald B. Fitzgerald, op. cit., p. 34.

The Work-Leisure Dichotomy

LEISURE AND NON-WORK OBLIGATIONS

In his study of the Equadorean Indians, Salz concluded they have no leisure in the Western sense of the term. They work steadily when necessary but not in the Western tempo. He noted that all their time is used, if not in work then in other 'structured activities'. However, in their non-work time he found that they enjoy life often with drinking and hilarity.[1] The Indian works and saves as if weddings, Christenings, birthdays and fiestas were the main reason for living. Salz holds that they do not regard such fun-making with the attitudes that Westerners have for leisure.

Lewis, who studied life in Mexican villages, also wrote about their pastimes, using the term 'diversion'. A fiesta people no less than the Equadoreans, the Mexicans may also neglect other needs to spend their money on these cermonials. Lewis noted that such holidays are looked forward to as occasions for fun, but the social duty element is not absent. These holidays are shared by all age groups and classes.[2] Such festive occasions in families and communities are common to most pre-industrial people, and universally they seem to have an obligatory character, but they seem to serve as leisure activities as well.

As Salz observed, Equadorean Indians seem to have no concept corresponding to the Western idea of leisure, but he hesitated to give a name to those playful activities from which they have fun. If they are not called leisure then another name meaning the same thing must be found. Here we are tempted to observe that the French have no word meaning 'home', but they do have homes. And, speaking of the French, Larrue found that among the French steelworkers in the Toulouse area, where he made a study of leisure, he found that the term 'leisure' is seldom heard. Instead, the workers speak of vacations and even a single holiday is a vacation.[3] It would be equally surprising if Parisians did not know the word '*loisir*'.

In the industrial urban society non-work obligations are not

---

[1] Beate R. Salz, 'The Human Element in Industrialization, a hypothetical Case Study of Equadorean Indians', *Economic Development and Cultural Change* Vol. IV, No. 1, Part 2, October 1955, pp. 100—2.

[2] Oscar Lewis, *Life in a Mexican Village*, Tapoztlas Revisited, Urbana, 1951, pp. 208-9

[3] Janine Larrue, 'Loisirs ouvriers, chez les metallurgistes toulousains', *Esprit*, 27 annee, No. 274, juin 1959, p. 955.

only distinguished from leisure, but they are known to fall into recognized catagories such as these:

Gardening   Informal group duties
Shopping   Fixing things around the house
Political party work   Helping children with their lessons
Church work   Visiting or helping a sick friend
    Doing part-time work for pay, a second job

It is in performing such obligations that one gets his status as a good spouse, good parent, good neighbour, good citizen, good friend and so on, all roles in which status must be earned, and the effort may be highly satisfying. The effort may be equally as satisfying as leisure activity.

The one indefinite item included in the above list tends to be controversial; doing extra work for pay, even holding a second steady job. Among American trade unionists, who scorn the practice, it is called 'moonlighting'. Moonlighting is often practiced by younger workers who need money to furnish the house, to buy an automobile, etc. Some may take extra work because they are bored with leisure, which they have not learned to use except in pastimes that may also become boring. Writing about the rubber industry in Akron, Ohio, Swados reports that some 30,000 workers in that city are on a six-hour day and six-day week schedule. He estimates that no less than forty per cent of these do extra work for pay.[1]

Holding an extra job would properly not be included among the non-work obligations, unless the work is of particular interest to the individual and allows him a measure of freedom not possible on the regular job. The extra job may even offer possibilities for creativity. It must be added that much of the work done around the home is a form of earning money, for

[1] Harvey Swados, 'Less Work—Less Leisure', *Nation*, Vol. 186, No. 8, 22 February 1958, pp. 153–8. In the week of 6–12 December 1950, the Bureau of the Census did a special canvass for the Bureau of Labour Statistics to determine the number of employed workers holding second jobs. The main results: 2,966,000 were holding two or more jobs, which was 4.5 per cent of total employment. A similar census had been taken in July 1958, and an earlier one in July 1957. The July 1957 enumeration showed 3,570,000 employed workers holding second jobs, 5.3 per cent of the total labour force. The higher percentage in summer was mainly due to working youth not then in school. Workers at all levels engage in this 'moonlighting'. Gertrude Bancroft, 'Multiple Jobholders in December 1959, *Monthly Labor Review*, Vol. 83, No. 10, October 1960, pp. 1045–51. Lafitte found that 27 per cent of Australian industrial male workers did home work to save spending money, and some held second jobs. Paul Lafitte, op. cit., p. 172.

The Work-Leisure Dichotomy

money is saved if family members do the necessary tasks at home. Much of the do-it-yourself work is of the money-saving character.

Do obligations interfere with one's leisure? That would depend on the individual, the circumstances and his interests from day to day. That people now speak of obligations as interfering with leisure suggests that competition for space on the clock is now less between work and leisure than between obligations and leisure. Thus Meyersohn wrote, 'What often gets into the way of an appreciation of leisure is an overextended sense of duty; everything is done for the sake of somebody—the children or the neighbours or the community—on the mistaken premise that it is expected of you.'[1] One may become like the mother, so involved in dedicated activities that leisure is all but excluded, or it ceases to be desired.

But leisure, say the Neumeyers, is 'time that is relatively free from obligatory pursuits'.[2] Could it be that one may find all the satisfactions of leisure in his obligatory pursuits? We know that a person who is absorbed in his work may even be bored if he is pressed into leisure activity. His problem is not one of finding time for leisure, but finding time for his non-work obligations. One may also become so involved and interested in his obligations that taking time for leisure may seem an intrusion. We find many such people who, besides their home duties, are members of different organizations, perhaps leaders in some of these. If asked, they will say they have no time for leisure.

Those who feel that too many people have too suddenly received more leisure than they know how to use, would do well to consider how many non-work and non-leisure demands are made on the time of most of us. It is in relation to these obligations, even more than in leisure, that we might look for the measure of social integration. In the performance of his obligations the individual is integrated into family life, group life and into the life of the community, participating variously in the community with interest.

---

[1] Rolf Meyersohn, 'Leisure is What You Make It', *House and Garden*, Vol. 115, No. 4, April 1959, p. 209.

[2] Martin H. and Esther S. Neumeyer, *Leisure and Recreation*, New York, 1949, p. 20.

The Work-Leisure Dichotomy

WHERE RECREATION COMES IN

By many Americans, and to some extent by the British, the terms 'leisure' and 'recreation' are used interchangeably. Most writers on recreation, even when using the terms synonymously, 'leisure and recreation' in the same sentence, are fairly agreed that leisure is free time and recreation concerns the uses made of such time. But often the use of the term, as remarked by Denny and Riesman, carries connotations of what recreation should be.[1] The term perhaps acquired such meanings as part of its Puritan heritage from a time when leisure was less plentiful, and mostly it was devoted to rest, re-creation. Many who interested themselves in the matter then were motivated by reform purposes, disturbed as they were about the way some people (in the lower social classes) were using their time. They did not speak of leisure, but of using idle time for recreation to be more fit for work, or for good works. They saw work and recreation as supplementary, one whetting the appetite for the other. Mead is of the opinion that such associations still cling. 'The linkage effects both joy in leisure and joy in work, or good works; one *should* have some recreation. And the minute that it looks as if there would be more time in between work and good works than the amount needed for "healthy recreation", alarm spreads over the country.'[2]

During the past two or three decades, while not losing all of its earlier sentimentality, recreation has acquired new meanings, especially among those who think about it professionally. Here we quote Butler:

> Expressed in terms of activities, recreation has been defined as an activity which is not consciously performed for the sake of any reward beyond itself, to which we give ourselves in our leisure time, which offers man an opportunity for his mastery, or in which man engages because of inner desire and not because of outer compulsion. In short, recreation may be considered as any form of leisure-time experience or activity

---

[1] Reuel Denney and David Riesman, 'Leisure in Industrial America', see Eugene Staley, Editor, *Creating an Industrial Civilization*, New York, 1952, p. 246.

[2] Margaret Mead, 'The Pattern of Leisure in Contemporary American Society', *Annals of the American Academy of Political and Social Science*, Vol. 313, September 1957, p. 13.

The Work-Leisure Dichotomy

in which the individual engages from choice because of the enjoyment and satisfaction which it brings directly to him.[1] Again we meet the thought that a recreational activity 'is not consciously performed for any reward beyond itself,' which was questioned earlier in this chapter. It overlooks how practical people use leisure activity to advance themselves. Otherwise, Butler's definition of recreation has much in common with Dumazedier's definition of leisure adopted above.

Recreation means activity, activity in fact that tends to become institutionalized to such an extent that some of its advocates feel there is no other way to use leisure time. One must play the game, not merely look on while others play. Not to participate means to vegetate. Nash puts it this way:

> The application of the abuse of rest to the problem of leisure time is obvious. Recreation should mean participation, adapted to strength and age, but participation. Rocking-chair sitting before the radio and television is not enough. Motion pictures, where others act, is not enough. Sitting in the stadia watching sports is not enough. Getting second-hand thrills in race-track gambling is not enough. Recreation means staying in the game.[2]

Recreation is also a type of movement devoted to finding ways of getting more people into leisure activity and in finding the means for providing all sorts of facilities. It is devoted to the values that are hoped for from such participation but, as the Neumeyers indicate, it is not promoting relaxation.[3] Those engaged in recreation professionally now regard this speciality as one of the service sciences. As a service, public or private, in the words of Fitzgerald, 'The early, outmoded concepts of recreation, namely to keep children off the streets, and to prevent juvenile delinquency, are no longer advanced as recreation's basic purpose by right-thinking people.' He apparently means that in addition to the early objectives the recreation movement now has wider objectives, serving all sorts of people in all sorts of activities.[4]

Recreation, then, means activity; it means a service movement to promote activities in recreation, but it also means

---
[1] George D. Butler, *Introduction to Community Recreation*, New York, 1949, p. 8.
[2] Jay B. Nash, *Philosophy of Recreation and Leisure*, St. Louis, 1953, p. 175.
[3] Martin H. and Esther S. Neumeyer, op. cit., pp. 21-22.
[4] Gerald B. Fitzgerald, op. cit., p. 32.

The Work-Leisure Dichotomy

organization and administration. In the great city the organization side of recreation includes, on the one hand, a wide variety of public facilities; playgrounds, playfields, beaches, swimming pools and the like staffed with trained leaders and instructors. Privately it means an equally large variety of facilities and services provided by churches, industries, welfare organizations and others. If private groups such as trade unions do not have outdoor facilities they may have programmes of other sorts, lectures, theatre groups, or organizations may do recreation planning.

However critical some may be of certain types of reformers in the recreation movement; organized, administered and institutional recreation is a logical and essential phase of modern life, and it would be difficult to imagine Western society without it. It not only supplements the various types of commercial entertainment which make up the amusement industry but it represents community conscience in setting standards for commercial entertainment. We may add that instututional recreation is perhaps the principal influence in defining for people what leisure is and how it should be used. This influence on the whole is a conservative one, although it is by no means static. Many would hold that such a conservative force is a wholesome and balancing influence in the realm of leisure where innovation is chronic.

PLAY AND AMUSEMENT

As some speak of recreation as if it were synonymous with leisure, others think of the wide area of leisure in terms of play. To Mitchell and Mason the term play is used because it affords easier conceptualization. Play, they hold, involves attitudes of mind as well as action. 'If one runs a foot race, drives a car, rows a boat, or reads a book, it may be play or not, depending on the way he thinks and feels about it.'[1] They add that one may feel differently about the same activity at different times.

Play is activity enjoyed by the performer and into which he enters with freedom and spontaneity. It may alternate between reality and fantasy, which to the child are not always distinguishable. Play and art, Dewey observed, are much akin. Both

[1] Elmer D. Mitchell and Bernard S. Mason, *The Theory of Play*, New York, 1948, p. 18.

The Work-Leisure Dichotomy

are moral necessities in caring for the 'margin that exists between the total stock of impulses that demand outlet and the amount expended in regular action. They keep the balance which work cannot indefinitely maintain.'[1] In this sense play and art find expression when the individual has a surplus of time and energy, above that needed for his work.[2] Some have maintained that play, when the individual has surplus energy, facilitates the growing and maturing process. It makes learning a natural interest.

Much of the research about play has been focused on children; how they grow into social beings, and here we need not digress to examine the various theories about play. What is important is that they evolved mainly in relation to education and interest in such research was very great about the turn of the century when American educators were reading the translated works of Groos who had written a book on the play of animals, and his *Die Spiel der Menschen* had a very wide reading.[3] His American counterpart was Hall who saw in the development of the child the stage by stage evolution of man, and Hall too was concerned with the use of such research in guiding education.[4] Thus play found a place in American education while recreation was finding a place in the school, more so than in the schools of other Western countries.

There was much resistance to bringing play into the education process. It went against the prevailing association of learning with work. Supervised recreation in the schools was also objected to by many. It was a challenge to the Puritan bias against play which was tolerated for younger children but for older children it was deemed a waste of time. As Erikson observed, play was permitted if one earned the right to it, even a child. 'The playing child, then, poses a problem; whoever does not work shall not play. Therefore, to be tolerant of the child's play the adult must invent theories which show either that childhood play is really work or that it does not count.

---

[1] John Dewey, *Human Nature and Conduct*, New York, 1922, p. 160.

[2] For one of the later views of the surplus of energy theory of play see Thomas M. French, *The Integration of Behavior*, Chicago, 1952, p. 150.

[3] Karl Groos, *The Play of Man*, New York, 1901.

[4] G. Stanley Hall, *Youth*, New York, 1906. For a review of the more important theories of play, see J. C. Flugel, *A Hundred Years of Psychology, 1833–1933*, 1933, pp. 135 ff.

The Work-Leisure Dichotomy

The most popular theory and the easiest on the observer is that the child is a *nobody yet*, and the nonsense of his play reflects it.'[1]

Nonetheless, following that burst of research into play there has been a growing receptiveness to it. The American school has become in many places the community centre for play and sport. Moreover, the ventures into the study of play afforded encouragement to guided recreation, as those who had experienced play at school increased in the population. By 1920 Dewey mentioned that many work-dedicated adults were still self-conscious about playing.[2] Such an observation could not be made today, most everyone is able freely to play. But the complaint now is that too few engage in play, they want to be amused.

Play is one way of using leisure, amusement is a somewhat opposite way. One participates in play, but for amusement he may watch others play. He may engage in some pastime alone for his amusement, reading, playing solitaire, singing in the bathroom or promoting some hobby. When he buys a ticket to visit a movie he may also pay an 'amusement tax'. We speak of public facilities for leisure; bathing beaches, parks, stadia and the like as amusement places. Often, too, commercial pastimes are identified as amusements, but so are public spectacles, like fireworks on a holiday.

IDLENESS AND UNEMPLOYMENT

Puritan doctrine branded idleness a grave sin, and one might be called idle even if he was having fun in some innocent game, or if he slept too much. Of Samuel Smiles, his granddaughter wrote that he would say, 'six hours sleep for a man, seven for a woman and eight for a fool.' She said he worked twelve hours, slept six and had six for food and his pastime of writing books.[3] When work was such a virtue, any avoidance of work for play was evil. This view was not unlike the doctrine of German Protestantism which held that idleness was neither a service to God nor to man.[4] Even sickness was not always a valid reason for absence from work.

But the idler was not condemned if he had social position

---

[1] Erik H. Erikson, *Childhood and Society*, New York, p. 187.
[2] John Dewey, op. cit., p. 158.
[3] Eileen Smiles, *Samuel Smiles and his Surroundings*, 1956, p. 20.
[4] Klara Vontobel, op. cit., p. 66.

The Work-Leisure Dichotomy

and wealth, as if he were beyond the pale of the worker for whom idleness was a badge of guilt. Thus under the puritan code one worked and learned to feel virtuous about it, and who did not was a sluggard. It often happened that one was idle because he could not find work; still the stigma of the sluggard was on him, and he knew it. Such attitudes took deep root in Western thinking and are still with us. As Durant concluded, one in our society acquires such attitude toward idleness from his childhood on.[1]

Sloth and idleness have always been a concern for those who work and in the Middle Ages those who sank into such a condition of lassitude were said to be sick. Monks so afflicted in ancient times were thought by their fellows as having been possessed by a demon, taking away their lust for labour and replacing serenity with attitudes of doubt and cynicism. This condition was called 'accidie', a reason for pity. In any society the loafer is a friendless one. But unemployment is something else; the idle one looks for work but cannot find it. It illustrates individual helplessness in the industrial labour market. One knows that he is seen as an idler. He has free time, but not leisure. He is insecure, as Beveridge put it, for he is outside the production process.[2]

In countries that have systems of unemployment insurance, the unemployed person is enabled to feel that he has status and rights, a factor for holding morale up, at least partially, while waiting for the next job, keenly aware all the while that the bias against idleness lingers on. Perhaps this serves to emphasize the positive relation between work and leisure, leisure being something earned, as against the negative relation between unemployment and leisure. We are learning, however, that if idleness is a fault, it is of individual volition; unemployment is an economic and social malady, dreaded alike by the idler and the enterprising worker.

When unemployment is present or threatening, however few may be affected, it chills the social atmosphere and slows down the tempo of leisure activity. This is well known among those who experienced the Great Depression when leisure activity was muted. The opposite has been true for the full employment years since World War II. With work for all, leisure activity

[1] W. H. Durant, op. cit., p. 5.
[2] William H. Beveridge, *Full Employment in a Free Society*, 1944, p. 20.

The Work-Leisure Dichotomy

has expanded as if out of control, and many wonder if we are really ready for leisure.

SUMMARY

Western civilization evolved under the injunction to work, and with that evolved the Puritan ideology of success through work; man must work out his salvation. Man invented capitalism and put it to use in evolving the industrial system of production. Capitalist industry was fashioned into a system for using the work of man, as of machines, in terms of money value, and man became a seller of his labour; his time. As a result of this general development, man produces more with less work and in the process he gets more goods, more conveniences, and has time left over for leisure.

This development has been taking place mainly in the course of a century, putting society in a condition of gradually increasing abundance, of having leisure and trying in a fumbling way to make use of it. The scholars, looking at these changing phenomena, were becoming aware of the social and economic importance of the emerging leisure. It was seen as time not worked, not paid for, and yet having value when measured against wage-earning time. Even they had no other answer but that such time should be used in practical ways, which meant the ways understandable to a work-dedicated society.

Today it is recognized that leisure is surplus time not needed in the production processes, but it may properly be used for relaxation, diversion and development of the personality. Leisure activity may be oriented to the world of work but it does not readily mix with work on the job. One who is occupationally motivated, whose job offers possibilities of creativity, may find some of the satisfactions of leisure in his work. Such possibilities are hardly present in most modern work. One who is motivated by ambition to rise occupationally may utilize leisure activities to advance himself, either through off-the-job study and training, or as he uses leisure contacts in various ways to promote himself. It is being increasingly recognized that leisure activity may point to goals quite separate from work, for example, as it is used in personality development and other pursuits of individual interest.

Recreation is usually associated with programmes for using

The Work-Leisure Dichotomy

leisure time. Attention is focused on people with free time, and on activity programmes in which they might be induced to join. Recreation is associated with guidance in the use of leisure time in socially approved activities. It may be a public service provided by the community or a private service, a professional and somewhat institutionalized service to leisure, highly necessary in the modern community. The professional recreationist aims to extend his service to all ages and classes of people, whatever their individual leisure preferences.

Some recreationists and others interested in play may use the term in lieu of leisure. Play is seen as the most natural of leisure activities, being common to animals as well as humans and serving the same basic needs in both. It is activity for its own sake, whereas much leisure activity may have ulterior motivations, although play elements may be present in all forms of leisure pastimes. In play as in art, reality and fantasy may be interwoven. Play has been contrasted with amusement in that one participates in play but in amusements he is entertained watching others play; but mentally he may be one with them.

One's free time is not always occupied with leisure activity, but may be used in performing non-work duties and obligations at home or in the community. These obligations may partake of leisure interests and yield similar satisfactions. The socially integrated individual may be occupied much of his time with such obligations rarely feeling the need of leisure, being in much the same position as the occupation-centred worker who 'never plays'.

Idleness is not synonymous with leisure, even though some would think of leisure as idleness if not used for socially approved ends. Idleness is the avoidance of work. But a distinction must be made between *idleness* when work is available and *unemployment* when work is not available. Bias against sloth and idleness is often so great that the distinction is ignored. Idleness is individual, a voluntary matter. Unemployment is a social and economic condition and is seldom voluntary. One may enjoy idleness for brief periods, but not unemployment, which confirms in part the linkage between work and leisure. Leisure as free time is positive, unemployment is negative.

3

SOME DIMENSIONS OF TIME

How one uses one's days and one's years is perhaps for no people more of a concern than for Western man. His main preoccupation has been to use his time to his advantage for material gain, for advancing himself in one way or other. At least his material civilization is witness to the effectiveness of his efforts. Some have reasoned that these achievements are due to the fact that Western man lives in a stimulating climate; that if he had not worked he would have frozen or starved in winter. Whatever the explanation, Western man has not only worked, he has evolved a cult of work, and he has become the most time-conscious of humans. He invented clocks and watches so he could work more effectively.

Because he has worked to advantage in the accumulation of material goods, Western man has won free time when he can turn from his work. How this has come about is one of the themes of this chapter. We will also consider how man in his striving for progress has surrounded himself with a civilization in which time acquires new meanings for him, which change during the cycle of his life.

THE TIME-INVESTMENT CULT

Vontobel, in her study of German Protestantism, was impressed with the importance placed on time, of which man had a limited measure and his salvation depended on the good use he made of it. In the later life time may be without end, but in this life, according to Protestantism, the shortage of time made the wasting of it a sin. The little given to man for his life cycle was

Some Dimensions of Time

like money on loan, a loan he could repay only with work and good works.[1] Max Weber, speaking of Protestantism, observed, 'Not leisure and pleasure but only deeds serve the unequivocal revealed will of God for the increase of his glory. Time wasting is the first and heaviest of all sins. The time span of life is infinitely short and precious when one may perform his work. Time loss through socializing and lazy gossip is a luxury.'[2] It was Weber's well-known thesis that the ethic of Protestantism formed at least a good share of the ideological basis of modern capitalism. Its advocacy of serious and continuous work and its intolerance of idleness was matched by Puritanism in England. But Puritanism in its later development was not entirely a religious ideology. As noted by Lewis and Maude, it stood for thrift, diligence in work, frugality in spending time and money and sobriety in living habits, especially for the working classes. Too, it was a cult of work.[3]

Puritanism began before the Industrial Revolution as a religious and moral reform movement, but even then it had its practical aspects; time was for work and good works, but the money values of work were not overlooked. This may be seen in John Wesley's sermon on money. The first rule of money, he said, was to 'get all you can', but he added that one must get money honestly and with a clear conscience. However the keeping of the conscience was an individual matter.

John Wesley's second rule of money was 'save all you can', and he advocated frugality in living in order to save the more. By saving, one would not be in want if ill fortune befell him.

Wesley's third rule of money was to 'give all you can', which contradicted somewhat his second rule. In saving one was avoiding the temptation to 'gratify the desire of the flesh, the desire of the eye or the pride of life'.[4] In giving one satisfied the soul. Again, it was left to the individual conscience to determine how much such satisfaction one needed for his soul.

These three rules of money, in Wesley's thinking, rested on a more basic rule that one must work continuously and wisely, being severely diligent in the use of his time. This was the

[1] Klara Vontobel, *Das Arbeitsethos des Deutschen Protestantismus*, 1946, p. 71.
[2] Max Weber, 'Die protestantische Ethic und der Geist des Kapitalismus', in *Gesammelte Aufsatze zur Religionssozeologie*, 1947, p. 17.
[3] Roy Lewis and Angus Maude, *The English Middle Classes*, 1950, pp. 37-40.
[4] John Wesley, *Sermons on Several Occasions*, 1746, p. 583.

basis of the time-investment cult that evolved with industrial enterprise. This fundamental doctrine of work and time was carried from England to New England where it flourished. John Wesley himself took it to Georgia, but his ideas of work and life were so strenuous and he was so unpopular that he was glad to return to his more sedate England.

The work-centred time-consciousness of both Englishmen and New Englanders was doubtless stimulated from about 1800 by other forces as well as by the ideology of Puritanism. In England where industry was then getting under way and where towns and cities were beginning to grow; also where much work had to be done, such a doctrine was highly useful. Two centuries after Wesley the time-investment cult had become more of a business than a religious ethic. It was less related to preparation for heaven than to personal advancement and security. The greatest apostle of the time-investment cult for nearly half a century in England was that untiring purveyor of inspiration for success, Samuel Smiles.

We mention Smiles because his writings on work and success were widely read in the United States, especially his *Self Help*, which was translated into several languages between 1860 and 1900. It preached the gospel of success through individual effort, every man for himself. He said of time:

> An hour wasted on trifles or in indolence would, if devoted to self-improvement, make an ignorant man wise in a few years, and employed in good works would make his life fruitful, and death a harvest of worthy deeds. Fifteen minutes a day devoted to self-improvement will be felt at the end of a year. Good thoughts and carefully gathered experience take up no room, and may be carried about as our companions everywhere, without cost of encumbrance. An economical use of time is the true mode of securing leisure; it enables us to get through business and carry it forward, instead of being driven by it. On the other hand, the miscalculation of time involves us in perpetual hurry, confusion and difficulties; and life becomes a mere shuffle of expedients, usually followed by disaster.[1]

To Jean Calvin, Martin Luther and John Wesley time and work were seen in fairly general terms. Theirs was the easily

---
[1] Samuel Smiles, *Self Help*, 1859, p. 236.

Some Dimensions of Time

understood, although strict proposition, that man must work and do good works, that being the way to serve God. All three were pre-industrial and for them most work was on the land or in the handwork shops under guild supervision. The factory with its division of labour was yet to come. Workers had not yet become mere sellers of time. The system under which time is sold in units measured by the clock, when selling and buying units of time became a transaction in terms of units of money, had not yet taken form. When that system arrived it brought with it different time values for different kinds of work, which meant that those who bought or sold time had to think precisely about it.

THE NEW TIME AWARENESS

Gradually, without plans to that end, industry developed means and goals within itself, and time acquired meanings quite removed from the transcendental meanings of earlier periods. It was oriented to industrial work, and industry, as an earthly institution, became the core element in a new way of life.

From the outset, the Industrial Revolution was little more than a variety of independent efforts by private enterprisers to find new ways of organizing the work of others and of making goods with their labour. They had to make goods faster, hence cheaper than could be done with hand labour. But each effort to operate a factory was an experiment. Capital was scarce and risks were great. Experience was lacking, and was only gained through trial and error. This fumbling beginning of enterprises is often overlooked by the chroniclers.

On the one hand, the emerging factory system was a venture in technology, one of making machines and using the machines to multiply the effectiveness of labour, for then the cost of labour was the chief outlay in making goods, or generally so. On the other hand, the factory system was a venture into using labour *en masse*, so the product of one worker would be equal in quality and amount to that of another. Effectiveness required that the tasks of all workers be linked into a single production process, something new in the history of work. Work time paid for had to be used so the employer would gain. Ways had to be found to measure work effectiveness, even though labour then was cheap.

Some Dimensions of Time

Labour was often exploited to the extreme of human endurance. Often to earn a bare subsistence, both father and mother, sometimes even the children, had to sell their labour to the factory. The work day was perhaps not longer than sometimes under the old guild system, but the guild system of security was lacking. For most workers economic security was about down to zero.[1]

But the factory, as it gained in the efficiency of its equipment and its organization, brought about a division of labour that was hardly possible in the beginning. Now there were different types of work calling for different degrees of skill. Some work called for high degrees of speed of deftness, some for strength and endurance. Some work called for more initiative than others. Thus developed scales of pay according to the nature of the work, and with this increasing refinement in the division of labour, more precise methods of measuring work effectiveness were developed. The workers found themselves in a labour market where different types of labour are bought and sold in units of time for units of money, but for different amounts of money.

It is not pertinent here to do more than mention that, paralleling the evolution of industry, there was a corresponding social evolution. Industrial working conditions were improved. The work day and the work week have been shortened from the extreme of fourteen hours to eight and from seven days in many cases to five or five and a half. It is hardly necessary to add that this and other changes for the better did not result without continuous struggle on the part of the workers. In the process of advancement, in addition to the shortening of work hours, wages have increased and levels of living have risen. It turns out to be necessary that workers enjoy higher levels of living so they can buy the products which industry turns out in greater quantity using less labour than ever before.

The result of this evolution which is pertinent to our present chapter is that all work, or almost all, has come to be visualized in terms of the time dimension, and the time dimension is concretized in money terms. These two common denominators cut across all the activities and interests of modern industrial urban

---

[1] For the story in England where industrialism began, see Sidney and Beatrice Webb, *History of Trade Unionism*, 1920; also J. L. and Barbara Hammond, *The Town Laborer*, 1917.

Some Dimensions of Time

man. Each of these denominators time and money tends to be the yardstick for measuring the other. Judgments boil down to such questions as: Is it worth the time? Is it worth the cost? The worker, and his employer, count the hours and minutes when he works, the minutes and even seconds needed for performing a specific task. The worker usually knows in terms of minutes the time needed to go from his work to his home. Often the time-consciousness which marks his pace in his work follows him when he turns from his work to leisure or to various non-work activities.

Whether the modern Western man any longer behaves as a Puritan towards his work is doubtful, but he has become more strict than a Puritan about the use of time. Whether at work or away from the job he is continually thinking of time in precise terms. Even when he takes a vacation he continues to wear his wrist watch, as he must, for all others do the same.

THE COMING OF CLOCKS

It is pertinent here to digress briefly to consider the role of the clock in the evolution of industry and the urban way of living. The clock, by which our day is dominated, is relatively new in the history of cities. Although cities got along for centuries without the clock, today it would be a calamity if suddenly all the clocks should stop. Many of our mechanisms, especially systems of communication and transportation, could hardly operate, and the co-ordination of mechanisms would be difficult.

In order to afford some regularity in the comings and goings of people, many of the medieval cities made use of sun dials. The church found need for correctly marking time and, quoting Mumford, it had the 'Collective Christian desire to provide for the welfare of souls in eternity by regular prayers and devotions', and it took the initiative in the promotion of 'time-keeping and the habits of temporal order' in the minds of men.[1] The need for temporal order in religious affairs was matched by an increasing temporal precision in secular matters, especially with the increase of commerce.

Those first clocks were mechanical devices that marked the time when church bells would be rung, and they appeared

[1] Lewis Mumford, *Technics and Civilization*, New York, Harcourt, Brace, 1934, p. 14.

during the 10th century. By the 14th century tower clocks with systems of wheels appeared and these were later supplemented with faces and hands. By now clocks had become a recognized necessity and the smaller models were being made, but it was not until about 1500 that a clock small enough to put in the pocket was made. In 1590 clocks measuring the seconds were achieved and this, as Sombart observed, was highly important to the development of industry. He also mentioned that the clock became increasingly essential to the measurement of money values.[1] Mumford wrote this on the technically strategic position of this mechanism:

> The clock, not the steam engine, is the key machine of the industrial age. For every phase of its development the clock is both the outstanding fact and the typical symbol of the machine: even today no other machine is so ubiquitous. Here at the very beginning of modern technics, appeared prophetically the accurate automatic machine which, only after centuries of further effort, was only to prove the final consummation of this technic in every department of industrial activity.[2]

More than the essential device for measuring the work of machines and the appointments of man, the clock freed man from the clumsy limitations of natural time. It enabled him to conceive time as an abstraction by which meaning was added to man's understanding of other abstractions, for example, space, distance, and speed. He can thus better measure other quantifiable values. To a degree, this has always been done with natural time, but the precision provided by time-measuring mechanisms was hardly necessary. To mark time into periods and to give meanings to the particular days, weeks, months or years facilitates social living, and affords order in sequences or durations of time, which also involves abstraction. Durkheim wrote about man and time with these social implications in mind, and he understood how peoples develop time rationalizations.

> It is an abstract and impersonal frame which surrounds, not only our individual existence, but that of all humanity. It is like an endless chart, where all duration is spread out before

[1] Werner Sombart, *Der Bourgeois*, Munchen und Leipzig, 1923, p. 421.
[2] Lewis Mumford, op. cit., p. 14.

Some Dimensions of Time

the mind and upon which all possible events can be located in relation to fixed and determined guide lines. It is not *my time* that is thus arranged; it is time in general, such as it is objectively thought of by everybody in a single civilization. That alone is enough to give us a hint that such an arrangement ought to be collective. And in reality observation proves that these indispensable guide lines, in relation to which all things are temporally located, are taken from social life.'[1]

Pre-industrial man with his natural time[2] did not have to be concerned with exactness as when the pulse is counted or when marking the revolutions of a wheel or the speed of a machine. Modern industry could not cope with some of its problems if it did not have the stopwatch to measure fractions of a second. And now the stopwatch has become the necessary device in leisure, for timing races, etc. The clock becomes a universal instrument because, as Walker observed, it enables man in all activities to dissociate time from human events. Moreover, it helps to 'create a belief in an independent world of mathematically measured sequences'.[3]

Once man achieved these precise temporal measurements, he was able to measure work in meaningful units; his own work and that of his machines, and to project these measurements into the future. The builder of an apartment house or a factory can estimate with impressive accuracy the amounts and costs of the many types of labour needed. The experienced operator of a movie theatre, once informed about the coming and going of people at different periods of the day, can estimate approximately the number of patrons to expect at different hours between opening and closing time. One can communicate by mail, telegraph or telephone with anyone anywhere on the globe with time precision, and just as precisely keep appointments, knowing that others are equally clock-regimented.

[1] Emile Durkheim, *The Elemental Forms of Religious Life*, 1915 (translation from French by Joseph Ward Swain), p. 10. For analysis of time in the modern world, see Alfred North Whitehead, *Science and the Modern World*, 1925, especially p. 184.

[2] Jean Daric, in a discussion of '*Milieu technique et milieu naturel*' (see Georges Friedmann, Editor, *Villes et Campagnes*, 1953, pp. 416–18) described machine time as 'pure', and he observed that work under pure time results in nervous as well as muscular fatigue, but work under natural time in muscular fatigue only. He held that nervous fatigue is less easily relieved than is muscular fatigue, hence there are more nervous illnesses under industrial urbanism.

[3] Patrick G. Walker, *Restatement of Liberty*, 1951, p. 61.

Some Dimensions of Time

This means that over all in this man-made environment people are pacing themselves in work and leisure to the ticking of clocks, and they are severely inconvenienced if they do not. If industrial urban man wishes to go to work an hour earlier in summer, he cannot unless all others in his general region do the same. Hence a law must be passed requiring that all the clocks must be moved an hour forward or backward. Thus urban man gets daylight-saving time. But the farmer, who is said to be regimented by natural time, must also set his clock even though he may be opposed to the idea, regarding it as another evidence of urban inadequacy. Thus even the farmer must adapt to the urban clocks.

TIME, WORK AND TEMPO

There is an uncompromising relentlessness about mechanical time which is very different from that of natural time. The mechanics of transportation and communication may slow down with the coming of night, but they do not stop. The factory must operate whatever the time as marked by the presence or absence of the sun. It is too costly to close down the plant and start again, so work continues around the clock. This relentlessness of the clock has so impressed Fearing that he wove the thought into one of his stories. He saw the Big Clock as more powerful than the calendar, something to which every man adjusts his entire life, a great impersonal machine.

> The machine cannot be challenged. It both creates and blots out, doing each with glacial impersonality. It measures people in the same way it measures money, and the growth of trees, the life span of the mosquitoes and morals, the advance of time. And when the hour strikes on the Big Clock, that is indeed the hour, the day, the correct time. When it says a man is right he is right, and when it finds him wrong he is through, with no appeal. It is deaf as it is blind.[1]

And the clock is always near; there on the tower, on the mantel or on the wrist. While he is dominated by it, man enjoys the illusion of being in control because he winds it himself. As Blum noted, there is nothing transcendental about mechanical time, that element has 'disappeared slowly under the blows of

---

[1] Kenneth Fearing, *The Big Clock*, 1948, p. 146.

Some Dimensions of Time

the rising industrial system'. Man's attention is fixed on the immediate world and what he is about as he strives to get somewhere or to get something done. He is relieved of the need to contemplate for 'the emphasis on the immediate result minimized contemplation and channelled human energy toward activity, toward work'.[1]

His energies so channelled and paced, industrial man is so preoccupied with immediate goals that mansions in heaven lose importance. He is driven to activity by the dread of empty time, which unfortunately for many is what leisure often turns out to be. One can be so perfectly regimented in his work activities that when he turns to play with the same tempo consciousness the result is often boredom. In leisure activity one must find his own interests and take command of himself. Leisure calls for a degree of casualness, which is foreign to the tempo of work. With leisure comes a restlessness which is not satisfied with driving to far places on a holiday or going to ball games. Leisure becomes what MacIver calls 'the great emptiness', a gift many are not prepared to use. 'Time is theirs, but they cannot redeem it.' They seem to have no choice but to escape the great emptiness. There are different escape routes but none a cure for the great emptiness. MacIver mentions, for example, the plight of the go-getters.

When they are efficient or unscrupulous or both, they rise in the world. They amass things. They make some money. They win some place and power. Not for anything, not to do anything with it. Their values are relative, which means they have no values at all. They make money to make more money. They win some power that enables them to seek more power. They are practical men.[2]

The great emptiness is a social malady which would not matter in the stereotyped preindustrial society, but in the modern society where one must be somewhat of an individual, being an individual is more of a challenge than many can meet in leisure, but they can meet it in the regimentation of work. Again quoting MacIver, 'They have never learned to climb the paths leading to the pleasures that wait in the realm

[1] Fred H. Blum, *Toward a Democratic Work Process*, New York, 1953, pp. 193-4.

[2] Robert M. MacIver, *The Pursuit of Happiness*, New York, 1955. Chapter 6, 'The Great Emptiness'.

of ideas, in the growing revelation of the nature of things, in the treasuries of the arts, and the rich lore of the libraries.' They keep the pace and tempo in work but cannot in leisure, as one must at times do, set their own pace and tempo; but more important still is that above work and leisure there is lacking life goals and interests.

This proclivity of Western man for work activity was remarked by Sombart in the 1920s and he wrote about 'tempo' and feverish effort. People hurry from appointment to appointment feeling that they must. One hurries even when he wishes to pause, but to pause would be to feel guilty. 'He will do more economic activity every minute of his life.' Sombart thought this lust for activity is so great that the Westerner seems without balance and the values of literature, art, and nature vanish into nothing. 'He has no time.'[1]

Sombart was very right when he added that this life of hurry is not something which can be blamed on the industrialists. Employer and worker alike are in the same treadmill. He apparently considered the situation one in which everyone is stimulated by everyone else, and there is no curb except the physical and nervous capacity of the individual. Sombart ended his thought with 'Tempo! Tempo! That is the watchword of our time.'[2]

Much has happened since Sombart wrote about tempo; in fact, the tempo of his day, compared with today, would seem tame. Wages have increased and relatively more workers have moved out of the unskilled into the skilled catagories. More people have moved into the higher levels of living. Veblin today would say that there is even less incentive for the 'instinct of workmanship', but he would find that the 'instinct' has not vanished, only it is found, as Arensberg noted, not always on the job but often in one's non-work activities.

> The instinct of workmanship flourishes now, we are told, in leisure. If flowers in the endless do-it-yourself work, the care of cars and hobbies and mechanical toys, the inventive puttering of life after work. Inventiveness, once a part of every artisan's work, has become instead the career job of the technician and the research man. The loss for work

[1] Werner Sombart, op. cit., p. 454.
[2] Ibid., pp. 228-9.

Some Dimensions of Time

democracy, and even work interest is clear, and no one denies it.[1]

This trend, taking interest and personality out of the job for many workers, has also gained momentum since Sombart, perhaps a necessary accompaniment of the increasing tempo. In the meanwhile the individual finds his deep interests in leisure and non-work activity. It does not mean that work has become dull and without interest, instead, other interests have gained importance. But the time consciousness and the tempo are not limited to work activities, they are seen in leisure and non-work activities as well. They belong to the industrial urban way of life, as the clock by which they are paced.

The tempo problem, if we may call it that, evidences the inherent cosmopolitanism of modern life in which man is behaving much of the time, at work or play, in relation to his own creations in the mechanized environment. It is a curious relationship in which he seems impelled ever to be in motion and he is ever short of time.[2] Even if he hurries all his waking hours, keeping the tempo, still he does not have time enough.[3]

MONEY VALUES AND TIME

Sumner was of the view that the modern civilization can be sustained only if man works wisely, but he must also accumulate if he would live well. 'This can only be true, however, when

---

[1] Conrad M. Arensberg, 'Work and the Changing American Scene', see Conrad M. Arensberg, *Research in Industrial Human Relations*, New York, 1957, p. 63.

[2] This thought is expressed in the following verse from '*Der Arbeitsman*', by Richard Dehmel, *Gesammelte Werke*, Berlin, 1915, Band II, p. 170
   Wir haben ein Bett, Wir haben ein Kind,
   mein Weib.
   Wir haben auch Arbeit, und gar zu zweit,
   und haben die Sonne und Regen und Wind,
   und uns fehlt nur eine Kleinigkeit,
   um so frei zu sein wie die Vogel sind;
   Nur Zeit.
(We have a bed, we have a child, my wife. We also have work, we both, and we have the sun and rain and wind, and yet we lack just one small thing if we would be free as the birds are, only time.)

[3] Hawley indicates what time, rhythm and tempo mean in relation to the ecological processes in nature, tempo being the number of events per unit of time and rhythm is the periodicity with which events occur. 'Rhythm, tempo and timing, therefore, represent three different aspects in which the temporal factor may be analysed, especially as it bears on the collective life of organisms.' Amos H. Hawley, *Human Ecology*, New York, 1950, p. 289.

labour is crowned with achievement, and that is when it is productive of wealth. Labour for the sake of labour is sport. ... Labour in the struggle for existence is irksome and painful, and is never happy or reasonably attractive except when it produces results. To glorify labour and decry wealth is to multiply absurdities.'[1] But Sumner also saw absurdity in the American passion for labour merely to gain wealth. This thought has been expressed in different ways by many others; one should work as much as he needs to that he may live well, and it is a senseless thing for one to force more work on himself merely for the sake of gain.

Sumner did not recognize that most men who work are really selling their time and few could accumulate wealth through that means alone, although most of the work he knew was marketed much as it is now. This is one of the unique characteristics of industrial work, that man sells or invests his time. He invests his time when he studies or submits to training in order to be advanced in his work, as the apprentice who gives three or four years of his time at a miserably low pay in order later to come into the state of the artisan with reasonable job security and good pay. For years American colleges have notoriously been proclaiming how 'higher education pays off', and the professor can prove it with pencil and paper. But the best evidence of this investment concept of education is the popularity of 'practical' compared with 'cultural' courses in American colleges. Engineering students feel apologetic if required to take advanced courses in English. But the investment of time takes other forms, in one's savings, for example, and in his life insurance.

There are still those to whom the idea of selling time seems a little vulgar. They like to think of work as being a source of joy, and they remind us of the artist or the inventor and the sacrifices they sometimes make in order to carry on their creative activity. All work can be so if we will it.[2] But even the artist blesses the day that he sells his first painting or his first piece of

---

[1] William Graham Sumner, *Folkways*, Boston, 1906, p. 162.

[2] On this thought Jacks wrote, 'A master in the art of living draws no sharp distinction between his work and his play, his labour and his leisure, his mind and his body, his education and his recreation. He hardly knows which is which. He simply pursues his vision of excellence through whatever he is doing and leaves others to determine whether he is working or playing. To himself he always seems to be doing both'. Lawrence P. Jacks, *Education through Recreation*, 1932, pp. 1-2.

Some Dimensions of Time

music. Most ordinary folks are satisfied to stand in line at the hiring office and they are pleased if later they can line up at the pay office to receive their 'time'. Time to ordinary workers means the pay they receive for the service hours they have sold. The ordinary worker tries to find in the labour market the job that will pay the most for the bits of his life that he surrenders. What he wishes, quoting Soule, is 'less *work* and more time of their own, time not for sale'.[1]

Employers, customers, clients, patients or spectators at a ball game are the buyers of this time. It comes in goods or services. They try to get as much value as possible for the least cost. The major part of all consumer expenditures for food, housing, clothing, transport, entertainment and so on move through the channels of trade to pay for work. The pay is also for the skill invested in the work as manifest in the quality of the goods produced or the excellence of the service rendered. It matters not whether the time finally paid for is that of the manager or mechanic, the doctor or nurse, the shopkeeper or errand boy, the baseball player or radio entertainer.

TIME, MONEY AND LEISURE

Working and earning money is time-passing activity, and most forms of consuming or spending money is also time passing. When one buys a ticket to a concert or a movie he pays to be entertained for about two hours. It is no mere coincidence that concerts, movies and ball games usually last two hours or so; apparently that has come about through long experience with audience behaviour. It is not that people could not endure longer, but they usually have other things to do. The two hours of entertainment fits into the average daily time schedule. Remember also, entertainment is business. For the ball-player, a two-hour game with all the before and after work that has to be done comprises a fair day's work. For the owner of the movie theatre the two-hour show permits the same programme to be repeated four to six times in a day.

Time and cost considerations are especially present in radio and television programmes. In countries where these are private enterprises, air time has high value. A programme of fifteen, thirty or sixty minutes might end a few seconds short, but it

[1] George Soule, *Time for Living*, New York, 1955, p. 94.

Some Dimensions of Time

must not extend longer to encroach on the next programme. When this time must be divided between entertainment and commercial announcements there is competition for time between the sponsor who wants to sell soap, cigarettes, dog food or what not, and entertainer who must get as much 'show' as possible into the few minutes allowed.

Under such circumstances, the entertainer is forced to pack as much as possible of humour, sentiment, thought and whatever else into his time. Thus we get songs including the melody, one verse and the chorus a couple of times. Jokes have to be to the point and quickly over with. Conversation must move fast, touching only the high points. Discussions and speeches must be stripped of all except the bare essentials. The leisurely manner has no place except to stimulate wit. These observations would be less pertinent if the programmes were merely heard or seen and then dismissed from mind. On the contrary, radio and television tempo enter into daily communication. In contrast to richness and mellowness, humour must be sharp and quick. Conversation becomes sketchy and the story is glossed over. It perhaps contributes to the glossing-over tendency in our reading. Other factors are certainly involved, but the influence just mentioned doubtless contributes to making so much of modern leisure a pursuit, a prusuit not related to anything in particular. This charge must be made with the reservation that it applies to only some of us much of the time, but it does apply to most of us some of the time.

It is often said that leisure time and spending are excessively set apart from work and the confirming evidence is that workers put the job out of mind as soon as they leave the work place. They hardly mention their work when they are about their non-work activity. Blum found that to be true of workers in a packing plant, 'work has no meaning for their life off the job'. But they talk about their leisure and non-work interests when they are at work. And if a worker is forced to stay away from the job a few days because of illness he is not only restless to get back to work, but he talks about the job.[1] Otherwise, work holds a neutral position so long as there is no worry about losing one's job. Since one does not plan the work or guide it, it would be an idle waste of time to talk about it. This is the pertinent point; the worker does not need to worry about wasting time

[1] Fred H. Blum, op. cit., pp. 95–97.

Some Dimensions of Time

on the job. That is left to management. But he does concern himself about the waste of time in his non-work activities. That is, if he worries at all about time, this is the time that gives him concern, and he rarely has time enough for all he would do.

Mills observed that a man's attitude toward his work may be determined by his leisure values. He may also be an effective worker and not mix his leisure values at all with those of his work, although if he is ambitious he may learn to use non-work time for advancing himself in work, while keeping non-work time in a realm apart. Most people acquire some capability for keeping work and leisure interests from intruding upon each other, even those who seem at times disorganized in their use of non-work time or leisure.[1]

WORK AND LEISURE IN LOCKSTEP

Time for hire has one value for the seller and another for the buyer, who must use it to gain some economic worth. Time not for hire, meaning leisure, also has economic worth and for industry this time is a resource of emerging importance. The importance emerges from the increasing amount of leisure that people have and the increasing amount of money available for leisure spending.

We have already noted how leisure made possible many productive enterprises; the entertainment industries, tourism, professional sport, the mode industries in dress and cosmetics and many special industries. Other industries may be less directly involved, including automobiles, boatbuilding, house furnishings, liquors, fancy foods, transportation and communication. All depend on leisure spending.

With the rising prevalence of vacations with pay, each industry becomes a major contributer to leisure spending from which others benefit. But each enterprise must find ways to carry on work with no additional money cost or loss in output while members of the work force take vacations. This very

---

[1] '...while men seek all values that matter to them outside of work, they must be serious during work: they must not laugh or sing or even talk, they must follow the rules and not violate the fetish of "the enterprise". In short, they must be serious and steady about something that does not mean anything to them, and moreover during the best hours of their day, the best hours of their life. Leisure time thus comes to mean an unserious freedom from the authoritarian seriousness of the job.' C. Wright Mills, *White Collar, the American Middle Classes*, 1951, p. 236.

important concession to leisure by the world of work is but one among many; the many concern the new markets opened by leisure upon which industry generally must depend.

We know how modern industry, American industry in particular, takes pride in its technical achievements and high productivity. Largely this advancement has been forced upon industry by competitive necessity. Not the least of the complicating elements in this continuous competition has been the changing position of labour. The industries that point with pride to their rapid evolution and mention the high living standards of American workers are the same that resisted every step of the way all efforts by labour to diminish hours of work and to increase wages. While insisting that the concessions could not be made, industry was able to find some new adjustment. Each adjustment has meant a more efficient use of labour and greater productivity.

One day, to be sure, the limit of this spiral will be reached and both labour and management will be faced with diminishing returns or some form of dead level, but that point is still not in sight. In the meanwhile, more workers have been winning more leisure time and more money for leisure spending. The worker has become infinitely more important as a market than in the era of the 14-hour work day; in fact, he has become a variety of new markets to which industry must cater. The new markets in many respects are the more colourful. They take up more space in newspapers and periodicals and of radio time than all other markets combined.

These new markets may be more fickle and less predictable than, for example, such markets as oil, rubber, steel or machinery, but they are not less profitable. We can estimate how many workers in a given country will have vacations with pay next year and how much money they are likely to spend. We can be sure that perhaps a fifth of all consumer money will go into some form of leisure spending, but there is so much opportunity for individual choice and, since choices change radically from year to year, we can hardly predict the where and how of spending.

What is pertinent here is that, while industry is watching and cultivating the leisure markets, it is also forced by increasing leisure time to be equally diligent in the use of the diminishing amounts of work time. As total work time becomes less plentiful

Some Dimensions of Time

and more precious, it must be utilized with greater skill. In the plant or office the work of each must 'gear in' more precisely with the work of others. The work of related departments and plants must be co-ordinated, so also the work of related industries, so the inflow of raw materials and the outflow of goods and services.

While industry must do this to survive, moving in the direction of automation, the trend is often seen as de-humanizing or regimenting, but if modern man wants more leisure and a higher standard of living, he has no alternative. Industry is accepting leisure and adjusting to it. Forced to use less work time, it is also forced to use that time more effectively. Unwittingly industry, in adapting itself, contributes to a new conception of time use, an example of what Blakelock calls an interdependence of a concept of time and regular collective activity'.[1]

HABITUAL TIME-USE PATTERNS

We mentioned above that it was necessary to pass a law in order to realize the idea of daylight-saving time. Clocks must be moved forward or back in unison, enabling us to start or leave work an hour later or earlier. This illustrates how all people are linked in our civilization. Whether in work or leisure, the coming and going of the individual depends on the coming and going of others. Work time is said to be *liquid* in that it can be exchanged for money which, in turn, can be used for many things. But Blakelock reminds us that time may have the qualities of *flexibility* and *rigidity* in that certain units of time may be put to any of several uses, or rigidly assigned to a specific use.

It can be seen that not only the length of time an activity takes but also its flexiblity is important in determining the demand it makes upon one's supply of time. The least flexible

---

[1] Edwin Blakelock, 'A New Look at the New Leisure', *Administrative Science Quarterly*, 4, 4, March 1960, p. 451. Without recognizing industry's own adjustment, managers worry about the lack of worker interest, but workers also make their adjustment, being indifferent to the job without diminishing their work efficiency. The worker has, says Dubin, 'a well-developed attachment to his work and workplace without a corresponding sense of total attachment to it', Robert Dubin, 'Industrial Workers' Worlds', *Social Problems*, 3, No. 3, January 1955, pp. 131-42.

Some Dimensions of Time

activities, perforce, structure one's other activities, which must be fitted around them. If the least flexible activities take up an individual's time of greatest liquidity, he may be relatively poor in time. The night worker gives an example of this.[1]

The night worker is exchanging time for money during some of the hours when most other workers are exchanging their leisure-time money for fun, but during the day when he has free time most of his friends are at work. Unless he has a very individual pattern of time use, he is likely to feel that much of his free time is lost; he cannot use it as he would normally wish.

Time uses tend to be structured into collective patterns. Whether working, shopping, going about his leisure or some other activity, the individual tends to behave in concert with many others doing much the same thing at the same time. What he does in the forenoon, afternoon or evening is largely influenced by what others do, which itself may be a source of satisfaction. Here we can point to an experiment undertaken by an industrial establishment in California where a new work-leisure time schedule was adopted with the approval of the labour force.

Briefly stated, the plan was this: for the first and second week-ends of each month the workers would be free on Saturday and Sunday, the usual schedule. At the third week-end workers would be free on Saturday, Sunday and Monday, deemed to be an opportunity for a three-day trip to the mountains or some other family activity. On the fourth week-end the workers would be free on Sunday only, working Saturday to 'pay back' for the previous Monday.

The experiment proved to be unsatisfactory for all concerned. On the free Monday management personnel had to be at work because other firms were working. Goods and messages had to be sent and received. Few took advantage of the three-day week-end. For most of those who looked forward to the extra free day few were able to use the time, especially on Monday which is washday for most housewives. Workers were free on Monday when all others were working and they worked on a Saturday when the neighbours were having a free day. Family schedules could not be adjusted.

[1] Edwin Blakelock, op. cit., p. 452.

Some Dimensions of Time

It might have been otherwise had all the workers been neighbours, but almost all owned their automobiles and they lived scattered over a 20-mile area. Few lived near enough together to take advantage of the new schedule. Surprisingly, none of the difficulties had been anticipated. After some months the scheme was rejected by the workers almost as unanimously as they had approved the idea when it was initially proposed.[1]

TRADITION AND TIME-USE PATTERNS

If any place could be called traditionless, it would be California, yet people there behave *en masse* even though the behaviour is ever changing. The compelling force is the mode, not tradition. If the time- and tempo-conscious and novelty-accepting Californians had been more tradition-directed (Riesman's term), they probably would not have accepted the new work-leisure experiment described above. Tradition-consciousness finds expression in fears that new ways may disturb the old ones. This is illustrated in a report by Vito describing resistance to change in communities on the Island of Sardinia. Here were old communities of small peasants and shepherds settled in their generations-old way of life, and now they face change.

In their long isolation these Sardinian communities had achieved a total adaptation to the situation and they needed little from the outside. The old nature-oriented time-use patterns there came to be challenged by different influences from the outside; new work, new goods and services and new forms of leisure activity. These were resisted by those of the old order.[2]

The shepherd's garb, Vito observed, is one of the symbols of the traditional way of life, as the overalls are the uniform for the new town worker and his ways of life.

The young man dressed in overalls working in a carpentry firm, watching television, criticising or approving such or such a singer or programme, thinks in political or trade union terms, while the young man in the shepherd's uniform

[1] Rolf Meyersohn, 'Some Consequences of Changing Work and Leisure Routines', Paper at World Congress of Sociology, Stresa, Italy, September 1959.
[2] Francesco Vito, 'A Sociological Survey of the Cultural Factors of Economic and Social Development', Paper before the International Social Science Council, Paris, 19–25 March 1959, p. 5.

represents the proud outlaw who refuses the State, its laws and instruments of mass media, free of all constraint, authoritative and autonomous in a classless society. In this same area economic development impoverishes, in fact and especially relatively, the traditional forms of wealth and prestige.[1]

This economic development coming to Sardinia means more than economic change; it also means quickening the tempo of one's daily round. The young man in overalls must carry a watch, something the shepherd never needed. Whether he likes it or not, the shepherd's tempo must also quicken. In his traditional way of life he could foresee his work for tomorrow, next month or next year, and the pace of his work had become habitual as the work itself; one was geared, as Vito noted, to 'subjective time'. Not so for the man in overalls; his work may change from day to day and his way of life can hardly be predicted in long-term perspective. These elements of uncertainty are now entering the way of life of the Sardinian shepherd.

According to the traditional way of life the work of the parents, their songs and dances would be repeated by their children. The time-use pattern of the parents for the days and seasons would not be changed by the children. But the man in overalls can pass little of traditional ways on to his children. In the changing situation they will have their own time-use patterns.

The situation of the Sardinian shepherds is unique, but it is not basically different from that of other isolated peoples who have had to adapt to change influences from without. They offer various degrees of resistance and display degrees of what Dumazedier calls 'inadaptation',[2] but little by little the old time-use patterns are changed for new ones.

OF MAN'S TOTAL TIME

Seen in religious terms, man's life cycle is given to him that he may work and perform good works and thus gain salvation in the life to come. The life cycle is a prelude to eternity, a period of preparation and continuous effort. The first concern of the

[1] Ibid, p. 8.

[2] Joffre Dumazedier with G. Friedmann and E. Morin, 'Les loisirs dans la vie quotidienne', *Encyclopedie Française*, T. 14, 54. 9.

Some Dimensions of Time

good Christian, according to the plan of life and salvation, is to live his days in this life so he will store up treasure for enjoyment in the next life. The key to this plan is work, and the worth of a man is that he works his entire life span and performs good works.

Without doubt, Western man has been influenced by one religious ideology or another in becoming the worker that he is, the saver of money and the investor of his time, although not always for next-life goals. Thus, too, he may have been stimulated to viewing his life in long-term perspective. Other influences have contributed as well to this way of thinking, perhaps the fact that the very existence of industrial urban society depends on long-term thinking and planning has been a factor. However much he may still be motivated by transcendental considerations, Western man is seriously preoccupied much of his time with the life-span implications of his earthly existence.

Perhaps in no other civilization has so much emphasis been placed on private insurance, on schemes of public insurance or on saving for old age. And perhaps in no other civilization has so much emphasis been placed on the life investment importance of education. Even more essential than for cultural reasons, education is seen as a way to economic advancement and final security. Perhaps, too, no other people have equalled Westerners in working to gain more leisure, only to insist that leisure must not be wasted but should be used for self-improvement. Even participation in play and sport is often justified with arguments that it develops useful skills and traits of personality which one can use to advantage in his work.

It is Western man who developed the clock and found hundreds of ways to use it in the perfection of his work. The benefits of these achievements he tries now to pass on to other peoples who are less clock-conscious. In his striving for precision in the use of time he has surrounded himself with a clock-dominated environment to which he tends to be subordinated whether working or at leisure. In these efforts he is finding new and still newer ways of using his time and his work to greater advantage, that is greater productiveness, only to become the more encased by the time and tempo demands of his mechanized environment. That same time-consciousness he devotes to his work is carried over to his uses of leisure.

This urge to Western man to keep occupied and use his time to advantage is no mere day to day interest, it extends across the years ahead, of which he is reminded again and again from childhood on. His code of life through the years has imposed on him the responsibility for his own life-span security, although in most industrial countries public insurance programmes are coming to the rescue. Yet most of the responsibility for getting educated and trained, for advancement in his work and for accumulating material reserves still rests with the individual himself.

This individual responsibility for security during one's own life span is something new in human history. It hardly exists among truly rural people and it was not a problem of older societies. The security of the individual was a group responsibility, but even the group did not plan for the future, storing away material things. The pattern of living was so established that the young had only to follow day by day into the steps of the old. Perhaps the individual carried charms to safeguard himself against unseen evils that might assail him today or tomorrow, but he took no personal precautions for his own life-span security.[2]

The life span for modern Western man is a procession of starting or terminal dates, with full measures of activity packed between. It is certainly a full measure for the child to learn all that is expected between kindergarten and his graduation from the primary school. In the next phase of his education he is again loaded until his exit from high school. There may be many starting and terminal dates in his work life as he moves from job to job or from one promotion to another. So he moves through the cycle of his private non-work life. Slowly he comes to the point when he dreads the approach of the terminal dates; he is entering the short end of his life span. All along, as he lives through one phase of his life cycle to enter another his way of living must change accordingly. His problem of total time is ever before him.

We can do no better in our examination of the phenomena of work and leisure than to consider these types of activity and

[1] See Clellan S. Ford, *Smoke from their Fires*, New Haven, 1941. An Indian chief tells his story to Ford. Especially pertinent are the chapters in this narrative about the childhood of the old chief, the magic performed in his infancy to protect him against evil. Much of his preparation for his work life was gained through play. No thought was given to his future economic security.

Some Dimensions of Time

interest in relation to man's life cycle. That is the approach which will be used in Chapter 6 which concerns the beginning or youth years of the cycle, in Chapter 7 which relates to the active and productive years, and in Chapter 8 in which the declining phase of the life cycle will be seen.

SUMMARY

Perhaps never in human existence has it been so necessary for man to be so time-conscious as Westerners are today. Man marked the seasons as they came and went and he counted the years, but he had no need of a watch for dividing time into tiny fractions. Western man not only counts time in tiny fractions but he measures the hours and minutes against money much as he measures goods and services against money.

Through the different religious ideologies, Western man has learned well the injunction that life is a period of probation, that life is short and one must invest his time in work and good works, thus to gain salvation. The minimum of work for a livelihood is not enough, he must do effective work and create surpluses. Under the pressure of such motivations, modern industry emerged and flourished, creating in turn a new time awareness co-ordinated to the on-going demands of co-ordinated mechanisms and to the equally insistent demands of a co-ordinated division of labour.

It was no accident that the clock came on the scene in the urban milieu. Rural man could not have invented the clock, which he did not need, any more than he could have invented centuries later the gang plow, the reaper and the cream separator, which he did need. It was both coincidental and providential, however, that the clock came on the scene ahead of the factory and mechanical power. It was the clock that made possible the co-ordination of mechanisms on the one side, and the co-ordinated division of labour on the other, a combination that placed man in a new and more precise relationship with time.

This new relationship with time, if we may over-simplify it, manifests itself in two overlapping activity spheres: the individual as seller of his work exchanges time for money, and the individual as buyer in his leisure exchanges money for time; time already invested through work in goods and services.

Some Dimensions of Time

In both spheres the relationship with time is competitive, having taken to itself the success and progess motivations of the religious ideologies which originally stimulated the work-dedicated way of life. Success and progress mean getting more product out of work and more value out of time. The tempo of this efficiency-mindedness carries over to the use of leisure.

Efficiency-mindedness in the workplace, while creating leisure, also not illogically excludes leisure from the work sphere. Sellers of time are, however, left to their own devices in using their own time. The minority who work are responsible for efficiency and the tempo of production. Those of the majority, while performing their work well, share no responsibility for it, or very little They turn elsewhere for their interests in living and social intimacy.

The mechanisms of industry have not destroyed the workers, as many feared a generation ago. Without planning or guidance, those of the majority are learning to meet in full the demands of work while centring their life interests in a sphere apart, submitting to management's time control at the workplace but in command of their own time outside. It may be true, as many claim, that they have yet to learn to use their own time, but the learning process goes on. In the meanwhile they are still tempo-dominated in their leisure.

While learning how to use his own time from day to day, modern man from childhood to old age must also be concerned about the total time of his life span. The individual in earlier civilizations merely followed the footsteps of the generations; he was not confronted with major choices along the way. For modern man time has a different meaning with each phase of his life span. Decade by decade his style of life changes and through his own efforts his fortunes may change. Depending on the converging of influences, changes take place in the roles of this living worker, spouse, parent, neighbour, citizen and so on. He must be continually conscious of short-time and long-time goals and make decisions accordingly. The span of his years, which science has been able to extend somewhat, is a continuous challenge to his time-using ability.

4
THE PROVOKING GIFT OF LEISURE

AS the views people have about leisure change they often reflect changing views about work. Moreover, as views about work change these may also be reflected in changing views about leisure and its uses. We know, too, that one's views about either work or leisure may change with his personal fortunes, as when he moves from one occupation or class to another; up or down. It is also expected that views about work and leisure change for the individual as he moves from one phase of his life cycle to another. Particularly does his leisure behaviour change with the phases of his life cycle.

These observations are commonplace, but even so are often not considered when views differ about leisure. Another commonplace is that people frequently endeavour to transmit their views about work and leisure, especially about leisure, to others. Views in these matters are not infrequently loaded with moral evaluations, with the 'should be' of work and leisure. These differences in our modern society stand out sharply partly because the pressures for change of views is great and partly because some are more susceptible to these pressures than others; they turn readier from old ways, more in leisure than in work.

In this chapter we will examine some of these views about work and leisure, although our attention will be mainly on leisure, for the controversy in viewpoint is ever stronger here.

The Provoking Gift of Leisure

LEISURE, THE UNINVITED

Mitchell and Mason called attention to the frequent pessimism among American writers on leisure and recreation; some claiming that people have more leisure than they can use, or more than is good for them, or that they use this precious free time in foolish, if not in evil ways. Such writers have their counterparts in other countries, although the Americans may express themselves more vigorously. Some go so far as to say that the American culture is on the way to ruin and will fall like that of Rome. To Rome 'leisure meant idleness, meant doles, meant free entertainments, meant license and orgies, and corruption'.[1] Mitchell and Mason do well to call such thinking to our notice. There is much more of it than is sometimes realized. We are often told how the Romans were softened by too much leisure, when they probably had very little in the sense that we know leisure. Meerloo is not alone in pointing to the dangers of the easy life and now we increase the danger by making machines that are called 'brains'. Incidently, brains are needed to make the machine and to effectively use it. We quote from Meerloo:

> The dangerous paradox in the boost of living standards is that in promoting ease, it promotes idleness and laziness. If the mind is not prepared to fill leisure time with new challenges and new endeavours, new initiative and new activities, the mind falls asleep and becomes an automaton. The god Automaton devours its own children. It can make highly specialized primitives of us.[2]

Others would argue that the dangers in leisure do not relate so much to ease as to pointless activity, or they mention the absence of social values that enable us to utilize ease in personality development. Then there are the views that relate to

---

[1] Elmer D. Mitchell and Bernard S. Mason, *The Theory of Play*, New York, 1948, p. 209.

[2] Joost A. M. Merloo, *The Rape of the Mind*, 1956, p. 216. Cutten wrote a generation earlier, 'The possession of surplus time, in the use of which one has not been trained, is more dangerous than surplus money under the same circumstances'. George B. Cutten, *The Threat of Leisure*, New Haven, 1926, p. 40. Quoted by Florence G. Robbins in making the point that, wisely used, leisure is man's opportunity for raising the level of culture. See her *Sociology of Play, Recreation and Leisure*, Dubuque, Iowa, 1955, p. 3.

The Provoking Gift of Leisure

the moral motivations of leisure activity, one must do good and avoid evil.

The moral views are not new to us. Let us go back, for example, to Richard Baxter (1615-1619), sometimes called the first Puritan, one who did not even spare himself in making of life an ordeal. His autobiography contained only a few pages on his childhood of which he was not proud. He confessed that at times he had been a very wicked little boy. Some of his juvenile sins confessed in his old age were:

> I was somewhat excessively addicted to play; and that with a covetousness for money.

> I was excessively bewitched with a love of romances, fables, and old tales, which corrupted my affections and lost my time.

> I was guilty of much idle foolish chat, and imitation of the boys in scurrilous foolish words and actions, though I durst not swear.[1]

Baxter lived a dedicated life and he dared to risk his personal safety for his convictions. He knew not leisure and there could have been no place in his thinking for it. He could accept the idea of bodily rest, but indulging in rest beyond need was to waste God's time. He declaimed against idleness as the great tempter. He tolerated, but only somewhat, the idleness of the rich and well-born, when they should be performing good works. Again from his autobiography: 'I more than ever lament the unhappiness of the nobility, gentry and great ones of the world who live in such temptations to sensuality, curiosity and wasting of their time about a multitude of little things, and whose lives are so often the transcript of the sins of Sodom; pride, fulness of bread and abundance of idleness, and want of compassion for the poor.'[2]

Some writers of today, looking back to that time when the nobility was the class with a monopoly on leisure, hold that the old nobility had lived with leisure a long time and had learned how to use it well. Baxter seemed of the view that they had too much leisure and had not learned to use it. Actually, the leisured ones then had work to do, but they also had much more leisure than any in the common classes. It is questionable that they

---
[1] Richard Baxter, *Autobiography*, London.
[2] Ibid., p. 241.

The Provoking Gift of Leisure

had more leisure than industrial workers today. Judged by the standards Baxter used, most people today would be judged much as he judged the nobility then; unready for leisure and not able to use leisure as they should.

Leisure today is called a gift, sometimes a challenge or a threat, a bane or an opportunity. Say Mitchell and Mason, 'leisure can take us along the road to new heights of happiness and attainment, or to the road that spells ruin to ourselves and our civilization'.[1] This implies that even they regard leisure (and they say nothing about work) as a problem, something to be concerned about. Often this attitude of concern is not expressed by some observers, but concern is often implied in their use of the term 'surplus of leisure'.

There are those who feel that if leisure seems to be so much of an obsession for some it is because work has lost its attraction. Modern work has been depersonalized, rendered routine or dull and people who must work welcome an opportunity to get away from it. Cleeton, who writes almost nothing about leisure, puts up a strong argument for making work human. 'To be human, work must become play, a game, an adventure.'[2] He thinks this can be done if everyone makes up his mind to take a zestful interest in his job and in pride of workmanship. He is asking for what many will call the impossible.

What must be recognized is that leisure is here and the amount of it in our lives is increasing. While increasing to this point, leisure was not planned for, and its coming in abundance was hardly expected. Being unprepared for it, and not knowing how to receive it, we have also lacked a capacity for understanding its meaning and potentiality. We have learned little about it, for our attention has been on other aspects of the rapidly-emerging new civilization. While we looked and marvelled at progress leisure was arriving and making itself at home, uninvited and not entirely welcome.

It was not entirely true that the coming of leisure went unnoticed for people of religious interest saw in the increase of free time more opportunity for service to God in performing good works.[3] Also there were those religious thinkers who saw

---
[1] Elmer D. Mitchell and Bernard S. Mason, op. cit., p. 210.
[2] Glenn U. Cleeton, *Making Work Human*, Yellow Springs, Ohio, Antioch Press, 1949, p. 10.
[3] See Klara Vontobel, *Das Arbeitsethos der deutschen Protestantismus*, Bern, 1946, p. 44.

The Provoking Gift of Leisure

in more free time more opportunity for man to develop spiritually, not necessarily in good deeds for others, although that was praiseworthy, in quiet prayer and contemplation by which the soul is enriched.[1] And the practical people urged the use of this time for self-improvement, as when one learns skills or engages in study to advance himself. Whether these views were religious or merely practical, the idea was that this extra time should be used diligently and not to do so was to lapse into idleness.

LEISURE MUST BE EARNED

There were others who saw the coming of leisure in what might be called social conscience terms, and their numbers tend to increase. As they see it, leisure is a gift to man because he has worked and worked to advantage; it is free time he has earned. They go a step further in their thinking, holding that if one has not worked he has not earned leisure and hence is not psychologically or morally prepared for it. The lazy man or the rich idler who has not worked may have free time, but he does not have leisure. This view has been expressed by Lindeman, among others. He regarded leisure as opportunity for personal development, but only for the man who worked and earned it.[2]

The idea that leisure belongs to those who work and who have earned it is not unrelated to the Puritan doctrine of using leisure for personal advancement. One difference is that the earned-leisure advocates recognize that leisure is time for fun as well as personal advancement. Only one can relish the fun more if he has earned it by the sweat of the brow. The worker enjoys his leisure because it supplements his work in making his life complete. It puts him in a mood for work later. Conversely, work tends to ready him for the later enjoyment of leisure.

The earned-leisure concept is also different from Puritanism in that it recognizes leisure not as an uninvited guest, but rather as something which man has developed, however unintentionally, by his work; a by-product. Our problem is to find ways of making sane uses of it, for leisure becomes increasingly important. Sussman wrote:

[1] This view is expressed by Josef Pieper, *Leisure, The Basis of Culture*, 1952. Translation by Alexander Dru.
[2] Eduard C. Lindeman, 'Recreation', see George B. Galloway, Editor, *Planning for America*, New York, 1941, p. 448.

The Provoking Gift of Leisure

In looking at leisure we cannot ignore its relation to work. Leisure today is superseding work in importance in our society. This shift of orientation from work to leisure has been long in coming. The changes during the last thirty years should have prepared us to meet the new life interests of people. Agencies devoted to the recreation, welfare, and social needs of people have given little provocative thought or creative action to meet this need.[1]

THE DO-SOMETHING COMPLEX

To say we were unprepared for leisure is to say mainly that we had not, until very recently, seen leisure in wider perspective. We have looked at it, perhaps, too much as a problem, even in terms of evils that were often enumerated; gambling, drinking, public dances, horse races, child gangs. As Sussman noted in the item just quoted, welfare and other agencies had done nothing to prepare the way for the reception of leisure. Too many agencies were seeing leisure as idleness and their attention was on the excess manifestations, not on total leisure.

Until at least three decades of this century had passed many Americans, as well as British who wrote and talked about leisure and recreation, concerned themselves with what they saw as wrong ways of using free time. Tropp made this observation of the British then:

> In Britain, until comparatively recently, leisure has been treated by most social investigators in its pathological aspects —as a 'problem'—and social surveys have tended to concentrate on betting, drinking, gambling, and sexual delinquency. Frequently spectator sports, ballroom dancing, popular music, cinema, radio, television, the popular press and popular periodicals have been included in the pathology of leisure. British sociology has always been strongly reformist in orientation while British sociologists have been mainly middle class in origin and 'intellectuals' by education. These factors *together* have hindered the proper understanding of the role of leisure in the people's life and the nature of popular culture.[2]

---
[1] Marvin B. Sussman, 'Leisure, Bane or Blessing?' *Social Work*, July 1956, p. 11.
[2] Asher Tropp, 'The Study of Leisure in Great Britain'. Paper presented at the Fourth World Congress of Sociology, Section on Leisure, Stresa, Italy, September, 1959, Mimeographed.

The Provoking Gift of Leisure

American sociology was also reformistic during its early decades and American sociologists worked closely with people and organized groups that concerned themselves with such social problems as the slums, housing, low wages, health, the vices and such leisure activities as Tropp mentions. They, too, were thinking as Smiles did about right ways to spend money and time and would agree with his rule of life to save the pennies and the minutes, and stay out of the 'beer shop'.[1]

Also in the United States as in Britain, there were studies in the areas of leisure, except that attention was on recreation, leading to proposals of one sort of recreation programme or other. There was great faith in the idea that when people are not working, then they should be active in some wholesome recreation, else they would fall into evil ways and find themselves in the wrong company. There was an awareness of leisure but it was not talked about because one talked about recreation, and recreation meant being active. Recreation always had to have a purpose that tied into work and life. Steiner described these views as the 'cult of recreation' whose object was 'physical, mental and moral efficiency'.[2]

If leisure was thought of at all in this context it was seen as empty time with nothing serious to think about and nothing for the hands to do, as an invitation to evil thought and action. The solution? Keep busy, do something that is useful and necessary. Nash put it this way:

> This leisure must be made to contribute to man's advancement, to aid him in his pursuit of happiness, and to give him a sense of worthwhileness. Otherwise it will be a liability and lay the basis for his destruction ... For fullness in living, man must go on doing, achieving and creating. He must be challenged and he must struggle to gain the satisfactions of mastery. He must pursue success to higher and higher levels of accomplishment.[3]

What does one do if he is a professional recreation worker in a community, and if he is guided by the thinking expressed by Nash? He tries to find more and more ways of getting more

---
[1] Samuel Smiles, *Self Help*, 1859, p. 259.
[2] Jesse F. Steiner, 'Recreation and Leisure Time Activities', in *Recent Social Trends in the United States*, 1934, p. 913.
[3] Jay B. Nash, *Philosophy of Recreation and Leisure*, St. Louis, 1953, p. 63.

people to participate in recreation activities. He knows there are many kinds of activities to suit the taste and age of the individual. He is likely to feel very uneasy if he sees increasing numbers of people lying in their hammocks or sitting in rocking chairs. Fortunately the thinking of leaders in the recreation profession tends to be away from that do-something ethic. In fairness to Nash, we must add that he also recognizes that cultural development may call for a certain amount of sitting, or reading or of just talking.[1]

Behind this urge to keep people active during leisure is the idea that recreation is good social medicine, especially for the young, and this is the motivation for much of the organized recreation in the modern community. Private organizations in their appeals for funds use the argument that they perform a stopgap service against delinquency. They provide programmes, and sometimes facilities and places to which youth may turn during free time. Much of this work is becoming a public service through playgrounds, swimming pools, recreation halls, sport fields and so on. The organization and direction of play becomes a professional service for all and no longer focusing its attention on merely combatting delinquency.[2]

PROTEST AGAINST PASSIVITY

Quoting Meadows, 'The new model of industrial man is likely to be less rational, less aggressive, and above all less certain than his predecessor.'[3] Support for this thought was found by Meadows in a group of books reviewed by him, all of which were concerned with the behaviour of man in the industrial urban society. In one way or other, the reviewed books conveyed the idea that modern man is becoming passive. He is less the slave of his mechanized environment than the pliant conformer to it, subordinating himself to whatever forces press upon him. He floats or drifts. The machine civilization, while giving him comfort, has taken his spirit and initiative. As he works so also he plays, in a passive way.

[1] Ibid., p. 21.
[2] Professional recreation workers argue that their service must have a wider base. They are not as policemen standing on guard or as doctors prescribing medicine, but must serve the community positively. See Gerand B. Fitzgerald, *Community Organization for Recreation*, New York, 1948, p. 43.
[3] Paul Meadows, 'Dynamic Technology and Psychic Passivity', *American Journal of Economics and Sociology*, 14, No. 2, January 1955, p. 207.

The Provoking Gift of Leisure

Modern man can be seen as the victim of passivity, and those who hold this view find ample supporting evidence. All about us we can see how people in their adaptation to situations seem to be governed by considerations of expediency and convenience. One avoids discord by taking the easiest course when a more rugged choice might ultimately be more satisfying. At work he looks for the task that calls for no decision-making and at play he would rather while time away on the strand than climb a mountain.

It may be that Riesman had passivity in mind when he classified personalities as being 'tradition-directed', 'inner-directed', and 'other-directed'. The other-directed person is one who, like a receiving set, behaves in terms of promptings and stimulation from without. The inner-directed person is one who is more likely to be guided by his own rationalizations. Some are much more inner-directed than outer- or other-directed, while many more are largely other-directed. It all adds up to a stereotype many hold of the American: shallow in his thinking, free with his money, automatically friendly, and yet not quite sure of himself and his values. This stereotype in many respects 'resembles the kind of character that a number of social scientists have seen as developing in contemporary, highly industrialized and bureaucratic America'.[1] He is active and ever moving, but passive in his choices.

As Riesman recognizes, other-directedness is not peculiarly American, it is a charcteristic of our industrial urban civilization. It is global and, because he is active, the other-directed man is more visible than are his various inner-directed brothers. They are more contemplative while he is more expressive and more happily active, especially in his leisure. He is the happier if he can get others to join him. In his leisure activity he is not likely to be much concerned about meanings, rather, his test of value is likely to be the cost, miles per hour, number of places seen, number of people in the crowd, how loud the applause, etc. For all forms of spectator amusements he is the principal customer.

Touraine made a study of work and leisure in France. He came to the conclusion that passivity must be seen in relation to the commercialization of leisure. The choices of the passive ones

[1] David Riesman with Nathan Glazier and Reuel Denny, *The Lonely Crowd*, 1953, p. 35.

are prompted by the offerings of the leisure market. In this market, Touraine observes, the consumer exercises but a feeble control over the producer and seller. The consumer lacks *sales resistance*; his only sanction being his refusal to buy the leisure goods and services. He accepts the films prepared for him as he accepts the clothes designed for mass consumption, and just so he accepts the mass-produced offerings of the publishing industry. He submits to being a stereotype. This behaviour in. France has been characterized by Touraine as 'le retrait culturel'.

Touraine also observed that those catagories of people most attracted by the 'loisir de masse', are also likely to be little interested in matters of wider community concern. They know well how to circulate in the wider community but have no interest in understanding it or in any active participation in community life. They have their small groups with which they are intimately associated and their main loyalties are to family and friends.[1]

One observation must be made in response to the protest against passivity; namely, that passivity may at times be more apparent than real, and there may be less of it than sometimes appears. To live in a civilization so intensively stimulating as ours one needs to acquire a degree of passivity or immunity. Some degree of passivity is good, but who can say how much?

Another observation is that passivity is native to men in most if not all societies. Otherwise the individual in the primitive or peasant society, where thinking and behaviour are traditionally uniform, would be unhappy indeed. Perhaps the protesters against passivity, like the Puritans before them, expect more individual intiative than is possible. We know that in those days when the leisure class was a small privileged minority, that only a small minority of that minority had initiative and creativity.

CULTURE AND MEDIOCRITY

Somewhat akin to the protest against passivity is the complaint that there is a poverty of imagination in much that most people do and that stupidity characterizes much of leisure activity. Domenach thinks such is to be expected of 'workers chained to the machine nine hours a day, for families living in one or two

[1] Alain Touraine, 'Travail, loisirs, societé', *Esprit*, 27 année, No. 274, juin 1959 p. 999. This entire issue is given to articles reporting on leisure research in France.

The Provoking Gift of Leisure

rooms'. For them the amusement industries offer an artificial paradise to which they may escape and experience something opposite to work. They behave in leisure as in work with attitudes of conformity and irresponsibility. The workers are seen as victims of some organized evil. Domenach asks if we may not say that capitalism, after colonizing the real world, is now colonizing the world of dreams.[1]

Crozier made a study of clerical and other white collar workers in the Paris region. He endeavoured to secure information about their leisure activities and interests, and the cultural level of their interests. Percentagewise, he found that the white-collar Parisiens fall into four categories: 1. High level of culture, 15 per cent; 2. Medium level of culture, 20 per cent; 3. Low or feeble level of culture, 40 per cent, and 4. Lowest or most feeble level of culture, 25 per cent. In arriving at this classification he took account of the types of reading reported, the types of films preferred, and preferences in music, theatre, etc.[2]

With respect to participation in various leisure activities Crozier found that the respondents in his sample could be classified into six groups which percentagewise were: 1. Those with no cultural interests, 11 per cent; 2. Those interested in the cultural forms which included light music, sentimental films and heartthrob reading, 13 per cent; 3. Those with somewhat sedate or traditional cultural interests, 14 per cent; 4. Persons interested in cinema and theatre, in best-selling novels and fashion magazines, 31 per cent; 5. Persons favouring the better films and readers of such works as Steinbeck, Tolstoi, Zola, etc., who rarely buy magazines, 20 per cent; and 6. The group with discriminating cultural interests who read poetry and who read critically such writers as Gide, Claudel, Saint-Exupéry, etc., 11 per cent.[3]

Three conclusions yielded by Crozier's study should be noted:
1. persons least active in their leisure and having fewest social interests were also least integrated in their work enterprises.
2. They tend to be of lower social origin and of less education than the other categories, and their degree of integration into

---

[1] Jean Marie Domenach, 'Loisir et travail', *Esprit*, 27 année, No. 274, juin 1959, p. 1104.
[2] Michel Crozier, 'Employes et petits fonctionnaires parisiens. Notes sur le loisir comme moyen de participation aux valeurs de la societe bourgeoise', *Esprit*, 27 année, No. 274, juin 1959, pp. 947–8.
[3] ibid., pp. 943–5.

social groups was low. 3. But these respondents of lower cultural level and interests tend to be less dissatisfied with their work than are persons of higher cultural level and interests. They are more stable than higher cultural level persons.[1]

Those who concern themselves about the level of taste and thinking of people find support in such studies for their conviction that the cultural level is tending toward mediocrity. The usual conclusion is that education is failing to lift the cultural level, or that commercial pastimes, expecially the mass media, are too effective in promoting mediocrity. The fear, as most Western intellectuals express it, is that the masses have more leisure than they can use, more at least than they can use well. They indulge incoherently in various meaningless activities, crude and mediocre activities. This threatens to pull down the cultural level of the entire society. They will admit that in the random efforts of the masses there is some cultural advance; the 'low brows' are lifted up somewhat, but against that the 'high brows' are pulled down a little. This may be done through the efforts of the lower classes to imitate upper-class culture, or it takes place in the offerings of the amusement industries: 'They cheapen culture.' Or the worker may intrude upon an upper cultural level if he wears the clothes and assumes the manner but lacks the graces of those of better background among whom he presumes to walk along the avenue.

Like the protest against passivity, the complaint about mediocrity assumes that people are being swept along. The difference is that the protesters against passivity see too little individual initiative in the masses while the complainers about mediocrity see too much initiative, most of it meaningless and crude, as measured against the best cultural standards. They not only see excessive random activity, but much of it appears to be pathological. They would probably accept Schelsky's term *Freizeitsüchtigkeit*, which means free-time sickness or mania. Its cultural manifestations are an eager, excited and superficial imitation of the real thing.[2]

'SPECTATORITIS' OR PARTICIPATION

We have already noted the concern of those who feel that leisure is time for self-improvement, the do-something complex. It is

[1] Ibid., pp. 939–40.
[2] Helmut Schelsky, *Die skeptische Generation*, Dusseldorf-Koln, 1957, p. 360.

The Provoking Gift of Leisure

not time to be frittered away in meaningless activity, one should study, acquire skills, read good books, put himself into good company and so on. Closely related to this viewpoint is the opinion of many who see with concern the great number of people who engage in mass pastimes. They sit silently in the movies or they sit shouting at the spectacles, watching football or baseball games, horse or dog races, prize fights and the like. They do not get into the game, their thrill comes from seeing the experts perform. This, Nash holds, is an unproductive use of time, or 'thousands of hours are spent each day listening to others or in trivial reading', another way of watching life from the sidelines.[1] This alleged social sickness is called 'spectatoritis'.

This growing tendency of people to avoid activity and to join the crowds at spectacles is thought to be devitalizing. Again we are reminded that this is what happened in Rome. The population was weakened by spectacles. People had leisure but used it badly. The moral is to turn from spectatorship and join the game; participation awakens the imagination and gives zest to life. Jacks put it this way:

> There is one form of sportsmanship which we don't think it necessary to encourage, that of merely looking on from the sidelines while the game is played by selected teams of professional experts. We are not opposed to that, but we are not contented with it. We want to persuade as many people as possible to play the game themselves, to play some game, instead of merely paying gate money to see a combat btween experts—a state of things which leads to the commercialization of sport.[2]

Jacks was making in the 1930s the same argument that Nash was advancing a generation later. In the meanwhile spectator amusements bounded forward into the ranks of big business. The Neumeyers, looking closer at such amusements, seem less alarmed about them, 'People are really never passive so long as they are alive and paying attention.'[3] Shouting and arguing at a ball game, or intently observing at a movie is often the most precise and critical form of mental participation, no less so than

[1] Jay B. Nash, op. cit., p. 64.
[2] L. J. Jacks, *The Revolt Against Machines*, 1934, pp. 145–6.
[3] Martin H. and Esther S. Neumeyer, *Leisure and Recreation*, New York, 1949, p. 269.

observing the opera or live acting on the stage. The latter would not be called spectatoritis.

The spectatorititis complaint is really a protest against certain types of mass leisure participation, so necessary for agglomerate living. There is no space for everyone to get into the game, and there would be little incentive for many to get into the game if there were no prospect for an audience. It is exactly because there are spectators willing to pay that the game is improved. Most of those who shout at the football game have played the game themselves at some time. They know the game well, else they could not enter with such spirit into this form of psychological participation. Moreover, only a small part of the individual's total leisure is so used.

ON VIEWING WITH ALARM

These fears about leisure and these worries about how it is not being used, in most cases, are serious efforts to understand leisure, often by persons who are judging leisure behaviour against standards of conduct that they feel are being lowered. It is not merely that too many people are having too much leisure too quickly, but they behave like animals turned loose in the spring, and this may pull down the level of culture. This appears to be the view of Toynbee who sees the right use of leisure as something that must grow with time, but the world moves too fast for any ripening. 'At a crisis in its history the Western Society was clipping the wings of a creative minority of a leisured minority and was lavishing leisure on a majority that had not yet had time to grow a new creative core. The immediate cultural effect of this equitable social revolution was as plain as it was deplorable.'[1]

Behind this observation is Toynbee's recognition that the old leisure class had become sterile and the creative minority of that class had apparently got lost in the milling crowd. It is not a complaint against leisure as such but a judgment that the new mass leisure is chaotic and lacks quality. There is not yet what he calls a 'creative core', but it may turn out that the creative core is there, dispersed perhaps in many creative cores which those of that viewpoint would not rate as creative. Is jazz creative? It depends on who is judging it, and when, 1920 or 1960.

[1] Arnold J. Toynbee, *A Study of History*, London, 1955, Vol. IX, p. 611.

The Provoking Gift of Leisure

Soule finds perhaps too much concern among the aristocracy-minded lest culture be vulgarized, making aristocracy less distinctive. The classical aristocrat would have expected this turn of events to debase taste, vulgarize intelligence, and make life easy for the demagogue, because he thought those engaged in work and trade were by birth inferior beings, not just adversely affected by their circumstances. Democracy would dilute the cultural brew to insipidity, perhaps even poison it. Traces of this attitude are often found in modern critics of American society, though usually these critics are too well informed—or too discrete—to put the matter in such crude terms as supposed lack of blue blood in the multitude.[1]

Soule is looking at critics of mass leisure who are concerned about its quality. These are the critics who see the quality of leisure in books of quality, in music above a certain level, in communing with nature instead of sleeping under the apple tree. Here we are confronted with issues involving high and low taste and quality levels, about which the advocates are usually fiercely divided and sometimes so focused on a set of values that they cannot understand that the same person may get a kind of enjoyment out of reading at different levels.

The high-brow versus low-brow issue is less involved among those who worry about the moral implications of certain leisure-time activities as against others. In general, there are two very distinct reasons for moral concern: 1. time is for work and leisure should be used to further one's work; and 2. time if for the enrichment of the personality in the spiritual sence and for good works. The two are often interwoven.

Criticizing British melancholy in the 1860s, Stephen wrote, 'To live without work is not supposed to enter into our conceptions.' Hence the French even then could not understand the serious purposefulness of the English.[2] Work-dedication, so deeply rooted in English culture (and American) a century ago, was the attitude that created so much leisure in the intervening time. To set such attitudes aside or to modify them is a slow process, the more so since they are also linked with the morals

[1] George Soule, *What Automation Does to Human Beings*, London, 1956, p. 151.

[2] 'A Cynic' (Leslie Stephen), 'Vacations', *Cornhill Magazine*, Vol. 20, No. 116, August 1869.

of religion which assume that virtue is not endangered so long as the hands are at work.

The moral fear of leisure is that in certain activities one loses control; if one plays cards one may gamble and gambling may lead to drink or to stealing; if young people dance they are playing in the realm of sex, who can tell to what ends such bodily contact may lead? One must cultivate good thoughts and this is deemed to be impossible if one abandons himself to certain types of play activity. Needless to say, these attitudes change and are changing fast at this time. This applies to critics with moral reservations as well as those with intellectual reservations. Among the intellectuals, for example, folk dancing and folk music are held in high esteem, but the intellectuals of a century or so ago held opposite views. Those same long-dead intellectuals regarded onion soup as something quite plebeian, but today onion soup is served in most 'Left Bank' restaurants of Paris.

AMBIGUITIES OF LEISURE

There is emerging, so Wolfenstein believes, a new attitude toward leisure which she designates 'fun morality', a new sort of compulsion of which people are becoming aware. They must not be mere stay-at-homes, they must join in the life about them. They may feel guilty at the party if it seems they are not having fun. They must be able to let themselves go. But many are held back by something, as Wolfenstein recognizes. They must cultivate a capacity for fun, which means they have reservations blocking them.[1]

Fun morality calls for more of a surrendering of the self than is compatible with Western culture, and many try to ease the process with alcoholic beverages to quiet the censor within. The idea of fun morality, a new tolerance for leisure, does seem to be taking hold. It has become fashionable for leaders in business and industry to look upon leisure with favour, as a sort of medicine for relieving the strains of work. Therefore the 'organization man', as portrayed by Whyte, must have his leisure. He must go through the motions and seem to like it, or risk being regarded with disapproval, if not pity. One must play

[1] Martha Wolfenstein, 'The Emergence of Fun Morality', *Journal of Social Issues*, Vol. 7, No. 4, 1951, pp. 3–16.

The Provoking Gift of Leisure

but not too much. One may lose himself in fun but not dive too deep. He dares not neglect the job where his real interest lies, or is supposed to, else he might not move forward and upward occupationally. Quoting Whyte: 'The "broad gauge" model we hear so much about these days is the man who keeps work separate from leisure and the rest of his life. Any organization man who managed to accomplish this feat wouldn't get very far. He still works hard, in short, but now he has to feel somewhat guilty about it.'[1]

The dilemma of the organization man, the little manager aspiring to become a big manager, is not unlike that of many another lesser worker of energy faced with an open-ended future. He is still a Puritan in his philosophy of work and success, but he is expected to become a little less than a Puritan in his philosophy of leisure. He must be a work-centred and duty-conscious person on the job, but he is supposed to put on another coat and another manner away from the job. Common workers do that anyhow.

That is one of the ambiguities of leisure. Another concerns saving and accumulation and another concerns the 'constructive' use of time. Both, if strictly followed, would redound negatively for leisure.

The doctrine of saving has ever been basic to capitalism. But if all people did all the saving possible under this Puritan mandate they would have to forgo much of their spending for leisure, and limit themselves in other forms of consumption. Industry would suffer. If all people are to have full employment there must be full consumption. Consuming and spending has become a modern virtue. Actually, few people save very much; it is being done for them in the accumulations of corporations and in the social security programmes of governments. There is less need to save against old age if the individual is assured of a pension.[2]

As for the use of time for self-improvement, the Puritan mandate calls for a serious goal-directed use of free time. If he reads, he should gather from the printed page good thoughts and bits of wisdom which might be used in bright conversation, or his reading should be study for improvement, then he will be

[1] William H. Whyte, Jr., *The Organization Man*, 1956, p. 18.
[2] Alessandro Pizzorno, 'Accumulation, loisirs, et rapports de classe', *Esprit*, 27 année, No. 274, juin 1959, p. 1014.

ready when opportunity comes. If he plays, it should be to keep physically fit or to gain skills. In part, the complaint against spectator amusements reflects this view about using leisure. Having fun unrestrained is contrary to this idea of using leisure.

Regarding the first-mentioned ambiguity in which the manager expects his staff to make use of their leisure, putting work out of mind, the interest in leisure is utilitarian; it affords change and relaxation. There is little or no interest in learning how to use leisure. In the second two ambiguities mentioned, leisure is rejected except as it can be used for getting ahead. Puritanism offers little in the way of preparing the individual to use leisure in the development of interests and in a balanced way of life. Hence the individual in a leisure-rejecting culture is left to his own devices. Understandably, Mills sees much emptiness in the efforts of most people to make use of their leisure time.

> The amusement of hollow people rests on their own hollowness and does not fill it up; it does not calm or relax them, as old middle-class frolics and jollification may have done; it does not recreate their spontaneity in work, as in the craftsman model. Their leisure diverts them from the restless grind of their work by the absorbing grind of passive enjoyment of glamour and thrills. To modern man leisure is the way to spend money, work is the way to make it. When the two compete, leisure wins hands down.[1]

The hollow people of today are probably no more so than were the grandparents in the days of 'old-fashioned frolics and jollification', but then they were not spending time and money in a competitive leisure market where the choices are largely individual and where different people hold different views about the leisure choices of others. The choices in old times were those of the community. If we judged the fiestas of Latin-American communities by the same standards, much of the activity seen there would have to be called hollow. As Lewis describes these festivals in the villages and towns of Mexico, they are the 'main source of diversion for all groups' and there are different ways of enjoying a fiesta from dancing to contests such as riding, from parading and singing to furtive lovemaking and less furtive alcoholic excesses. The spirit of festival is one of

---
[1] C. Wright Mills, *White Collar, the American Middle Classes*, 1951, p. 238.

The Provoking Gift of Leisure

temporary tolerance for all sorts of fun. But the fun is shared in various ways by the community.[1] Out of this setting, in a more sophisticated environment, much of it might seem hollow and crude.

This brings to a fourth type of ambiguity of modern leisure, one mentioned by Touraine; it does not fuse people into a single 'homogenous public', rather it permits and promotes separateness. This had been one of the functions of village festivals, they fused all the people into a fun-making aggregate. People are isolated into fragmented groups or by class.[2] Fun-seeking is a social activity and it can be found in small groups as well, and this ambiguity to which Touraine points is less serious than may be assumed. Community-wide homogeneity is not possible in the heterogeneous community. It may not be necessary that the cultural values associated with leisure be the same for all classes. Cultural values between classes have apparently always been different, but in the modern community there is more competition between classes, which makes us more aware of the contrasting values as demonstrated in leisure-time activity.

NEW THINKING ABOUT LEISURE

It is to be expected that responsible people, today as formerly, will have wide differences of opinion about how leisure should be used. It is nothing new that social reformers and intellectuals should have different views on this subject, but the views change in both groups. Social reformers today hold views about leisure which would have been heresy to social reformers of 1850 or even 1900. Intellectuals, to use the term loosely, are ever changing their views, both about work and leisure. Between the two stands the practical man who holds with neither the reformers nor the intellectuals, although the American practical man has usually been more sympathetic with the reformers. He is better able to understand what they are getting at, although he may not hold their objectives in very high regard but, as Cohen observed, he has ever been sceptical of intellectuals.

In no other country is the word *intellectual* so often used as a term of derision and opprobrium. This is true, not only of the

[1] Oscar Lewis, *Life in a Mexican Village, Tepoztlán Revisited*, Urbana, 1951, p. 208.
[2] Alain Touraine, op. cit., p. 999.

The Provoking Gift of Leisure

backward rural regions where, under the influence of poverty, ignorance and fundamentalism, intellectual enlightenment is generally feared. It is also true of the supposedly more advanced Eastern states where to be called a *mere theorist* is likewise to be damned. As a people we do not enjoy reflective thinking for its own sake as a noble way of spending our leisure.[1]

If there is any doubt about Cohen's observation, one needs but to remember the contempt with which the Roosevelt Administration after 1932 was held because a flood of trained persons were brought into the government, a course that city governments had already taken and state governments were soon to follow. These new public servants were called 'brain-trusters'. Since that day the universities have had to add many special courses and some departments to train specialists in new fields for business and government.

Since that time many who might even now be called reformers have also become intellectuals of a kind. There are now sorts of intellectuals, types which were only coming on the scene a generation ago. Intellectualism, however defined, becomes widespread and diffused.

A wide range of these intellectual élites now turn their attention to the phenomena of work and leisure. Taken together they present a spectacle of seeming confusion, especially as they turn their critical focus on leisure. Even though this new thinking about leisure has not yet resulted in a solid front, the direction is away from the old stereotypes. The problems are not being solved, that is true. As Brew observed, leisure is still big business and the young are caught in a situation involving strain and stress and they need wise guidance.

> They are frequently left to cope with the question of social adjustment, on the physical and emotional level, with problems of behaviour in work and leisure, and as if this were not enough, with religious and ethical conflicts, with almost no adult guidance. Meanwhile the press, the cinema, the club, the uniformed organizations, the church, the dance hall, the pin-ball saloon, the public house and the home are competing for their bodies with all the desire to exploit them which characterized the body-snatchers of a more downright

[1] Morris R. Cohen, *American Thought, a Critical Sketch*, Glencoe, 1957, p. 18.

The Provoking Gift of Leisure

age, when they at least waited for death before engaging in their grim work.[1]

Actually, the situation is not without encouraging trends and prospects. Much of the prudishness has vanished in the leisure relationships enjoyed by both sexes. Card-playing, removed from the sin category, is now a good way to spend a quiet evening, especially for those not good at conversation. There is much less bombast and pugnaciousness in sport, and now women can participate in sports without loss of lady-status. The old distinctions between upper-class and lower-class pastimes tend to disappear.

Much of the coarseness has gone out of public manners. On the promenade, at the theatre, on the beaches the classes can no longer be easily distinguished. There is much less of awkwardness among the working classes in their leisure-time activities, and there is a marked absence of the silly emptiness in their behaviour, so common a few decades ago. While people are not less fashion-conscious, much of the old garishness and loudness has gone out of the dress of women, The poor girl may even become a movie queen without undergoing a Pygmalian evolution. Even the bad manners of the rich, often paraded in the 1890s with extravagant display, have disappeared.[2]

Without the guidance of any central authority, industrial society is evolving new institutions of leisure. Reformers, intellectuals and others, differing though their views may be, contribute to this trend. The debate keeps the issues alive, and this is an educational force. Even the lowest common level of the culture is stimulated, but it is not today the lowest common level of 1850, nor of 1900. This social evolution is being speeded precisely because there is more leisure, and leisure is also a reformer.

SUMMARY

Most everyone agrees that man should work, but there may be different views about the work one person or another should do, or about how much work is enough. There is little dispute about the injunction that man should earn his bread by work,

---

[1] J. Macalister Brew, *Youth and Youth Groyps*, 1957, p. 18.

[2] Foster Rhea Dulles, *America Learns to Play*, 1952, is a good review of this evolution.

but many believe he should work for other reasons as well. Some see work as a religious duty, a sacrament. There are also moral arguments; one who works is not likely to be tempted into evil ways. Otherwise he might lapse into idleness which, in religious terms, is sin because idleness is time-wasting. Time, God's gift to man, must not be frittered away. Again, work is called a social good, because it permits the worker to feel a sense of self-respect in his community.

Opinions are far less unanimous regarding leisure. Many people still look with suspicion on even a little leisure, and they may hold very strict views about how leisure should be used; or more correctly, about how it should not be used. For many people, their attitudes toward leisure are of a piece with their attitudes toward work. Life to them is a continuous serious endeavour. For example, one may use leisure for rest, but if there is more than can be used for rest it should be invested in self-improvement, not irresponsibly spent in merely having fun.

This idea of putting leisure to work may not be used always to advance a religious argument. It may be promoted on very practical, although equally Puritan grounds. There may be no objection to man having ample leisure, but he should *do something* with it. Here is an opportunity to gain knowledge, develop skills, cultivate his social and artistic faculties and advance himself culturally, moving into a higher job perhaps.

The above viewpoints about leisure are essentially conservative in that they would, in most instances, conserve old forms and values. But they are less concerned about conserving old forms and values in work. Against these viewpoints there are others that are often critical of modern leisure. They would not go back to old forms and values, but ahead to new ones. Leisure is called opportunity for enlarging one's social and intellectual horizon. This criticism of leisure as they see it, often advanced by intellectuals of different kinds, finds expression in various complaints about growing passivity. People seem, these critics claim, to be living their days without zest or purpose. At work or play, they tend to be stereotypes. Perhaps they lack inner resources or they do nothing to develop themselves.

It is feared that a passive population of floaters, not swimmers, may plunge our civilization into non-creative sterility. Passivity in this sense is not new. Apparently a good share of the population has always been rutted into one stereotype or other, but

The Provoking Gift of Leisure

we see increasing variety among stereotypes. The élite is no longer a small group of noble birth, there are many élites and each has its influence of ways on work and leisure. The lowest cultural level for social and leisure life is far higher (by any standard) today than in 1900 and still higher than in 1850. The distance between low-brow and high-brow uses of leisure tends to narrow.

The debate about leisure and work, whether religious, moral or intellectual, has doubtless been very helpful to this evloution. The debate has been an important educational force. But leisure is itself an educational force. A people, normally creative in their work, if given free time will be equally creative in their leisure. This is not saying that there is no need for concern about how people use their leisure, or how some use it; that is a problem of control and guidance which will be more fully considered in Chapter 9.

5

SOME PERTINENT ASPECTS OF LEISURE

WHEN a man works it is usually possible in terms of quality and quantity to see what he has done. For any kind of work it is possible to visualize a man-day of labour. Work submits to measurement, leisure not. When work time is paid for the employer must be able to estimate in advance what he will get. Leisure has no standard measurement; its value changes from person to person and from one situation to another. Yet people continue their efforts to measure leisure activity. They count the hours people spent for a given period viewing television, listening to the radio, reading, gardening, attending spectator amusements and so on. One is not always sure what is being measured. While recognizing that these studies do have value for some purposes, they seldom tell us much about leisure.

In this chapter we will see our subject from a number of perspectives, considering only some of the aspects of leisure and obligated non-work time. The effort may perhaps indicate the complexity of the subject and bring to our attention in different ways the inter-relatedness of work, leisure and other life interest. Let us look first at the cost of such free-time activity.

LEISURE AS CONSUMER SPENDING

Lundberg observed in connection with his study of leisure in a New York suburb, that leisure is ever associated with spending money. 'Not infrequently the desire to buy more leisure becomes the primary incentive for more and harder work.'[1] We can hardly think of leisure activity that can be enjoyed without spending money; it may be from trifling amounts to much more than can be afforded. Even a stroll through the park is not free, the cost comes to the citizen on his tax bill.

If one is asked what part of his monthly or annual income is spent for leisure, he would find the answer difficult. He might have a problem making a list of his leisure expenditures over the past few days. For such reasons national estimates of the cost of leisure are highly uncertain. Saunders and Parker estimated that in 1953 Americans spent $30 billion on leisure consumption, 'which is half as much as the American consumer spends on clothing and shelter, and twice what he pays out for new cars or home goods'. The leisure market is a composite of many special markets, all of which overlap with other markets[2] The estimates, moreover, exclude such marginal items as liquors and tobacco, the consumption of which may or may not relate to leisure, and these expenditures are large ($6.5 billion for cigarettes in the United States in 1958), as are food costs, some of which relate to leisure.

The $30.6 billion estimated leisure cost for 1953, a year of full employment was a three-fold increase over the estimated $10.17 billion leisure cost for 1929–1930, a depression year. Steiner estimated that about two-thirds of the 1929–1930 leisure outlay went for travel and vacations,[3] but not more than a fourth of the 1953 leisure outlay went for travel and vacations,[4] yet more people had vacations in 1953. This is perhaps because in 1953 people had more money for other leisure expenditures. For 1957 an estimated $37 billion was spent by Americans on leisure and 80 million Americans took vacations at a total cost of about $12 billion.[5]

Even if we cannot estimate, except in fragmentary terms, the cost of leisure, we may be sure that relatively as well as abso-

[1] George A. Lundberg, Mirra Komarovsky and Mary A. McInerny, *Leisure, a Suburban Study*, New York, 1934, p. 85.

[2] Dero A. Saunders and Sanford S. Parker, '$30 Billion for Fun', *Fortune*, Vol. 49, No. 6, June 1954, p. 115.

[3] Jesse F. Steiner, 'Recreation and Leisure Time Activities', in *Recent Social Trends in the United States*, New York, 1934, p. 949.

[4] Saunders and Parker, op. cit., p. 119.

[5] These figures were received from the National Recreation Association Correspondence and Consultation Service.

lutely the figures are high, especially during times of full employment. It would not be excessive for the United States to estimate leisure spending at about 10 per cent of all consumer expenditures, which would include only the more obvious leisure outlays. The ratio would be about the same in other industrial urban countries. Such spending is something modern man feels impelled to do if he would enjoy life. It is for the enjoyment of leisure, as some see it, that man works. He sells time so he will be able to pay for his fun. We quote Mills:

> Each day men sell little pieces of their lives in order to buy them back each night and week-end with the coin of 'fun'. With amusement, with love, with movies, with vicarious intimacy, they pull themselves into a sort of whole again, and now they are different men. Thus the cycle of work and leisure gives rise to two quite different images of self; the everyday image based upon work, and the holiday image, based upon leisure.[1]

For many people work and leisure stand in some such opposite relation to each other; each represents one phase of a double transaction. Work is the treadmill one enters to earn his money, and leisure is the house of fun where he spends it, usually all he can afford. From this level of strenuous leisure to that of casual leisure a variety of work-leisure linkages may be found, but at each point or linkage or level, leisure calls for some spending; we can only guess how much relatively this is.

INVOLVEMENTS IN LEISURE SPENDING

We can name four reasons why estimates on the cost of leisure are usually uncertain. These serve to remind us how overlapping leisure activity is with other activities which are marginal to leisure. Just so the costs of leisure are mixed with other costs.

1. *Public Costs.* In many ways the cost of leisure activity is included in the tax bill. All levels of government provide free-time facilities: parks, playgrounds, promenades, beaches, ski-jumps, wild-life areas, dancing pavilions, theatres, museums, libraries, the list is long. In these facilities services are provided: play leaders, teachers, life guards and various attendants

---

[1] C. Wright Mills, *White Collar, the American Middle Classes*, New York, Oxford University Press, 1951, p. 237.

Some Pertinent Aspects of Leisure

including those who keep order. Since millions use automobiles, the public roads become an important leisure facility for those who would go to public camping places or forest preserves, or even for the pleasure of driving.

2. *Mass Media Costs.* Radio listening and television viewing are often seen as low-cost leisure activities; one needs but to buy the receiving sets and maintain them. Here is mass entertainment that the individual privately could never afford. Actually he pays the cost each time he buys tooth paste, razor blades, cigarettes, gasoline or other article advertised over the airways. Even at that the cost is not high because it is shared with millions of other listeners and viewers. In countries where these facilities are owned by government the user pays a tax on his receiving sets. In Germany the tax is about six dollars per year, which is low cost entertainment.

3. *Mixed Costs.* The family automobile is a facility for leisure use as well as a utility for work, but who can say what part of the cost should be charged to leisure? The family has guests for dinner or there is a birthday party; leisure is mixed with ceremony and family obligations. So also are the costs mixed. Social occasions may be costly but they are not included in the estimates of leisure cost. Another area of mixed costs includes clothing for parties, sport clothes and personal decorations. A family with no leisure interests would also spend much less on house furnishings. These mixed costs tend to rise with one's income and social class.

4. *Transferred Costs.* Leaders in business or industry tend to enjoy certain privileges while travelling for the firm. The manager may take his wife along. She can visit friends, see the sights or go shopping while he keeps appointments and they can have their evenings together. His work finished, the manager may stay a day or so longer, charging it to his vacation. This is not a 'swindle sheet' technique, but the manager and his wife have a short holiday and part of the cost is paid by the firm. Public officials may do the same and still not be guilty of misusing public funds. In some European countries the firm may own a number of automobiles which are assigned to the employees and they are often used for all purposes as if they were privately owned. The reasons for the practice have to do with saving on taxes. Or the firm may contribute money for various types of leisure activities for the work force, excursions,

Some Pertinent Aspects of Leisure

picnics, Christmas parties and so on. These are but a few of many ways that the cost of leisure is transferred.

Assuming a year of full employment, such as 1960 is, and assuming that 1960 level of living, it would be safe to estimate that the usually listed leisure expenditure, plus leisure-related expenses would total about 15 per cent of consumer costs. This, we add, would be a conservative estimate.

TIME GIVEN TO LEISURE

It is hardly necessary to give more than passing mention to the shortening of the work day and work week. Around 1850 the seven-day, 70-hour week was not unusual. Even in 1900 the six-day week of 72 hours prevailed. (This writer's father worked the 12-hour shift seven days per week in an iron furnace in Michigan as late as 1911). By 1950 the work week in most industrial countries came down to about 44 hours and is now approaching 40 hours. This means that industrial urban workers have gained from twenty to thirty hours of time from their work over the past five or six decades and, reckoned in terms of money values today, wage and salary incomes have more than doubled.

On the basis of such figures, observers come to various conclusions about the abundance of leisure most workers have gained during about a half-century. How much leisure time has been gained is worth noting. The California Department of Water Resources in 1958 had a study made to determine the uses to expect of the Cache Creek Basin recreation area fifty

TABLE 1

Work and non-work time for a worker in 1958

Uses of time	Days		Hours	Total hours
Work week	240	×	8	1,920
Sleeping	365	×	8	2,920
Eating, commuting	365	×	$3\frac{1}{2}$	1,277
Weekday leisure	240	×	$4\frac{1}{2}$	1,080
Weekend leisure	104	×	$12\frac{1}{2}$	1,300
Holidays	11	×	$12\frac{1}{2}$	138
Vacations	10	×	$12\frac{1}{2}$	125

Some Pertinent Aspects of Leisure

years hence. Table 1 shows the estimated work and non-work time of a worker in 1958, a total of 2,643 hours of leisure. The forecast for 2010 was 3,261 hours of leisure, an anticipated gain of 618 hours per year at the expense of work time.[1]
Lundberg found that leisure time varied among suburban dwellers. It was 438 minutes per day for male white-collar workers compared with 399 minutes or about six and a half hours, but this included eating time. Executives reported an average of 401 minutes, while the leisure for housewives was about 330 minutes per day. These were middle-class housewives most of whom had maids, still they had less leisure than their husbands.[2]
For most people who work the distribution of weekly hours would be about as follows:

Work	44	Eating, personal care	17
Work-connected travel	6	Leisure or free time	45
Sleep	56	Total	168

This means forty-five hours, more or less, of free or non-work time. Over the year this would be increased by holidays and vacation time. It is loosely called leisure, but actually much of it is not.

NON WORK OBLIGATED TIME

In their estimate of leisure costs in the United States, Saunders and Parker excluded activities carried on at home; cooking which 'to some few people is both an art and a job', and do-it-yourself activities. They excluded gardening as being work as well as leisure. These are but a few of the many activities one engages in at home. He may also use his free time for club work, especially if he is an active member of organized groups.[3] Lundberg rated suburban housewives as conspicuously in the leisure class, but:

> They are also the most ready to assure the investigator that they 'have no leisure at all'. It is clear that, just as the paid work of the gainfully employed is frequently mixed with

[1] Figures provided by the National Recreation Association Correspondence and Consultation service.
[2] Lundberg, Komarovsky, and McInerny, op. cit., pp. 100–1.
[3] Saunders and Parker, op. cit., p. 115.

leisure and recreational elements, so the leisure of such groups as housewives is frequently occupied with more or less obligatory activities which no longer yield the peculiar satisfactions which we associate with leisure pursuits.[1]

Of such duty-oriented activities during non-work time, Pipping wrote, 'In active minds leisure means anything but idleness. Club meetings, "going places", and visiting parties are no longer—and probably never were—ends in themselves, but have always become part of the obligatory activities of life and lost their essential nature as leisure.'[2] These obligations are often continuous; they may be repeated as chores each day or they may continue for many days as when a man bit by bit paints his house.

Dumazedier would include as free obligated time the hours a worker may give to an extra job, work for pay in addition to his regular job. During his study of leisure at Anecy, France, he found that 25 per cent of the workers were doing such extra jobs, and 60 per cent of these regarded the second job as a source of pleasure. He reasoned that for many such work was satisfying because workers had the opportunity to perform tasks with their hands and as individuals, a relief from the regimented work at the work place. Dumazedier suggests that in modern society a new type of *Homo Faber* is developing, one who earns his living in a routine industrial job, but part of his own time is used for doing work that he enjoys. He may put the extra earnings to good use, but he earns his living mainly on a regular job.[3] When such extra work becomes chronic, however, it is regarded by the trade unions as unfair. In some European countries it is called 'black' because it is not reported to the employment offices. American trade unionists call it 'moonlighting'.

Much of the work done during free time is performed at home. It may at times be a type of recreation and again it may be an economy effort to save the cost of hiring work done. This is nothing new for Americans. On the frontier and on the farm still people know how to use handtools and work in the house

[1] Lundberg, Komarovsky, and McInerny, op. cit., p. 99.

[2] Hugo E. Pipping, *Standards of Living, a Concept and its Place in Economics*, Copenhagen, Munksgaards Forlag, 1953, p. 1958.

[3] Joffre Dumazedier, 'Realites du loisir et ideologies', *Esprit*, 27 année, No. 274, juin 1959, p. 879.

Some Pertinent Aspects of Leisure

or around home has never been anything unusual. But among most urbanites, few of whom know how to use handtools even a simple task like mending a chair or making a window screen is a major undertaking. This helplessness when confronted with simple tasks that wait to be done has stimulated enterprising firms to prepare do-it-yourself kits with tools and full instructions; how to paint furniture, how to paper a room, how to make a bookshelf, how to make a stone garden seat, how to cultivate a flower bed, how to grow vegetables; the variety is great.

The United States Department of Commerce in 1954 issued a business information pamphlet which indicated that do-it-yourself in 1954 was a $6 billion market and growing, another cost not included among leisure expenditures, as was noted above. Here we are informed that do-it-yourself falls into six areas of activity:

1. Structural home improvements (building a garage)
2. Home decoration (painting, wallpapering)
3. Home furnishing (making or finishing furniture, slip covering)
4. Gardening and maintenance of grounds
5. Home dressmaking and sewing
6. Hobbies (model-building, cabinet making)[1]

It may be that leisure, as it is seen by many (free time for enjoyment unrelated to work) is an abnormality. At any rate, it seems that the more integrated the individual is in family life, in the life of formal and informal groups and with other duty activity the less leisure he may have. Like one who is personally immersed in his work, he thinks little about leisure. Or if he engages in leisure even that may contain an element of obligation, as when the father of the family goes once a week to bowl

---

[1] Robert J. Bond, 'Summary of Information on the Do-it-yourself Market', *Business Service Bulletin No. 84*, U.S. Department of Commerce, November 1954. Do-it-yourself, as leisure-time venturing into special kinds of work, has also reached England. We quote Brew: 'Coming to us as it has from America, a compound of financial stringency and the high cost of labour, it has given many people a high degree of creative satisfaction. Moreover, the do-it-yourself fashion has produced those innumerable and fascinating gadgets such as paint rollers which are fun to use and give the adolescent an opportunity to use tools which in the home are commonly the playthings reserved for parents who have developed the zest of children for splashing an infinite variety of colours on their walls.' J. Macalister Brew, *Youth and Youth Groups*, London, 1957, p. 248.

with his friends; he dare not be absent, or the mother of the family would be embarrassed if she failed to appear at the meeting of her social club.

LEISURE FOR WIVES AND MOTHERS

Much of the activity of the man at home, non-work obligations which may yield a leisure satisfaction, would be ordinary work for the wife and mother. If he helps care for the children, she is relieved of some of her work. For him it may be recreation to work in the garden, but for her it may be work, except as she may give time caring for flowers. In most industrial countries a fourth to a third of the wives and mothers have jobs outside the home. Girard reported on a study of the work time and free time of employed wives and women who were housewives only in the larger French cities. It was found that employed women, after doing their housework, had 3.3 free hours daily for the week and 7.8 hours of free time on Sundays. The women who were housewives only had 4.4 hours of free time daily and 7.2 hours on Sunday. For women in each group Sunday meant an extra hour of sleep.[1]

Table 2 shows work hours at home and on the job for each

TABLE 2

Hours of work weekly for French urban housewives, 1958, those with and without jobs, by number of children,

Number of children	Housewives with outside jobs			Housewives only
	Hours of housework	Hours for job travel	Total	
None	27.2	50.1	77.3	54.3
1	39.1	44.5	83.6	71.2
2	46.6	36.9	83.5	75.5
3 or more	49.7	34.3	84.0	77.5

group of women.[2] Each group is divided according to the number of children reported, or no children. We see that the married women with jobs but without children spent 50.1 hours weekly at work or travelling to and from work, and 27.2 hours

[1] Alain Girard, 'Le budget-temps de la femme mariee dans les agglomerations urbaines', *Population*, Vol. 13, No. 4, Octobre-Decembre 1958, p. 614.
[2] Ibid., pp. 606-7.

Some Pertinent Aspects of Leisure

on housework, a total of 77.3 hours. A wife without children and without outside employment gave 54.3 hours weekly to her housework. We note that the women with children and outside employment tend to diminish their employed time as they have more children and their hours of housework increase. The hours the working woman gives to the household is probably the bare minimum needed for comfort and appearance, but for each line the 'housewives only' women give much more time to their home work. There are some who would say that the employed wives accomplish more in their housework time than do non-employed housewives. They argue that working wives must apply themselves more systematically to their housework, while the non-working wives mingle their work with listening to the radio, talking with neighbours and other interruptions.

The study in France supports an earlier study at Bryn Mawr College which showed that housewives in American cities of 100,000 or more population devoted 80.6 hours per week to their housework, while housewives in cities under 100,000 averaged 78.4 hours of housework per week. The average for farm wives was 60.6 hours per week. And the urban housewive has the most labour-saving household equipment, but urban living is more complex and adds duties not essential in the country.[1]

HOLIDAYS AND VACATIONS

There is nothing new about holidays; they are found in all cultures. If they did not originate as religious ceremonials they may be of national origin. Of the first type, Christmas and Easter are examples, but many harvest and spring festivals are much older. Those of politcal origin are typified by Independence Day in the United States or Bastille day in France. In many countries May First is Labour Day, but Labour Day in the United States is the first Monday in September. The European May Day was an ancient spring festival which has since been urbanized by the industrial workers.

Not only were most of the old holidays of rural or primitive origin but they occur at times of the year when the conditions of nature or the work afforded free time. Often they served the purpose of release from periods of strict work application, as

---
[1] Reported by Margaret Mead, *Male and Female*, 1949, p. 332.

well as release from the various moral codes. As these old holidays have been brought into modern life they have become more formal and ceremonial, as carnival in some countries, although they have not been fully stripped of their initial fun and folly character.

The vacation, especially the vacation with pay, is a fairly modern institution, and a supplement to week-ends and holidays. With the coming of paid vacations it is becoming customary for workers also to be paid for holidays if they come on a normal work day. Holidays have always been occasions of collective relief from routine and of collective leisure; dancing, singing, feasting and even orgies. The vacation is more of an individual matter, although in the aggregate, particularly in summer, it assumes a mass character. Saunders and Parker estimated that in 1953 American workers had 60 million weeks of vacation time which resulted in about $8 billion of vacation spending.[1] For 1958, with longer paid vacations and more of them, Americans probably had close to 80 million weeks of vacation time.

Counting ten legal holidays a year for which workers are paid, counting fifty-two Sundays and the same number of half-Saturdays, and an average of fourteen days of paid vacation, most modern workers enjoy from 100 upward of free days during the year. It may be less for the diminishing ranks of unskilled workers, but it increases with higher level occupations. This is time the cost of which is paid for out of the total product of labour during the 250 or so work days of the year. For the less favoured workers it may be 265 work days and for the most favoured about 230 work days. This means that holidays and vacations become the major item in modern man's leisure-time calendar and the major item among his leisure-time expenditures. Often vacation spending, forces curtailments in other forms of leisure spending.

Because he makes effective use of science and technics, modern man makes industry more productive, which enables him to gain more free hours in the day and more free days in the year. Under the same influences, plus the stimulation of industrial urbanism, agriculture becomes more productive, and rural man is also gaining more free time. It all results in more holiday and vacation activity. A small indication of this growth

[1] Saunders and Parker, op. cit., pp. 119, 226.

Some Pertinent Aspects of Leisure

is given by Clawson who reports that in 1910 less than 100,000 persons visited national parks and forests in the United States, but since 1950 the visitors to these places exceed two million annually. In 1910 the problem was to induce people to visit these public recreation areas, now the problem is one of caring for the crowd.[1] Vacations and holidays are occasions for urbanites to go to the country, breaking in on the old rural serenity. In France immediately following the war some 400,000 youth went to the country on camping trips. By 1950 the number of youthful campers each summer was near 1,200,000. Urbanites, so Dumazedier observes, think unrealistically about the country. As they rush countryward out of the cities each summer looking for fun and freedom, they often become a great nuisance because they don't know how to behave. It adds fuel to the bias of country people against urbanites, believed by many farmers to be idlers even when they claim to be working.[2] In addition to families and youth camping, there are crowds of tourists who go to the conventional resorts in the mountains or by the sea where they enjoy all the urban comforts plus the illusion of contact with country and nature.

THE CONVENTIONAL VACATION

With the growing number of vacations and the growing length of the average vacation, with millions going here and there to find escape in vacation, it is to be expected that the leisure industries will make the most of this growing form of consumption. Here is grist and money for the popular magazines and the press. Vacation reading and advertising are enormous items not included in leisure cost estimates. Costs most frequently mentioned are those lumped under the term 'tourism', and tourism in some countries is a major item in the national budget. In 1957 European hotels and hostels reported 33 million tourist days. Many who travelled on bicycles or as hitch hikers and camping along the way were not included. Nor was it possible to keep a record on the increasing number of families travelling in their own automobiles and camping wherever

[1] Marion Clawson, 'The Crisis in Outdoor Recreation', *American Forests*, March–April 1959, p. 7.
[2] Joffre Dumazedier, see discussion in Georges Friedmann, Editor, *Villes et Campagnes*, Paris, 1953, p. 238.

convenient or living in trailers. Over 90 per cent of tourism in Europe is packed into the period between the first of April to the first of October, with the peak during the months of July and August.[1]

Vausson reported that in France in 1957 about 10 million individuals, nearly a fourth of the population, went on vacations away from home. The percentages ranged from about zero for rural villages to 44 per cent for larger towns and 72 per cent for Parisians. Vacations away from home were enjoyed by 82 per cent of the higher income groups compared with 23 per cent for workers, and 41 per cent of all Frenchmen took no vacation away from home for the want of money. Of the 10 million who took vacations away from home in 1957, about 1.3 million went to other countries. Vausson was able to get comparative figures for pre-war tourism of French abroad on but two countries. For 1936–1937 French vacationists spent 261,162 nights in Austria compared with 926,174 nights in 1956–1957, while in 1938 French vacationists spent 932,294 nights in Switzerland compared with 2,393,459 nights in 1957.[2]

The most sought tourists in Europe are the Americans because they bring the needed dollars, but the cost of travel brings down the number to less than half a million a year. Equally important are the Germans of whom about four million took vacations in foreign countries during 1958. According to the German Ministry of Transport, German vacationists spent about $511 million in foreign countries in 1958, while tourists to German spent but $477 million.[3]

Leisure activities of many kinds may figure in vacation time, in particular it includes the outdoor sports. It is part of the idea of vacation to engage in sports and other activities in the open. One may 'rough it' and go hunting or fishing, camping in the wilds. Boating and water sport figure in another type of vacation. One may go to a dude ranch and ride horses, dressing like a cowboy after the Hollywood model and behaving as a storybook cowboy should. If the vacation is spent in the mountains, one must make hiking trips or try mountain climb-

[1] *Tourism in Europe*, Paris, Organization for European Economic Co-operation, 1958, pp. 5, 19.
[2] Claude Vausson, 'Vacances a l'etranger', *Esprit*, 27 annee, No. 274, juin 1959, pp. 1023–5.
[3] Article by Robert Sage, *New York Herald Tribune*, Paris Edition, 6 October 1959, p. 3.

Some Pertinent Aspects of Leisure

ing. Other vacation spots may feature golf or tennis. The increase in the various outdoor sports in the United States since the war is phenomenal, paralleling the increase in vacationing. Typical of this growth in outdoor activity are the figures which follow. These are assembled by the Athletic Association of Chicago.

	1946	1956	1959
Boating	20,000,000	28,000,000	37,000,000
Fishing	13,100,000	20,813,000	25,620,000
Hunting	9,990,000	11,784,000	18,000,000
Ski-ing	1,400,000	2,180,000	3,000,000

The study from which these figures were taken shows striking gains in other sports most of which are not so related to vacation. For example, bowling showed an increase in participation from 12,500,000 in 1946 to 20,050,000 in 1956 and golf from 4,300,000 to 5,100,000 for the same years.[1]

We hear much about the inequalities in vacations, such as high-salaried persons 'who need it least have the longest vacations', a proper complaint, but it needs no elaboration here. We should mention another complaint about which too little is said; vacation as advertised is mainly for young adults. The pictures in the magazines not only feature young adults engaged in the conventional vacation activities, but they are always young adults from the middle and upper middle classes. No space is given to the great mass of ordinary people, and definitely no space is given for mothers with children, although some space is given to children in camps.

Kieslich found in his study of leisure in a German industrial city that, whereas 14 per cent of the men did not have vacations in 1955, of the women 63 per cent had been vacationless. Of housewives in the same city 79 per cent had no vacation in 1955. Vacations for workers of two weeks or more had been enjoyed by 63 per cent of the men compared with 62 per cent of the women.[2] German families with two, three or more children are much less likely to own automobiles than corresponding American families. It is the unusual American family that

[1] Figures received from the National Recreation Association Correspondence and Consultation Service.
[2] Gunther Kieslich, *Freizeitgestaltung in einer Industriestadl*, Munster, Wilhelm Universitat, 1956, p. 34.

Some Pertinent Aspects of Leisure

cannot load in the automobile and go to the open places, but it is not convenient for the American family to go to the conventional vacation centres, unless there are cottages which can be occupied, and these are expensive.

Regarding family vacations in England, where also mothers with children are disadvantaged, Beveridge holds that even if the family goes to some vacation resort, the mother cannot get rest.

This is one side of the defective appreciation of the housewife as an unpaid worker. Nothing short of a revolution in housing would give the working housewife the equivalent of the two hours additional leisure a day on five days of each week that has come to the wage workers in the past seventy years and nothing but a revolution in holiday accomodations can give to the housewife with children the essence of a holiday, that is to say change and release from normal duties.[1]

The conventional vacation, as viewed by Jelden, has economic meaning but little meaning for leisure. It is rarely a relaxing or recuperative experience, and it is not designed to serve the needs of families. He sees the vacation as a cluster of tensions which do not relieve the tensions of work, but he holds that this complaint applies to other types of leisure activity as well. When man learns the art of relaxing, Jelden argues, then he can enjoy leisure anywhere and he needs no vacation, and the family can enjoy free time in any sort of outing without going to conventional vacation places.[2]

Vacations are probably here to stay and there will be more vacations and vacation time, continuing to be the biggest item in the leisure budget. Vacation is also big business selling the idea that one must get away from his work for a few weeks each year, not to sit at home but to go to one or another of the stereotyped places where all the stereotyped services can be found and where certain stereotyped activities must be engaged in. Vacation has become a compulsion and each type of vacation is a cluster of special compulsions. If one lets a year pass without taking a vacation he must expect to be pitied or perhaps be regarded as somewhat odd. At the workplace,

---

[1] William H. Beveridge, *Voluntary Action*, 1949, p. 275.

[2] Helmut Jelden, '*Erholung, ein Lebensproblem der Gegenwart*', *Soziale Welt*, Jahrgang VI, 1955, pp. 110–16.

Some Pertinent Aspects of Leisure

however, it would be treason to express such a view; the idea is rooted that vacation is the kind of medicine everyone needs ever so often. The manager expects his understaff to take their vacations, to get away from it all for a while, and 'come back rested'. If one merely passes the time at home, that is not enough; it is likely to mark him as a person a little on the lazy side. These observations regarding vacations and self-deception can be encountered each year at the close of the summer vacation season, especially in the jokes found in the press or the post vacation cartoons. Stephen said of the English vacationist: 'Thousands of people at the present moment are enjoying or pretending to themselves that they are enjoying, a holiday. They will come back almost tired to death of their pleasures, and delighted to return to their business, and yet they will persuade themselves and others that they have passed an inconceivably agreeable vacation.'[1]

That was written almost a century ago when only the well-to-do in England could boast a 'holiday'. Stephen described in detail the typical day of the typical vacationist at the usual resort of that time as a venture into boredom. He was not complaining against vacations, nor do we, only calling attention to the inability of people to do anything but follow the pattern.

LEISURE PLANNING AND PREFERENCES

Vacations are generally planned for, especially conventional vacations. One saves to make the necessary purchases and he works out detailed time shedules. He takes pride in following the plans. Other types of leisure activity are rarely planned, or if plans are made they are seldom followed. In leisure one is tempted to let things drift, and when he does he need not be embarrassed. This indefiniteness and unpredicability in leisure is sometimes distressing to those who believe that such time is precious and should be used systematically for some good purpose.

If people are asked what they plan to do with their leisure tomorrow or next week, they are likely to be guided in their answers by social expectations. Clarke asked workers in different occupational groups (prestige levels) how they would

[1] 'A Cynic' (Leslie Stephen). 'Vacations', *Cornhill Magazine*, Vol. 20, No. 116, August 1869, pp. 205-14. On the British worker and vacations, see C. A. Oakley, *Men at Work*, 1946, p. 154.

use two extra hours each day.[2] The answers are summarized in Table 3. When the first four items for Level I are compared

TABLE 3

'What would you do with an extra two hours in your day?'
In percentages by prestige levels

Activity	Prestige level*				
	I	II	III	IV	V
	N.128	102	133	109	102
Relax, rest, loaf, sleep	24·7	31·1	26·7	32·9	39·7
Read, study	27·9	18·7	14·8	11·2	12·8
Work at job	19·8	13·8	14·0	8·3	9·1
Work around house	8·5	7·9	12·3	18·4	15·7
Enjoy family, play with children	4·3	11·8	7·3	7·5	4·9
Watch television	0·0	1·9	2·5	5·6	6·9
Other activity	7·1	4·1	10·8	6·1	3·2
Do not know	2·3	5·8	8·3	6·4	3·9
No answer	5·4	4·9	3·3	3·6	3·8
Total	100·0	100·0	100·0	100·0	100·0

[1] Level I, mainly professional workers; Level II, managers and proprietors; Level III, sales, clerical, other white collar workers; Level IV, mainly skilled craftsmen; Level V, semi-skilled and skilled workers.

with those of Level V the contrast is considerable. Level I, the better educated and better paid workers would do less resting than Level V (24.7% to 39.7%) but more study and reading than Level V (27.9% to 12.8%) and they would work more on the job than would Level V respondents (19.8% to 9.1%). Yet those of Level I would do less work around the house than those of Level V (8.5% to 15.7%).

Clarke's study also raises questions. For example, were the respondents influenced by social expectations about how leisure should be used, thinking the while about the ways they were using leisure? Would they make amends with more loafing in one case or more work and study in another? Did some feel they were neglecting certain activities and would use the extra two

[1] Alfred C. Clarke, 'The Use of Leisure and its Relation to Levels of Occupational Prestige,' *American Sociological Reveiw*, Vol. 21, No. 3, June 1956, p. 306.

Some Pertinent Aspects of Leisure

hours to make it up? At any rate, Table 3 makes it clear that attitudes toward leisure and how it should be used differ with occupational prestige levels.

Saunders and Parker touched on the subject of people's leisure plans and leisure practices and they cited a study by the National Recreation Association. Respondents were asked what they would do with their leisure and how they had used their leisure. The first column below shows the rank order of what respondents said they would do and the second column shows what they did do in rank order.

What respondents would do	What respondents did
1. Tennis	1. Reading magazines, newspapers
2. Swimming	2. Listening to the radio
3. Boating	3. Going to movies
4. Golf	4. Visiting or entertaining
5. Camping	5. Reading books (fiction)
6. Gardening	6. Automobile riding
7. Playing music	7. Swimming
8. Automobile riding	8. Writing letters
9. Theatre-going	9. Reading books (non-fiction)
10. Ice skating	10. Conversation

Of the ten activities in the would-do column, only automobile riding and swimming appear in the did-do column. Reading appears three times in the did-do column but is not among the items in the first column. Apparently, when people are asked about what they will do with leisure, they give answers in terms of social expectations, pious answers. Most of the would-do leisure activities call for planning, getting dressed, going to places and arriving on time; 'getting organized'. On the other side, most did-do activities called for little effort, little planning and also little cost.[1] To recreationists who favour purposeful leisure activity, most activities in the second column would be mere dawdling and wasting time. Who can say if they are good leisure or not?

Table 4 shows what adults in a German city said they would do with their leisure and what they did the previous Saturday and Sunday.[2] The rank order of percentages in the first column

[1] Saunders and Parker, op. cit., p. 118.
[2] Gunther Kieslich, op. cit., pp. 145, 148, 150.

TABLE 4

What Germans said they would do with their leisure and what they did the previous Saturday and Sunday

Activities	What they said they would do	What they did	
		Saturday afternoon	Sunday all day
	%	%	%
Sport (active, passive)	17	1	5
Work around home	15	10	5
Gardening	13	5	1
Attend lectures	11	11	7
Animal care (rabbits, pets)	9	1	—
Walking, strolling	7	8	17
Music, singing	7	—*	—
Rest, extra sleep	6	11	11
Modelling, crafts	4	1	1
Photography	2	—	—
Dancing	2	1	2
Auto, other riding	1	5	7
Radio listening	1	10	7
Parties, ceremonials	1	—	6
Movies	1	4	4
Television viewing	—	2	1
Informal visiting	—	7	11
Total	97%	77%	85%

* Dashes (—) indicate less than 1%

indicates what respondents said they would do with leisure and the leading item in this column is sport (as participants or spectators). The second two items; working around home (15%) and gardening (13%), would be non-work obligations, but the fourth item, attending lectures (11%), would be a leisure activity. These four items make 56 per cent of the total. When we look over the next two columns we find that the leisure activities of a Saturday afternoon and Sunday are heavily in favour of the easy pastimes, resting and getting extra

Some Pertinent Aspects of Leisure

sleep, walking and strolling, radio listening and informal visiting.[1] If one lives in a community where social expectations and social pressures in favour of certain 'right' ways of using leisure are strong, these attitudes are likely to find expression in any statement he makes about uses he expects to make of his own future leisure. It would be surprising if work-dedicated Germans and Americans did not at least give lip service to such moral expectations when asked to speak of their own leisure plans. It should not be surprising if the good intentions are not always carried out, if people fall back into relaxing activites, taking the easy course.

COMMERCIAL AMUSEMENT

Various charges are made that our changing preferences of leisure activity are defined largely by the diverse offerings of the amusement industries. Allegedly the commercialized amusements, designed to gain profit, resort to any appeal that will attract the largest number of patrons without regard for the quality of the entertainment or its moral implications. Commercial amusement is thus depicted as a creature with many false faces, as an evil about which something should be done. Actually, commercial amusement is not one thing, but a multitude of enterprises from a world-touring basketball team to the major baseball leagues, from the travelling theatre troupe to the movie industry or from the small dance orchestras to the radio and television industries. It includes the factories that make sport equipment and it includes whole communities like Atlantic City or Monte Carlo that cater to people with leisure on their hands and money in their pockets.

Commercial amusement, seen collectively, is not only big

[1] Steelworkers in the Toulouse area of France are fairly habitual in their leisure activities. All read and listen to radio. Other activities:

Trips to country	83%	Sitting in cafes	32%
Work around the house	79%	Gardening	27%
Sports (spectators)	70%	Theatre and music	24%
Movies	62%	Dancing	17%
Fishing	59%	Sports (participants)	14%
Playing games	49%	Artistic activity	13%
Marketing	45%	Hunting	12%

For vacations: 24% visited parents, 39% stayed home, 37% travelled, 20% own automobiles. Janine Larrue, 'Loisirs ouvriers chez metallurgistes toulousains', *Esprit*, 27 annee, No. 274, juin 1959, p. 956.

business, it is also not a new thing in the world. It goes back to the wandering troubadours and to the fun makers of the Middle Ages touring from one market or fair to another or from one carnival to another. Seen collectively, commercial amusement is not only big and old, it is integrated with other industries; steel, oil, plastics, instruments and most importantly with transportation. Besides being big and pervading, it is also versatile and creative, ever finding new areas for effort and new ways to entertain. Durant wrote:

> All forms of leisure have become commercialized, endless devices are offered to the idle person, each to be enjoyed only on condition that he has the money to pay. Without money he is condemned, unable to share in the pleasure and pastimes which press on him from all sides. But commercialization does not merely erect a gate through which only those with the necessary fee can pass. It has a profound effect also on the nature of the fare offered. The 'machinery of amusement' is run by business men actuated by business motives.[1]

Some would meet the threat of commercial amusement by going back to the simple pleasures. Ross lauded the good old times and home-made fun supervised in the community by parents, teachers, preachers and trustees. He wrote with regret that such amusements are no longer wanted. 'Thanks to good roads and automobiles, the country young people are turning from their home-bred fun to the professional amusement makers to be enjoyed in the town. Hence, as never before recreation is being supplied for money.'[2] Yet Ross did not object to the good roads and automobiles, or labour-saving machines that brought more leisure and other benefits to the farmer. He would have the farmer go forward in his work, but remain old-fashioned in his leisure. This 'back to the old pleasures' argument is also made for the leisure of urbanites.

A frequent complaint against commercial amusements is that they offer entertainment suited to the level of taste and appreciation that attracts the largest number of patrons. They encourage passivity and emphasize sentimentalism, in brief, they foster mediocrity. Nash wrote: 'Social organization and organized leisure should aim at the highest common denomin-

[1] H. W. Durant, *The Problem of Leisure*, 1938, p. 22.
[2] Edward A. Ross, *New-age Sociology*, New York, 1940, p. 352.

Some Pertinent Aspects of Leisure

ator, and in various degrees and ways bring the average human nature up toward highest human nature. Commercial amusement too often seeks out, exploits, socializes and makes dominant a low common denominator, and the masses, rendered passive, seem to be momentarily helpless.'[1]

What might be expected if the leisure industries, becoming less money-motivated, tried to design their offerings in the direction of what Nash calls 'highest human nature?' No doubt there would be many willing to give advice about highest human nature, although the advisors would differ widely about what would be included under 'highest'. The result might be a trend toward dullness in movie themes, radio and television programmes, music selections and the dances that would be encouraged. Many would object to dancing altogether. The clash about what should be would bring forth various moral views as well as various artistic or cultural views about what is 'highest'.

However it is defined, the 'low common denominator' is nothing new and it certainly was much lower when society was dominated by a leisure class nobility. Said Toynbee, 'In the days when leisure had been a monopoly of a minority, a minority of that minority had always misused it.' The great mass of people had no leisure and were not expected to have standards. Again Toynbee, 'Only a minority of that minority had made the creative use of leisure that had been the mainspring of Civilization.'[2] Yet Toynbee believed that the level of culture had been raised by the leisure class, and most scholars will agree. But he also seems of the opinion that giving abundant leisure to all classes can do no other than lower the general level of culture. The idea is that good culture is an inner growth, not something plastered on, and good culture is gained only by living with good culture.

The Neumeyers commented that not all leisure is used for the enrichment of life. Much of it is idled away or people 'turn to commercial amusements for pleasures'.[3] This observation is enlarged by some into the complaint that commercial amusements cater to idleness and induce the wasting of time, and leisure is time for the enrichment of life. This is a far cry from

[1] Jay B. Nash, *Philosophy of Recreation and Leisure*, 1953, p. 62.
[2] Arnold J. Toynbee, *A Study of History*, 1955, Vol. IX, p. 610.
[3] Martin H. and Esther S. Neumeyer, *Leisure and Recreation*, 1949, p. 19.

the moral of bygone days when old King Cole 'called for his pipe and he called for his bowl and he called for his fiddlers three'. Looking again at the people who had leisure in the bygone days we find that much of it was given over to concerns about court manners, dress, certain sports, the art of conversation and the niceties of social protocol; the game of snobbery.

The faults of commercial amusement can be freely admitted but with reservations. Consider, for example, the complaints about horror films which from time to time are offered by the movie industry. In one form or other, the horror film must have a monster; a giant, a witch, a man from Mars, a robot or other. With the aid of technology, the industry has invented other and equally terrifying monsters, like King Kong, the great ape. But the idea of the monster, as too many critics forget, is much older than the movies; for example, the witch in 'Snow White and the Seven Dwarfs', the giant in 'Jack and the Bean Stalk' or the genie in 'Arabian Nights'. Now we are told that only occasionally does the modern horror film make a profit, at least for cinema houses, although they may be produced by the industry at low cost. They go out of vogue and may return in some other form later.[1] However, they follow the same old pattern; the monster is destroyed, the hero wins and society feels free again.

Clarke makes the point that only a small part of the leisure of most people is spent in commercial amusements such as theatre, movies, bowling, pool or billiards, cafés and taverns, night clubs, dances, or sporting events. The percentage of time varies with occupational groups in this wise.:

Professional workers	3.8%
Managers, owners, officials	4.2%
Clerical, white-collar	7.7%
Artisans and other skilled	7.9%
Semi-skilled, unskilled	10.1%

By these figures, from 96.2 per cent of the free time of the professional workers to 89.9 per cent for the unskilled and semi-skilled levels is spent in other time uses than commercial amusement.[2] However in these other time uses they may still be

---

[1] On horror movies, see, 'Lovers of Frankenstein', *The Economist*, Vol. 189, No. 6015, 6 December 1958, p. 868.

[2] Alfred C. Clarke, op. cit., p. 305.

Some Pertinent Aspects of Leisure

customers of the leisure industries whether they engage in sports, go boating, fishing or hunting, ride in their automobiles or have guests at home.

As Clarke would recognize, the time spent in attending a commercial amusement is not a full measure of the time devoted to it. Two hours of the young lady's evening may be spent at a dance, but she may have invested many hours in preparations, enjoying the event in prospect as she may live through the experience many times in retrospect. Like certain movies a ball game or a vacation, the dance is remembered and talked about. In fact, much of the conversation when people stand at the corner, sit in cafés or visit from house to house, concerns the movies seen or to be seen, ball games, and other items which touch on commercial amusements. Much of the wit passed comes from the same source and much of our reading relates to the same amusements.

We may say that commercial amusements have a place in modern society, and in a sense they are public amusements. As such they come properly under public regulation, but that is a topic to be included in Chapter 9

LEISURE AND THE SEXES

Many of the oldest and most honoured of pastimes are for the men; sports, horse racing, the hunt, fencing, chess, and until recent times, card playing. The dance is perhaps the oldest pastime in which the sexes mixed, although in some cultures certain dances are for men only. In Western society, except as it was banned under Puritanism, the dance became a gracious performance, so much so that Western missionaries, going to the less advanced peoples, were shocked by the dances they found. Beaglehole tells of the missionaries discouraging the native dances of the Polynesians and how new pastimes were introduced without changing materially the human nature of these people.[1]

With the help of the British civil authorities, the missionaries to Trinidad banned the native dances. Even so, as Herskovits reports, the dances are still indulged in 'quietly and often secretly, in order to avert the public and private chidings of priest and parson'. Often such dances took on a happy wild

---

[1] Ernest Beaglehole, *Social Change in the South Pacific*, 1957, pp. 14-18

character leading to excesses. The natives accepted the religion offered by the missionaries but it was not easy to adopt the dignified British way of worship. For them the holy spirit did not merely abide within, it had to become active and vocal. The natives would jump and shout, but since 1917 'shouting' is illegal.[1] The shouting religious meeting assumes the character of a dance with singing, jumping, handclapping and emotional display. The sexes come into close smiling 'brother and sister' contact, religious ceremony shakes free of conventional stiffness to become play, and the assembly becomes a happy leisure-time activity.

Fiesta among Latin Americans, and its counterparts among other peoples, examplifies a type of leisure experience in which sport, dancing, drinking and laughter brings the sexes, the ages and the classes of the community into a single merrymaking unity. Fiesta people save and sacrifice for the next joyful ceremonial with as much anticipation as sophisticated moderns save and plan for their vacations. For some, perhaps, vacation holds the promise of a little clandestine sexual adventuring, but in fiesta time there is no need for clandestine sex play. Morality in the stern sense withdraws to the background, which does not mean that, while fun is the less conventional, morality has been abandoned. Fiesta, too, has its codes of conduct. For the young it means that the awkwardness of day to day contact between the sexes is set aside. They meet in the dance, hold hands in the crowd and steal embraces when the eyes of the elders are turned. As for the elders, they use the occasion for a little more drinking than they would approve at other times. Of festival drinking in Guatemala, Tax found it was very much of a social obligation.

In a particular ceremony the practice is such that an individual has no alternative but to drink his share. The participants are arranged in hierarchical order; a boy with a bottle and a single glass starts with the highest ranking person, and in turn fills the glass for each, which must be drained at a gulp so the boy can pass on the next. This is repeated over and over to the end of the ceremony.[2]

[1] Melville J, and Frances S. Herskovits, *Trinidad Village*, New York, 1947 pp. 274, 183-184.
[2] Sol Tax, 'Changing Consumption in Indian Guatemala', *Economic Development and Cultural Change*, Vol. V, No. 2, January 1957, p. 157.

Some Pertinent Aspects of Leisure

Carnival as it is found in many cities apparently came down through the years from fiesta-like origins. Although more under the control of convention, it is still an occasion for setting strictness aside. In normally staid Cologne it is expected at carnival time that people will disregard conventional manners. One sees kissing and embracing on the streets and strangers need not hesitate to join the merrymaking. But carnival in the city does not bring all sorts of people, including strangers, into a single homogeneous milling mass which characterizes fiesta in smaller places. Nor does carnival in the city pull everyone to itself. The young fellow with a motorcycle, with his lady sitting behind, may join other pairs for a trip to some dance place in the hills or at some lakeshore. Sex play in any situation will find its way.

To a high degree the services of the leisure industries cater to that part of the public in the sex play years, eager for novelty and variety and for opportunities to come together. As all generations before, they will be in close personal contact, for which the automobile is the modern convenience, but 'lovers lane' served the same function in years past. The dance serves this purpose for there they may be in close contact and still mingle with their own set, or in the movie they can be alone in the crowd.

Foote writes of sex as play, perhaps furtive play in the Puritan milieu, perhaps the most worried about and scrutinized form of play activity but, whatever taboos are imposed from without, sex as play is not balked. :

> For play—any kind of play—generates its own morality and values. And the enforcement of the rules of play becomes the concern of every player, because without their observance, the play cannot continue; the spoilsport is sternly rejected. To be sure, the development of rules intrinsic to the game itself does not guarantee that they will be the same rules outsiders would like to impose, and when outsiders repress the play itself as illicit, the development of rules can hardly occur at all.[1]

In the more urban community where strangers too may join the game the self-imposed rules on sex play are sometimes disregarded. And the rules that players make for themselves in

[1] Nelson N. Foote, 'Sex as Play', *Social Problems*, Vol. 1, No. 4, April 1954, p. 160

their romantic years they may fear to approve for their own children later.

ALCOHOL AND LEISURE

Alcohol is no longer merely another worry for reformers, but the concern of many others. It is true, as Patrick reminds us,[1] that in most cultures alcoholic drinks have served important social and ceremonial functions, but the old controls over drinking are losing their force, as among the fiesta-loving Latin Americans. With Western industrial man control is more an individual matter. He may turn to alcohol to relieve the awkwardness that leisure brings to many. It may loosen the tongue of one who lacks the social capabilities. It may dispel the stiffness that strangers feel among other strangers at a social gathering. Granted that most of these services are illusory, social drinking remains very much in fashion, perhaps less in connection with work than formerly, but certainly more in connection with leisure.

Excessive alcohol consumption is a menace to safe living in our mechanized environment. Concern about alcoholism goes beyond the argument of 'Ten Nights in a Bar Room', and we see instead a racing automobile with a drunken driver. The problem becomes one of serious research.[2]

In the Scandinavian countries a systematic programme of sociological and psychological research into alcoholism is under way. Under the old folk cultures there was drinking but not excessive drinking. With industrialization and urbanization, with people having more leisure and more money, the old controls tend to weaken. The idea of prohibition had been tried in places, but this could not be enforced. In Finland the government then took a middle course by making the sale of alcohol, a state monopoly with a rationing system. From Sariola's study of the drinking habits among Laplanders in the north of Finland we get this observation on the operation of state control:

> Statistical study of the consumption of liquors in Finland reveals a preference for the strongest alcoholic drinks. However, the tendency towards the use of better quality beverages is

[1] Clarence H. Patrick, *Alcohol, Culture and Society*, Durham, N.C., 1952, pp. 47, 59.
[2] On proposals for Britain see, Herman Levy, *Drink, and Economic and Social Study*, 1951, p. 123.

Some Pertinent Aspects of Leisure

becoming evident. There is also a very definite recent tendency toward the consumption of milder alcoholic drinks. The former tendency can be connected primarily with spontaneous changes in the customer's choice in the area . . . higher qualities sold in the liquor store.

The other tendency, toward milder drinks, is probably based more on the official alcohol policy measures adopted in Finland than on spontaneous trends among customers.[1]

The Laplanders, formerly moderate drinkers, have become heavy drinkers. Sariola relates this change to the industrial urban trends in Finland. The question is whether or not Finland with a policy of enlightened public control can give to alcoholic beverages a status in the modern industrial urban culture equal to that they had in the previous folk culture. Alcohol had its proper function then in most leisure occasions and it was not the frustrating role alcohol so often has in leisure today.[2]

READING, HIGH AND LOW

Reading is perhaps the most time-consuming of all leisure activities, but it relates to work as well as leisure. It is perhaps the most frequently crossed bridge between our different life interests. For education, for the development of personality or for amusement, modern man turns to reading. More than any other pastime, reading is a lone activity and people differ widely in what they get out of it. Because of this hidden element, many people for moral reasons may concern themselves greatly about the reading of others. Certain categories of reading are called good, and views are very different about what is good reading. Other categories of reading are called bad. There are many who deprecate much of the reading available now to children, like the comics.

Robbins enumerates at least nine types of comic books: Child life, Family life, Adolescence, Popular and appealing characteristics, Animal personifications, Crime (detection and punishment), Other-worldly, Fantastic adventures, Horror and sex,

[1] Sakari Sariola, *Drinking Patterns in Finnish Lapland*, Helsinki, Finnish Foundation for Alcohol Studies, 1956, pp. 23, 46.
[2] Although Britain has no alcohol control policy as Finland, the per capita consumption of bulk beer dropped from 28.8 gallons in 1913-14 to 18.4 gallons for the year 1951-2. During the same period the annual per capita consumption of whisky dropped from .71 gallons to .19 gallons. T. Cauter and J. S. Downham, *The Communication of Ideas*, 1954, p. 89.

and Burlesque. 70 million comic books are sold to Americans yearly and half of these are bought by children under twelve years, and 98 per cent of children from eight to twelve read such books.[1] And we must add that many are read by adults as well, and with the same zest that a philosopher may read detective stories.

Calling it no laughing matter, a British journal noted that 8.5 million English children between five and fifteen years of age read an average of three comic books each week. These books are exchanged or loaned from child to child. It is mentioned that comic books (for girls or boys) range in quality from those acceptable by the highest standards to those that are crude and objectionable by any standards. The article notes that views differ regarding the effects of comic books. Some hold that the comics provide literature for children who might otherwise not read anything, and they develop the reading habit. At the other extreme are those who would discourage such reading, claiming that better reading is available. The first viewpoint gets support from the fact that along with the increase in comic-book reading most libraries report an increasing demand for children's books.[2]

Allardt and associates studied the reading habits of Finnish youth to examine the proposition: 'It has sometimes been said that the reading of immoral or intellectually low books would hamper interest in more valuable literature; more generally, participation in "bad" activities would be likely to suppress interest in more valuable activities.' They found that youth reading no books at all, or very few, also read few comics or true story magazines. But youth who read up to ten recognized good books also read the comics and true story magazines. Youth with serious reading interests also read the less approved literature.[3] Allardt suggests that further study may reveal that a positive relation exists between all-around reading and all-around social adaptation; the all-around reader is the better integrated in his work and leisure.

It may be that in reading, the most popular and pervasive

[1] Florence Greenloe Robbins, *The Sociology of Play, Recreation and Leisure*, Dubuque, 1955, p. 303.
[2] 'No Laughing Matter', *The Economist*, Vol. 189, No. 6012, 16 November, 1958, pp. 579 ff.
[3] Eric Allardt, Pentti Jartti, Feina Jyrkila and Yrjo Littunen, 'On the Cumulative Nature of Leisure Activities', *Acta Sociologica*, Vol. 3, No. 4, 1958, p. 171.

Some Pertinent Aspects of Leisure

of leisure activities, the individual is guided in his choice of pastimes. Not only is he guided, but his taste in choosing may be rendered more critical. This may be one of the means of elevating the taste level of the mass; not the only one, of course, for there are other mass media, each of which in its own way performs a type of mass education service.

SUMMARY

This chapter concerns some pertinent aspects of leisure as a phenomenon in modern society. These in part underline the thought that leisure is more than time gained from work, but is intrically linked with various other life interests which are non-leisure in their essence. This we see when we ask about the cost of leisure; they interweave with social costs, body-maintenance costs and some may be included in the taxes one pays for the support of government.

In much the same degree leisure as time is hard to identify. It is certain that over the past several decades leisure has increased until one has more free hours than work hours in the course of a year, disregarding time needed for sleep, eating and body care. Counting holidays, week-ends and vacations, the American worker in 1958 had about eleven hours of free time for each eight hours of work time. According to some predictions, fifty years hence he will have about sixteen free hours to seven work hours. This is why many are concerned about modern man learning to use leisure.

The answer appears to be coming from a direction too little considered by leisure researchers. People are learning to use their own time less for leisure activity for its own sake and more on activity which we have identified as obligations. It is in such activity that he gains status as spouse, parent, neighbour, group member, friend, church member and citizen. Through them he gets involved in the life about him, and the more that is true the less he is concerned about the use of leisure. He becomes so much the socialized human being that no matter how much free time he has, he finds little time for leisure.

The work-leisure time pattern has evolved in relation to the needs and interests of those who work for hire, the men in particular. A woman who works for hire and must be a housekeeper in addition benefits very little from it, although she may earn a vacation. A woman who does not work for hire, who is occupied with being a wife and mother is most disadvantaged as far as leisure is concerned. These observations, of course, have been made many times, especially as they concern the vacationless existence of most housewives with children. Some argue that the problem is one that calls for some sort of public programme.

Holidays and vacations comprise the biggest item in both the time budget for leisure and the leisure cost budget. Holidays are taken when they come by everyone, but vacations are largely an individual matter left usually to the wishes of the individual. In different ways vacations tend to become fairly standardized. They are mostly taken during summer and for those who can afford it they usually involve going some place, perhaps to a foreign land, usually to some specialized vacation area or other, there to engage in the activities customary for vacationists. Especially since World War II the length of paid vacations has increased and so the number of persons being given vacations.

Normally the vacation is planned for, often in detail and well in advance but this is not true of other types of leisure. The ideal held up for most of us is that leisure should be systematically used for a purpose, establishes certain expectations of which most people are conscious when asked their plans about the use of leisure. It turns out that the uses to which people say they will put leisure are not always realized; they require planning and more 'organization' than many are ready to give and some are prone to use the time in easy activities, which may be all to the good. Perhaps a better basis for judging the use of the individual's own time should not relate to his leisure activities but to his non-work obligations.

We find that only a small part of the individual's total leisure is spent in commercial amusement, which is not surprising considering the cost. One may attend a ball game only occasionally and a movie only once in a week but this is not a full measure of the influence of such amusements in the reading, conversation and thinking of the individual. The baseball fan gives some time daily to reading about the game or listening to the radio. The importance of commercial amusements is not measured by spectatorship alone, but by the fact that commercialization enters most leisure areas. It is a permanent phase of our society and must be regarded as a form of public

Some Pertinent Aspects of Leisure

service. As such it must be subject to public guidance, as will be noted in Chapter 9.

Much of the emphasis in commercial entertainment as in leisure market advertising is focused on the romantic years, the song market in particular. Sex is the exploited theme in most selling appeals, and unrealistically so for sex play has figured prominently in leisure activity through the generations. However, the subject itself continues to be hedged about with taboos and obscured with evasive thinking and talking. Some hold that sex interest in most of its manifestations is play and, if left alone, would establish its own rules of conduct. How and when this may happen, if at all, is problematic. In the meanwhile, there is some evidence that the taboos are mellowing.

Alchohol and leisure have always been associated, but under folk cultures alcohol was rarely a problem. The opposite is true in the industrial urban society. For different reasons, persons who cannot use leisure find refuge in excessive drinking. The problem is no longer merely one of moral reform, alcoholism is a danger. For this reason, in the United States and other countries serious research is under way. Research in Finland shows that state control of sales is having some influence in changing the pattern of drinking. The problem is less one of prohibition than of establishing folk controls as effective as those in pre-industrial societies.

In some respects reading is the most universal of leisure pastimes for all classes, ages and intellectual levels. It is one of the solitary leisure pastimes. Since one is never sure what the reader takes from the printed page, many concern themselves about what others read. For example, comic books for children have been the subject of much worry. Recent studies point to the conclusion that readers of comic books and other light literature later move into more approved types of reading, and serious readers often turn to comic books for reading relaxation. The voracious reader, it seems, finds his way, which may mean that the non-reader is really the problem.

6

YOUTH AND THE LIFE CYCLE

THE major phases of the life cycle, youth, the middle years and the years of decline, will be considered in this and the two following chapters. The cycle begins with the individual's introduction to society, to work and living, and ends with his final decline. Each phase of the cycle imposes on the individual its own adaptation demands, and of these he is ever aware as he moves from phase to phase, as he is equally aware of the phases ahead.

Our attention in this chapter is on the preparatory years of physical growth when the young person readies himself for the first adult phase of the cycle. To some extent he may be led or pushed along as he confronts a whole series of tasks incidental to his upbringing. Some of these tasks in the learning process are traditionally defined, some are defined by the immediate situation. Thus the learning process may at times be confusing.

The overshadowing task for the young person is to grow up, physically and mentally. He must behave as one should in any situation. He must not only learn to talk, but when to talk and what to talk about. He must learn to use his hands, his feet and his face, and he soon discovers that these are instruments that can be used in wrong as well as right ways.

Most of the urges within the child, but still more of the urgings from without, focus his attention on the future. The image of what he must become is set before him continually, although as he goes along he actively visualizes the future in his own terms. As he gains experience his own conception of the future widens, perhaps to become more realistic and serious as he

Youth and the Life Cycle

moves into adolescence and then out of his teens. In this learning process, reality is often mixed with fun and fantasy. The control and guidance function of the adult world becomes more and more indirect as the young person gains self-discipline and confidence, as well as more knowledge and experience. Through all this learning, the model of what he might or should become is held up to him in long-term perspective. He is expected to keep his attention on the path that starts at his feet and extends itself far over the hill and down the other side. That is the life cycle, and he must never forget that one day he will enter old age and he must not be unprepared. Santayana asked: 'Why should a youth suppress his budding passions in favour of the sordid interests of his own withered old age? Why is that problematic old man who may bear his name fifty years hence nearer to him now than any other imaginary creature?'[1]

But the fact remains that the youth phase of the life cycle is much too brief for all that the child must learn and achieve. However diligent one may be, the learning can no longer be accomplished, as formerly, before the end of adolescence. For many, it now extends a decade or longer beyond adolescence. The child must apply himself; but childhood is also for play.

WHEN PLAY IS TOLERATED

In the natural state of organisms, for the lower animals at least, as observed by Huizinga, play evidences the overflowing eagerness for life, and play facilitates the development of the physical being. Co-ordinations are realized, skills are acquired and strength is tested. For the child the element of make-believe is added, his wits and imagination are tested, and in play he achieves social adaptations. The play of children demonstrates their viability, gives form to personality and affords ways to recognition.[2]

Even among the most severely work-oriented adults, there is a willingness to tolerate play in small children and it may be urged on very small children. According to these rarely-rationalized adult attitudes, not only is play expected of small children, but various efforts may be made to guide this play

[1] George Santayana, *Atoms of Thoughts*, anthology edited by Ira D. Cardiff, New York, 1950, p. 210.
[2] Johan Huizinga, *Homo Ludens*, 1938, pp. 12–18, 70–73.

through such devices as the selection of toys or guidance in the choice of playmates. This tolerance of adults for the play of children is apparently found in all cultures, but in Western society the period of tolerance ends sooner, when the child must begin the learning tasks.

In a common-sense way most people have understood the natural utility of play in growth and learning; even primitive people are aware of the development functions of play. It is now a preoccupation of educators to use play systematically in a guided learning process; they would put play to work in making lighter and quicker the task of learning. During the past half century the professional recreationists have developed a supplemental service to education. They would use play positively as a profitable pastime for adults as well as children in community recreation programmes. The normal would be occupied with approved leisure activities, while play would be used as medicine for those who tend to indulge in disapproved activities. In this sense play would be used for re-education, encouraging approved social values and activities.

Much has been accomplished by these efforts of educators and recreationists to utilize play, especially in the guidance of youth. The importance of this trend in the institutionalization of play should not be underestimated; it is a logical and necessary development in the organization of the modern mass society. Yet it must be recognized that play does not submit fully to being institutionalized. Its ways are too elusive and spontaneous, bursting forth continuously in unpredictable expression and, quoting Erikson, 'in its own playful way, it tries to elude definition'.[1]

However play may be utilized by adults in the upbringing of the young, it apparently functions most effectively in moments of release from adult guidance. Where the adult ways and values have not yet been internalized, then play may assume creative roles in what may be called the self-education of the young. It is pertinent here to consider the most cherished childhood memories of adults; the most cherished and often exaggerated memories relate to play episodes in their youth. They like to remember Tom Sawyer tricks they played on the elders, or situations involving harmless mischief, and there may be some recalling of the fantasy experiences of childhood play.

[1] Erik H. Erikson, *Childhood and Society*, New York, 1950, p. 185.

Most of these memories of childhood fun concern play free of adult supervision, or behind the back of the best-intended adult supervision.

PLAY AND SOCIAL DISCIPLINE

The childhood prank remembered by the adult may be sweetened if he can end the narrative with, 'and he never found out who did it', which means that the prank involved risk and punishment had been averted. Ford, in his report on the life story of an Indian chief, as narrated by the old chief, includes a chapter on the Indian's childhood. What seemed to be the brightest episodes in his period of youth related to play, much of it to mischief. In many respects the play activities of the chief and his companions related to the day-to-day living and work of the tribe.[1] In the step by step process of learning to be adults there was a mingling of work with play, play receding as years passed.

For the child in modern society much that goes on in play is quite unrelated to what he may later do in his work, although it may relate to his wider life interests. His time is divided somehow between three types of activities: work that he must do as required by the family, study and training for his later work life, and play. Each activity in different ways relates to the total process of growing up and becoming integrated into his society. Each is a phase of the social discipline, the evidence of growing up, to which the whole learning process is devoted.

While the child may find opportunities for play in work required by the family and in connection with his formal education, his most lively interests are likely to centre in play as such. Much that the child is required to do in learning and in work is not of his design or purpose; demands are imposed and gradually become internalized by him. But the dseign and purpose of play are largely of his definition, a definition that links him with the adult world and yet separates him from it. His play, whether guided or not, is 'preparation and practice' for the social discipline of adulthood.[2]

The play world of the child is one of rapid year-to-year

---

[1] Clelland S. Ford, *Smoke from their Fires*, New Haven, 1941, first chapter.

[2] On this thought see Edmund H. Volkart (Ed.), *Social Behavior and Personality*, Contributions of W. I. Thomas to Theory and Social Research, New York, 1951, p. 217.

change and each change means a slightly different identification with the work world of the adult which lies in the distance. It must be kept in mind, however, that the child in our time and society has almost no opportunity to be in personal contact with real work, in the sense that the rural child does. In the urban industrial community the child may have chores to do at home, or certain kinds of made-work which is seldom inspiring because it points nowhere. He escapes as he can into the play world where he finds reality in different sorts of fantasy, Cowboy and Indian games, for example.

Just the same, he keeps growing up and taking pride in it, scorning those who are less grown up and eagerly trying to qualify for the next phase of growth, but he has no contact with real work. That is against the law. First he must study and learn, grow up, 'produce himself'; then he will be ready for work. This phase of the individual's life cycle is one of impatient looking ahead, not to the 65.5 years allotted to him by the life expectancy charts, but to the first years of adulthood. He must 'get over the hump'. As he grows he leaves one kind of play behind to take up another. Not until he reaches adulthood when he doesn't play any more, or only rarely, does play have meaning. Now he looks back, enjoying play in retrospect with what Alexander calls a 'periodic desire for irresponsible play'.[1]

Some types of play do carry over into adulthood, and that is one kind of work inspiration that many youths have. Perhaps not one in four or five hundred aspiring baseball players ever gets into a major league, but it affords a worthy goal to strive for. The same holds for talented girls who dream of show business. All youth perhaps get much more out of play than we know how to measure. This is a thought Flugel leaves with us.[2]

THE EDUCATIONAL FUNCTION

Without venturing to say how the task should be done, or how well it is being done, let us ask where education comes in. The school is the one institution for youth, designed as adults with conflicting views think it should be. Whatever it has come to be, the school is the product of a long period of continuous trial and

---

[1] Franz Alexander, *Our Age of Unreason*, Philadelphia, 1951, p. 155.
[2] J. C. Flugel, *Men, Morals and Society*, 1948, p. 234.

Youth and the Life Cycle

error. It is ever under attack for being backward or being too daring in getting rid of backwardness. Some say, with approval, others not, that it has taken functions from the family, when actually the family alone never performed the whole function of rearing and training the young. It has always been shared by the neighbours, other children (according to the 'pecking order') and by the clergy. Until fairly modern times, the clergy claimed education as its own domain. The young were trained mainly by watching the elders or listening to them, not enough for modern educational needs.

The school emerged because education had to be more definite and systematic. What it had to do had never been done before. The public school, in particular, had to be a responsible institution, and because it has been responsible more and more tasks have been given to it. The public school belongs to all, and for that reason demands are made on it from all sides. This is to be expected, since it is set in the midst of a changing scene; while not scorning tradition, it must meet changing needs. As one educator said, 'We must have our coat off to the future and our hat off to the past.' The critics notwithstanding, the school, as Thomas indicated, tends to recognize that: 'The individual must be trained not for conformity but for efficiency; not for stability, but for creative evolution.'[1]

Thomas recognized that, while the school is never ahead of technological, economic and social change, it is never so far behind, and it is never ready for the surprises that the evolutionary processes bring. While on the one hand it has had to become more specialized in its training, it must not fail to be general in its education. It must train the young person for work, but also he must be prepared for social citizenship, for his entry and functioning in community life. He must sense responsibility and know how to choose. Child wrote:

> It is just here, in my opinion, that we have seen a tragic failure to educate for responsibility. There has been little or no real effort to teach the meaning of the free choice in a free society. Too often the educator has stood aside in an attitude of timid neutrality. The illusion of objectivity has been fostered. The passivity, the so-called objectivity, the timid neutrality in the teaching of the social and political sciences

[1] Edward H. Volkart, op. cit., p. 186.

have resulted in exactly the kind of response that might have been expected; an almost wholly negative response.[1]

What Child is asking for is teachers who can make choices and who are not neutral. Such personalities in most communities would not be wanted as teachers or, if selected, might not be retained. They don't fit the stereotype. We must add, as Child is aware, the school has no monopoly on the training of the young. It may have only a minor influence. On this Mannheim wrote:

> In modern society the machinery of formal education, including adult education, is one of the most powerful organizations for fashioning men's minds. Organized public persuasion is also gaining in strength. Functions formerly fulfilled by the priesthood alone are now shared by the educator, administrator, political propagandist, journalist and public relations counsellor. All of them use the modern means of mass communication and reproduction, press, radio, film, television, mimeographs, phonographs, photographs and the like, to implement policies of their own. They are partly co-ordinated and partly conflicting.[2]

The school is expected to be the principal carrier and transmitter of the culture. It symbolizes what the community stands for, and it must reflect the social values of the community; in fact, the teacher becomes a sort of symbol of these values. He tends to be one of the most stereotyped of public servants; even the security of his job depends on the skill with which he fits into the model. His personality becomes part of his professional equipment, the personality expected of a teacher.

Neither the school nor the teacher can be progressive in the sense that industry must be. Note, for example, how imaginative and resourceful the leisure industries have to be, and they compete with the school for the attention of the young. But these industries do not have the community responsibilities which the school cannot ignore. Progressiveness in education often relates to less dull ways of teaching but, however successful, the

---

[1] Marquis Child, 'The Meaning of Citizenship Responsibility in our Society', see Edward A. Richards, Editor, *Mid-century White House Conference on Children and Youth*, Raleigh, Health Publications Institute, 1950, p. 109.

[2] Karl Mannheim, *Freedom, Power and Democratic Planning*, 1950, p. 53.

learning process calls for work and discipline. The load must be delivered and time is short.

EDUCATION FOR WORK AND LEISURE

With the everyday worker for hire having much more free time than work time during his waking hours, people begin to ask what the school is doing to teach ways of using leisure. The Youth Advisory Council of the British Ministry of Education took the stand that something must be done to teach the use of leisure, implying that schools were over-dedicated to the teaching for work.[1] The British public schools have not gone so far as the American in bringing education and recreation together. American schools have been criticized by many for catering too much to play and programmes of recreation, to sports and games. For England, Barker expressed the thought even before the war that education for effectiveness should be:

> directed not only to the preparation of men for the effective doing of work, but also for the training of men for the happy and fruitful use of their leisure. Leisure is not easily used, unless we have learned to feel interests with which we can readily fill it; and it has often been remarked of our nation that, if it has any special attribute, it is that of a peculiar genius for being bored.[2]

The schools have had a century of experience in teaching for work and, whether they do the task well or not, the assignment is definite; teaching for leisure would be anything but that. Meerloo, looking at the American schools and, apparently against the background of the schools he knew in Holland, finds in them 'an atmosphere of compulsive regimentation' which imprints a 'sense of dependency and awe of authority'.[3] We mention this mainly to indicate how varied opinions about the school and education can be.

The American school has taken to itself the gymnasium,

---

[1] Reported by P. H. K. Kuenstler, *Youth Work in England*, 1954, p. 26. Tropp says of the English school system, it 'foils three-quarters of the child population at the age of ten and sends them out into the world with an inadequate and sketchy education at the age of fifteen'. Asher Tropp, 'The Study of Leisure in Great Britain', paper delivered in the Section on Leisure, Fourth World Congress of Sociology, Stresa, Italy, September 1959 (mimeo).

[2] Ernest Barker, *National Character*, 1949, 4th Ed., p. 238.

[3] Joost A. M. Meerloo, *The Rape of the Mind*, 1956, p. 268.

theatre, sport field, the swimming pool and the dance, not to forget a great variety of student social functions. Apparently Americans themselves are not always aware of the many ways that the school *belongs*. Still the complaint is heard that it fails educationally to keep up with technological progress. Siepmann holds it is being outdistanced by the mass media. More than that:

> For centuries the schools, together with the church, have enjoyed a virtual monopoly in the interpretation and transmission if cultural values, but that monopoly is at an end. Today both face the stiff and enterprising competition of the mass media of communication for the attention and loyalty of both young and old. The teaching world has failed thus far, either to avail itself extensively of these media or to acquaint itself with their cultural effects and provide proper antidotes where these run counter to educational objectives.[2]

Siepman concedes that the school may teach the technics of radio and film, but it does not use these facilities as it might, nor is it fully aware of their role as conveyers of culture. The school could hardly engage in such a competition without neglecting other tasks, and to 'provide proper antidotes' would be to engage in a fool's race, since the mass media in their leisure offerings change from novelty to novelty almost daily. Moreover, they strive to interest and amuse, not to educate. For them to educate would mean to introduce system and discipline into their programmes.

Developing in the American school, or in close conjunction with it, is a system of guided recreation, mainly sports and games. Seen in terms of end products, this is education for leisure. The effort is to teach one to play the game, to win or lose in good spirit, and there is a loosely though-out conviction that this is preparation for the 'game of life', which would be fine if sport and games were the only ways of using leisure. Such guided recreation, whether in the school or separate from it, is looked to for certain order-keeping, delinquency-avoiding, morale-building services, which are sometimes more highly considered than the simple service of helping people to enjoy themselves. Guided recreation is often seen as holding a midway point between the parent and teacher, parent and

[1] C. A. Siepmann, *Radio, Television and Society*, 1950, pp. 268-9.

preacher, and between all three and the policeman. Riesman objects to this.

Thus just as schools are asked to become quasi-parental, quasi-custodial, quasi-psychiatric, and quasi-everything else, filling in for tasks other institutions leave undone or badly done, with the result that schools often cannot do their job of education adequately; so leisure is now being required to take up the energies left untapped everywhere else in our social order, with the result that it often fails in its original task of recreation for most of us most of the time and creativity for some of us some of the time.[1]

We may leave institutionalized education and guided recreation for youth, believing they do fairly well, considering the task set before them and the ambivalent direction these institutions get from society. But what of the youth?

THE DISTANT GOALS

It is difficult for most adults to understand that rarely in this changing society do the children follow in the steps of the parents. If from today on that should be so, what would happen to the leisure industries? The parting of the ways begins unconsciously at an early age, perhaps when the young 'sprout' smirks a bored 'ha—ha' at a joke his father tells. Perhaps it begins when the teenage daughter wearily complains, 'Oh Mother, sometimes you are *so* old-fashioned.' The mother was a teenager only twenty years ago.

For the teenager, thinking back twenty years is a long time, but looking ahead twenty years seems much longer; that is time waited for. It's much more interesting looking ahead five years, or three, or two years when the model of one's self is designed to suit immediate values. But the young person is ever being stimulated by the forces about him to fix his attention on distant goals, beyond the striving to grow up and beyond his entry into work to the time when he will be firmly settled, when he will be a somebody. Most youth do that some of the time and some much of the time. For most youth, waiting for time to pass in

---

[1] David Riesman, 'Leisure and Work in the Post-Industrial Society', see Eric Larrabee and Rolf Meyersohn, Editors, *Mass Leisure*, Glencoe, Illinois, 1958, pp. 371–2.

that long-term perspective is tedious. They fix attention on the attainable goals and on the fun along the way.

The young person knows full well, and usually believes it, that before he reaches the distant goals he must do a lot of preparing. He must study and grow. Study is his work much as earning money is work for his father, but his work is different for work at learning does not pay off, if at all, until the distant future. Moreover, his work is different because he is told it is a way of making himself, developing his faculties, and so on; again, so he can earn more and live better sometime in the future. It is only the occasional child who can see the connection between his study and the distant goal and he may feel some incentive, but he may be interested in arithmetic although bored with writing themes or learning languages. Apparently with good reason, the school puts pressure on him to learn the other subjects also. The teacher must be the taskmaster, the symbol of authority in the name of the community. Here is work one cannot quit and look for a new job. This, he will learn in later years is some of the discipline that must be acquired along with other phases of growing up.

The school is only one of the forces impinging on the young person during this phase of his life span. So much of it seems not to count, and there is only one way up, to grow up. It he is very impatient, he may try to leave school as soon as the law allows to take his first real job.

WORK COMES TO THE RESCUE

The child in industrial urban society is set in an artificial situation, preparing for a life of work, but having no real contact with work. Depending on the sort of child he is and his circumstances, this waiting period may range from an existence like 'doing time', to the exceptional child who works out an orientation of his own.

The result is that two out of three or three out of four children leave school as soon as possible to find work. Work means to have fun and to *live*. Work means to earn money so one can buy things long desired. The majority exit from 'training for life' as soon as permitted, a minority goes on for more schooling and a small part of that minority tries for higher education. Of the situation in Britain, we read:

Youth and the Life Cycle

In 1957 over 3,000,000 girls and boys 16–21 in the United Kingdom were at work or in preparation for it. About 2,500,000 were on jobs, 250,000 were still in school or the university and another 250,000 were doing national service, to return to school of work later. Three out of four of those at work left school as early as possible, at 15 or 16 years. Of the boys, 37 per cent are serving apprenticements and will attend school a day a week for another four or five years. Only 8 per cent of the girls are taking such further training.[1]

Quite the reverse of the situation in Britain, 91 per cent of American youth of 15 years and 81 per cent of the 16-year-olds were still in school at the time of the 1950 Census. In 1957 of the 14–17 age group 89.5 per cent was still attending school, that is about 9,000,000 of the approximately 10,000,000 young persons within that age bracket. Of 41,166,000 young persons 5–34 years of age attending school in the United States in 1957, 70.6 per cent were in primary schools, 21.8 per cent in high schools and 7.6 per cent were in colleges or universities.[2] But even in the United States, although the young person may get two, three or four years more of schooling than in most other industrial urban countries, somewhere between two and three out of four discontinue their formal education when they complete primary school.

In a time of full employment, as since the war in Britain, the problem of young persons finding jobs is not difficult. Using 1938 as the base = 100, the index of earnings for the British girl in 1958 was 454 and that for a boy 402. Using the same base, the index figure for a British working woman was 387 and for a man it was 350. Part of the explanation is that in 1938 work for youth in Britain was scarce and the pay was very low. Comparatively then, working boys and girls in Britain are well-paid. They have their own spending money and, since their parents earn more than formerly, they are under very little pressure to contribute to the family budget. This gives rise to the British teenage generation called 'teddy boys' and 'teddy girls'. We quote Brew:

They spend their money freely on entertainment, on a great

---

[1] From an article on 'Gilded Youth', *The Economist*, 11 January, 1958, pp. 94–96. Figures on earnings which follow are from same article.

[2] *Statistical Abstract of the United States, 1958*, Washington, pp. 105–6.

deal of eating and drinking (mostly in ice cream parlours, milk bars and expresso cafés), on their clothes and on spasmodic saving for such things as motor bicycles, cameras, and holidays. If they are too well paid, it is not their fault . . . As for any wider purpose in their work, the majority of them are puzzled that there should be one. On the other hand, they expect to *learn* something at work and are dejected when they find that in many of their jobs there is very little to learn.[1]

Except in countries where apprentices must attend classes one day each week, it is not usual for the school to concern itself about youth after they have entered the labour market. This observation seems to hold for other agencies of the community organized to serve childhood needs. Such are likely to be concerned about their health, their moral surroundings, their free time (recreation) or their proper behaviour (juvenile delinquency). The youth and his job is usually a matter of minor interest. At the 1950 White House Conference on Children and Youth all types of American organizations were represented, but very little was said about either work or leisure. Regarding work, a statement of 'conditions which contribute to satisfying work patterns' was prepared. These indicate what ideals were held up.

1. Work must be rewarded in some fashion satisfactory to the worker.
2. Respect for human values should be a guiding attitude for both worker and those with whom he works.
3. The worker must be satisfactorily identified in the community structure.
4. Personality factors must be suitably assessed.
5. There must be freedom of choice.
6. The work must have a purpose.
7. Opportunities must exist for satisfying teamwork and individual participation.
8. Vocational guidance and individual counselling should be provided.
9. The individual's potential capacities should be used to the maximum.

[1] J. Macalister Brew, *Youth and Youth Groups*, 1957, p. 78.

Youth and the Life Cycle

10. Environmental factors—health, economic conditions, and vocational opportunitites—should be satisfactory.[1]

We recognize that these are 'target conditions', but even as such they betray a touch of innocence about the realities of the industrial urban labour market into which most youth enter after leaving primary school. They are not even met in European coal mines, always short of workers, where the employers use all devices to coax youth into apprenticeships and use every means to keep them happy while learning.

WORK AS THE YOUNG FIND IT

Often the introduction of the young person to a job is disappointing and uninspiring, although this may be less true for the disillusioned children of the very poor. The dullness and routine of much of the work given to youth have led some observers to see in it an incentive for escape into leisure. We quote an opinion of the Central Council of Education in England:

> On a broader view it seems to many of us that the amount of work demanded is not the whole of the trouble. The quality of it is as objectionable as the quantity. Here we are face to face with one of the inescapable facts of a machine age: young people inevitably spend much of their lives on work which is essential to production, but which does nothing whatever to develop their personalities and may indeed positively damage them ... If, as well may be the case, there is no solution of this problem inside working hours, so much more urgent is an increase in the amount of a young worker's leisure and the wisest possible use of it, to produce through genuine recreation the fullest flowering of every side of a developing personality.[2]

The British group just quoted not only recognized the uninviting character of most work given to youth, but recognized that it would be difficult for most employers to do otherwise. Hollingshead found that youth work was equally unattractive in Elmtown USA. He found among youth the same disinterest

---

[1] Edward A. Richards, Editor, *Mid-century Whitehouse Conference on Children and Youth*, Raleigh, N.C., 1950, pp. 268–9.

[2] Reported by Kuenstler, *Youth Work in England*, pp. 23–24.

in the work that most employers showed for the youth. For the youth the job was needed to get spending money and for the employer 'the kid' was tolerated because he could be assigned tasks others did not care for. As for these young workers, they endure the work as a means to having fun.

> From the stories they tell it is apparent that thoughts about these pleasures, flitting through their dreams while they work, often hinder the efficient exercise of their duties. But memories of past pleasures and dreams of those to come form a pleasant fantasy world which helps the time pass when one is forced to spend long hours alone cleaning house, cultivating corn, polishing cars, washing milk bottles, or one of a half-hundred other monotonous, always menial and often hard jobs these youngsters work at from eight to twelve hours a day, six days a week.[1]

This indifference to challengeless jobs may be no more or less than a healthy psychological adaptation. Here we must add the thought often neglected by some observers; namely, that the young person is not always so naïve as to be disappointed in his first employment. He understands, since he has perhaps often heard it, that 'one must eat his peck of dirt', he must show that he can 'take it', and he expects to be imposed on. He learns in time to cope with the impositions of the job and other workers. He learns that the older workers had travelled the same rough road when they entered the labour market. The challenge that he finds is not in the work itself but in the work situation.

While some elect to endure through on the same job, others try to meet the problem by moving. This was the case with 1,347 school-leaving Glasgow boys (a single school-leaving class) studied by Ferguson and Cunnison in 1950. Over a period of three years only 137 of these boys had remained with their first job, while 533 had had two jobs. Of the one-job boys 77 per cent were interested in their work and of the two-job boys 73 per cent liked their work. This attitude went down to 30 per cent for the 50 boys who had had six jobs or more during the three years since leaving school.[2]

But the Glasgow boys were in a favourable labour market.

[1] August B. Hollingshead, *Elmtown's Youth*, New York, 1949, p. 377.
[2] T. Ferguson and J. Cunnison, *The Young Wage-earner*, 1951, pp. 11, 14, 88.

Youth and the Life Cycle

It was possible to leave one job and find another, and perhaps some of these moves were well advised, not merely escapes from boredom. Bell studied some 3,000 American boys and girls during the Great Depression when jobs were hard to find and when there was little moving from one work place to another. He found that about 90 per cent of the boys wished to change their jobs. These attitudes ranged from 98 per cent of textile operatives to 85 per cent for certain clerical workers. About 85 per cent of the girls were dissatisfied with their work and these attitudes ranged from 98 per cent of textile workers down to 55 per cent for secretaries and 23 per cent for beauty parlour workers. In general, the higher the status of the work the less was the wish for change.[1]

Blucher, reporting on his study of youth, work and leisure in Germany, concluded that normally these young workers are given the least interesting, sometimes the heaviest, and often the most tedious tasks. Yet the youth seem willing to bear it as part of the initiation into the work world. In Germany the hours of work for youth are limited by law to eight per day and 48 per week. Yet about 10 per cent of the youth work 10 hours or more per day and 60 hours or more per week. In small establishments, not usually visited by the inspectors, 79 per cent of the youth work 10 hours or more per day and 60 or more per week. Complaints are rare. Apparently even the young person accepts the idea that this is the rough part of the road that all must travel, part of the entry test into work life.[2]

ARE NEW WORK VALUES NEEDED?

Generally in Western society a double attitude maintains toward work. On the one hand, one gets status from his work, if not for the kind of work he does, then status comes from the fact that he works. His status is often measured by the size of his income. But even if income is low, one has higher status if he works than if he does not. The other attitude is somewhat

---

[1] Howard M. Bell, *Youth Tell Their Story*, Washington, 1938, p. 135.

[2] Viggo Graf Blucher, *Freizeit in der industriellen Gesellschaft*, Stuttgart, 1956, p. 19. Wurzbacher found that German girls on their first jobs met the same adult indifference. Often the view was that work for teenage girls was for many a stopgap activity until marriage and housekeeping. Among many girls he found/depressed attitudes toward their jobs, 'it's only work, not an occupation'. Gerhard Wurzbacher, *Die junge Arbeiterin*, Munich 1958, pp. 61–76.

negative. Work may be recognized as necessary and status-giving, but work may also be heavy, dull and unrelated to the personality of the worker. It calls for continuous application, perhaps precision, perhaps speed, all of which make work a discipline.

For most workers who sell their time, work is intermediate activity, something one does to get money that he may engage in activity he likes, usually activity in which he must spend money. It is understandable, then, as Hollingshead found in his study of youth in Elmtown, that the social class of a family depends on its source of livelihood. It is equally understandable that, while parents in each social class expect their children to enter the work world, upper-class families make special efforts to have their children become active at the higher occupation levels where the work is easier, cleaner and more prestigeful. These attitudes, as Hollingshead recognizes, involve respect for some kinds of work and disdain for other kinds of work. These attitudes also mean respect for people doing some kinds of work and a low opinion of people doing other kinds of work. Thus upper-class Elmtown families wish their sons in positions 'apart from such contaminating odours as hamburgers and onions'.[1]

Such attitudes, as well as our attitudes toward work in general, prompt ten Have to call for a new approach to work in education. He holds that we must recognize the limited satisfaction one may derive from some kinds of work, while other work may yield diverse satisfactions.

> It may be rightly valued as a means of subsistence, as an opportunity to be bodily or mentally active, or as an opportunity to perform something or to function as a part of a whole. Work may be valued for these and many other reasons, and most likely nobody would contradict it, but it must be clear that work thus valued does not appeal to the total personality. It may be satisfying in some sphere or spheres of personal life, it may help to develop some potentialities or it may render a gratification of some vital needs, nevertheless, it means less than a vocation.[2]

---

[1] August B. Hollingshead, op. cit., p. 281.

[2] T. T. ten Have, 'Automation, Work and Leisure', *Range*, No. 15, Philips' Telecommunicatei Industrie, Hilversum, Holland, 1960 ff, pp. 8–9.

Youth and the Life Cycle

People doing the ordinary work that most workers are asked to perform, would not be normal if they did not fail to get satisfaction out of it. In ten Have's thinking, this fact needs to be recognized by educators and they should strive to educate, not for work only, but for the wide range of living. If one's work is not a satisfying and full vocation, the worker should be prepared to live at peace with his work while earning a living by it. This is not the preparation most young persons have who enter the labour market to become ordinary workers. It appears to be ten Have's view that the young person must be educated to use his time and to get satisfaction out of it, not his work time alone.

WHERE THE FUN COMES IN

Whether the child grows up in the village or a great city, whether in a better residential area of the city or in a slum, he is normally able to find companions and to have fun. Whether he belongs to one or another, or to none of the organizations designed by adults to serve and guide youth, he will in any event belong to informal groups. These informal groups will be very important to him. They will influence, as much or more than other factors, his choice of leisure activities, as they will also influence his thinking about work, leisure and other interests.

In fact we do not have much information about the influence that the formal organizations do have in role-defining for youth, and the reports of these organizations are rarely very helpful, Moreover, assuming that the influence is as great as sometimes stated, we must remember that the time of contact with such activities is not great, a few hours in the week, and often for no more than three or four years. The child is ever outgrowing the organization. A membership regarded highly by him at twelve may be of little interest, only 'kid stuff', two years later. Those sixteen or seventeen years of age prefer not to be in a club with a median age of fourteen years. They are looking to the groups with a median age of eighteen or nineteen years. Warner found that in Yankee City that sub-adult clubs (twenty years and younger) are usually short-lived and must continually be re-organized.[1] To recognize this element of transiency is in no

---

[1] W. Lloyd Warner and Paul S. Lunt, *The Social Life of a Modern Community*, New Haven, 1950 (1st Ed. 1941), p. 304.

Youth and the Life Cycle

sense a negative rating of the efforts of these organizations; we are merely recognizing the high transiency in the situation.

Added to the high transiency, there are other elements which in the urban environment render the situation more complex. The movement of people from class to class is one of the elements, but in a country such as the United States complexity is increased by the heterogeneity of the population. In Denmark, for example, the population is more homogeneous. There we find that the formal organizations for leisure are widely participated in and membership may continue a decade or more. Of the 4,448,000 people in Denmark about 700,000 belong to sport and gymnastic associations. In this small country in 1957 there were 4,736 athletic clubs to which normally both males and females belong. Membership begins at fifteen and one may hold his membership until old age, although activity is mostly among the young. Sport participants include 29 per cent of the female and 55 per cent of the male members. These clubs do not limit their activities to sport alone, they are social clubs as well and some are also political clubs. They afford one type of device for bridging the gap between youth and adulthood.[1]

Much of the play of the young is competitive. This seems to hold whether in sport, climbing trees, collecting stamps or sitting in groups and bragging. To no small degree, the success of the Boy Scouts, Campfire Girls and such groups stems from their systems of stages, promotions, tests and awards. The envied member is one with the most badges on his sleeve. Much of this competition in which personality is developed is consciously or unconsciously oriented to adult roles. Alexander observed that the adolescent 'feels obliged to play the novel role of the adult, and his prevailing state of mind is insecurity, which he tries to offset by comparing himself with others in competition'.[2] This sense of insecurity may be present in the

---

[1] Helga Anderson, Aage Bo-Jensen, N. Elkaer-Hansen and A. Sonne, 'Sport and Games in Denmark in the Light of Sociology', *Acta Sociologica*, Vol. 2, 1957, pp. 1–14. A book by Svalastoga was not received until after the above was written. Here we see that 85 per cent of the adult males and 69 per cent of the adult females belong to formal associations of all types. He does not give separate figures for youth. He does indicate that more than half of all free time activity is home-related. Kaare Svalastoga, Prestige, *Class and Social Mobility*, Copenhagen, Gyldendal, 1959, pp. 250 ff.

[2] Franz Alexander, op. cit., p. 157.

face of the adult's competition also, but he is more seasoned and resourceful and better able to recover from disappointment, at least supposed to be. The adult, in turn, may try in his leisure to recapture the competitive enjoyments of youth but, quoting Alexander further, 'we return to a period when competition was not so serious, utilitarian, and realistic as in the later struggle for existence'.

This element of competition is exploited by the commercial amusements; record-breaking in field athletics, 'statistics' in baseball and other professional sports, marathon dancing, beauty contests. One is dared to take the rides at the amusement park. Carnival directors say that the old thrillers like the 'ghost train' and the 'tunnel of love' have been replaced by rides that take one to the brink of life itself. They must seem hazardous, but legally they must be safe.[1]

For the smaller urban child going to a summer camp is an invitation to adventure. In most of the activities there he finds some element of contest. In the United States are thousands of such camps serving different types of children and several million children visit these places each year.[2] After two or three such experiences the child outgrows the camp idea. It is guided recreation much of which the young person tends to leave behind.

Going to work and leaving the diverse guidances of youth behind means that the young person has parted company with the juvenile estate. The point of exit is when he takes his first job with pay. Illusory though it may be, he has arrived at an important goal. He is now more free in his choice of fun and he has the money to pay for it. Much has been written on how boys behave on reaching this stage of imagined independence, especially those who entered the labour market in their middle teens. Here is a word from Brew on the behaviour of female teenage first-jobbers.

> Most of them are ridiculously efficient on a small scale and they are going nowhere. At this boy-mad stage, having been dominated by the male at home, at school and in the factory, they realize in a confused instinctive fashion that they can

[1] 'Gaining on the Roundabouts', *The Economist*, Vol. 186, No. 5985, 10 May, 1958, pp. 476-8.
[2] Raymond E. Carlson, 'Organized Camping', *Annals of the American Academy of Political and Social Sciences*, Vol. 313, September 1957, p. 83.

only dominate the male in their leisure, and as a compensation for all this submission, how they work to use their new-found power of attraction! This is the reason behind what so often seems the over-erotic attitude of so many adolescent girls. Hence their pathetic displays of finery and love of dancing, hence the loud shrieks of laughter at the street corners and the loud and competitive boasting of mild adventures.[1]

More than for the boys, the first job for girls also means escape from home supervision. They are less free than boys to come and go at will. They must help with the housework, which is seldom required of boys. Ernst Liebermann, at this writing is

TABLE 5

Rank order of leisure-time activities of teenage youth

Rank order	Boys Activity	Percentage	Girls Activity	Percentage
1.	Sport (individual)	22	Reading	35
2.	Reading	17	Dancing, dating	14
3.	Team games	16	Hobbies	13
4.	Loafing	13	Movies	12
5.	Dancing, dating	11	Sports (individual)	11
6.	Movies	9	Loafing	6
7.	Hobbies	5	Radio listening	2
8.	Radio listening	2	Team games	1
9.	Quiet games	1	Quiet games	1
10.	Other activities	4	Other Activities	5
	Total	100		100

making a study of youth in a German city. From some of the first results of this study we note that the time budgets for this group of 15–24-year-olds that girls have less leisure than boys. Time budgets for Saturday and Sunday show that girls had 8.4 (tenths) hours of leisure, while boys had 10.3 hours per day. But girls on Saturday and Sunday averaged 2.8 hours of housework while boys did less than a tenth of an hour. Boys on Saturday and Sunday averaged 8.7 hours per day for sleep com-

---

[1] J. Macalister Brew, op. cit., p. 26.

Youth and the Life Cycle

pared with 8.1 hours for the girls. For the two week-end days boys had 20.6 hours of free time, girls 16.8 hours.

Whether the young person is employed or not, as he advances in his teens play takes on new meanings. Love and romance begin to mingle with other leisure interests. This we see in Table 5, which shows the rank order of most-mentioned leisure interests of boys and girls, as reported by Bell in his study of American youth during the Great Depression.[1] These rank orders between the sexes tell more than can be said about them.

ADAPTATION AND CONFORMITY

At school or at work a young man or woman is inside a relationship which is based on authority. It may be—it often is—the case that the authority is very much in the background, and that neither the teacher nor the foreman has to wield a big stick, either literally or metaphorically. But the fact remains that in the last resort the relationship between teacher and pupil or between manager and employee is one which is based on authoritarian sanction. In a club or voluntary society the relationship is based on consent, and the relationship between leader and member is therefore different from that between teacher and pupil[2]

The above quotation is from a circular issued by the British Ministry of Education in 1945, and it was concerned largely with getting more youth into voluntary youth organizations where the relationship is one of consent and not authority. While the club does not exercise authority as the parents would or the teacher, using instead example and persuasion, it stands for the same social values as the home and the school. It may also promulgate the ideology of the church. True, the club does not resort to authority, but it does invoke, as it properly can, all available social compulsions.

In the life of the child, no less than in adult life, the social compulsions are probably much more important than authority as such. Authority does not insist that the child must be loyal

---

[1] Howard H. Bell, op. cit., p. 26. The German study by Liebermann, mentioned above, was made at a time of full employment for youth. Here, again, the time budgets show that the most engaged-in leisure activity for girls was dancing and dating, and again, the most engaged-in activity for boys was sport.

[2] Reported by P. H. K. Kuenstlet, *Youth Work in England*, p. 31.

to a friend but it may insist that he study his arithmetic. Authority does not tell the child that he must leave school at the age of sixteen and find a job, although that may be necessary in some cases. Normally parents would be pleased if the young person had the wish to remain longer in school to get a better job later. Social pressure from one's peers may have more influence on the school-leaving decision.

Without underestimating the influence of parents, we should not also underestimate the role of the peer group in defining the social values of the child and in helping him make decisions. This thought was forcibly emphasized by Whyte in his study of youth in a slum district. One may influence the compact little street-corner group, but he is also continually influenced by it.[1]

While the youth is very much under the influence of his peers, these peer groups in different ways, mostly unintended influences, tend to be guided by adults, certainly this holds in sport. It is also true that youth are often influenced by the example of others a year or two ahead of them in the growing and maturing process. Just so, they influence other youth a year or two younger. Much of this step-by-step learning comes down from the adult world. Whether it is conversation, dress or good manners and whether learned at home or in the movies, the source of the thing learned is usually the adult world. Thus comes much of the young person's code of right and wrong, but the peer group may apply the code differently at times than adults would.

How well youth learns from the adult world is well illustrated in a negative example. The young person learns mainly by observation that the codes of right and wrong are not always kept by adults, and they may need to become very wise adults later before they discover that all societies to some extent have their double codes. They learn to know certain adults who by the social conventions live one code, but privately and occasionally they practise another. They learn that one may speak somewhat freely among men but he must guard his language if women or children are present. These 'facts of life', known to most of us, were mentioned by Hollingshead in connection with his Elmtown study. He mentioned that 'bowling, roller-skating, attending motion pictures and dancing are defined as recreation. By way of contrast, smoking, drinking,

[1] William Foote Whyte, *Street Corner Society*, Chicago, 1943, pp. 208, 255.

Youth and the Life Cycle

gambling and sex play come under the heading of forbidden pleasures in the view of the adults'.[1]

Youth also learns that as between adults, also within strict rules, one tends to be tolerant of the sins of others. What one knows he keeps to himself in what Hollingshead calls a 'conspiracy of silence', knowing how privately one may pursue his forbidden pleasures. Youth learns that even in the adult world, especially in connection with having fun, there are times when he sees not, hears not and says nothing. Again Hollingshead:

> To illustrate, picnics are an approved recreation for boys and girls, and petting is generally an important activity sometime during the picnic. The 'necking' may be the most interesting, if not the most important, thing about the picnic, but, since it is pleasurable and involves sex play, the adolescent ignores this when he says he had a 'swell time' at the picnic.[2]

Thus the holiday phase of the life cycle is one of continuous adaptation and conformity, some of which is formal and guided but most of which is not. Sometimes old age is spoken of as the 'golden years', but the adult as soon as he leaves youth behind begins looking back. Consciously or not, he usually looks back with nostalgic sentimentality. Whatever the individual's own youth may have been, that very often becomes his model of what youth today should be. Moreover, whatever his youth may have been, he continues reluctantly to leave it behind; hence the spectacle of people trying to seem younger than they are, a more desperate effort often than that of children trying to seem older than they are. The 'golden years' are behind.

SUMMARY

Much of the content of this chapter on the youth phase of the life cycle can be summarized briefly with saying that youth is the period for growing up, for play and for learning.

Growing up is something the young human shares with all animals. It is nature's mandate to all creatures. First, they must grow so they will be able to forage for a living, only foraging for man is work. Second, and the most important part of the mandate, when they grow up they must produce the next generation

---

[1] A. B. Hollingshead, op. cit., p. 288.

of their kind. Mating is their first concern when they are old enough and big enough. This function for humans, which becomes a dominant interest in the final years of youth, is garnished with ideas about romanticism and hedged about by a great variety of guides and taboos. Sex with humans is also social.

Humans while growing up, like all animals, indulge in play. The infant is expected to play, but for youth play tends to be rationed. It serves in learning body co-ordinations, in gaining skill and testing strength. However adults may use play in guiding child development, some play seems essential to growing up. When the animal reaches maturity, play is left behind. The child, while growing up, each year or so changes to 'older' types of play, arriving at last to sex play and adulthood. The play urge appears in other forms during adult life.

While animals can learn, systematic learning is not part of their growing up. Without learning, the child could hardly enter society. He acquires all sorts of common knowledge, the cultural heritage and, since he must later earn his living, it is necessary to acquire special knowledge. Some of this learning is systematically acquired through education, but much of it is acquired through social contact and observation, or in connection with play.

In Western society this learning, excepting gifted children, is often a pointless, tedious endeavour to prepare for goals so far away. It is work for which the rewards will come years later, beyond the dream horizon of the child. The school was established and given the task of systematic education and of imparting discipline in thinking, as well as for performing other functions deemed necessary for child development, functions neglected or badly performed by other institutions. The task of the school is greater than the time allowed and the juvenile consumers are often interested in other things. As soon as the law allows, a good share of them try to get away from this educational treatment. They enter the labour market. The minority remains for more education and later enter the labour market under more favourable circumstances.

Some must leave school for work because of economic necessity, but this is no longer general in Western society. For many more work is an escape from a guided adolescence. And for those having the minimum of education, work means unskilled labour, the dull jobs that rarely offer promotion prospects. Often working conditions are worse than those on adult jobs. We must add, however: First, this has always been true of work assigned to youth. It is assumed, 'If he has the stuff in him, he will live it through.' The youth learns that. Second, industry is not organized so to provide learning work for youth, as some believe it should be. The industrial labour market is not a swimming pool with shallow water at one end.

The adult world in many ways endeavours to provide for youth leisure guidance and facilities for play. Even though these institutionalized services do not reach all youth, they do establish models and goals that most youth understand. But their contacts with even the most co-operative of young persons are only occasional, much of their time is filled with activities of their own choosing. Moreover, these services for guidance in recreation are ever being outgrown. The young leave for something else. They are also guided by the social values of their peers, usually those older than themselves.

The young person probably gives more thought to his growing-up problems than is often recognized, however unrealisitic his thinking at times may seem. Moreover, he is probably more influenced by the adult world than we know, sometimes in strange ways not in keeping with the guidance ideal. Also, he may be more dedicated to adult codes of right and wrong than is often realized, but the codes are applied according to the realities in his own situation. The codes to him do not rule out having fun. The goals that adults set for him may seem remote at times, and he takes short cuts, as when he becomes impatient with school and wants to find real work for money so he will have his own fun money.

While emphasizing the importance of play for youth, we have not in this chapter tried to de-emphasize the need for youth guidance. We have implied that these services and especially their motivations should be re-examined. Perhaps they are a little unrealistic and backward-looking. Certainly the years of youth should be used to prepare the young person for his life of work, but he also needs to be prepared for using leisure, and there is a tendency not to frankly face that educational need. Work is still more important for the work-dedicated adult world.

7
ACTIVE YEARS OF THE LIFE CYCLE

UNLIKE the tree or the animal, man knows he has a life span. He can be rational about it and do some planning for it. Within limits, he has been able to extend his expectation of life. His life at any point is a cluster of relationships, but he can look back on it, and he can visualize the future. The cluster of relationships changes with events in his life; leaving school, entering the labour market, entering adolescence, entering marriage, and there is finally retirement. The entries and exits are marked with uncertainties.

Of some things he is certain; for example, the serious beginning is when he becomes an adult worker, and equally serious is his entry into family life. This entire phase of his life relates mainly to these two roles, and to these other roles are related. In this connection we refer again to the classification of life roles offered by Havinghurst: Worker, Spouse, Parent, Homemaker, Leisure participant, Friend, Citizen, Group member, Church member. Each role has its own meaning and yields its own kind of satisfaction and each calls for its own type of performance. Each is a changing role.[1]

If these roles do not indicate family and home identification, at least in everyday thinking they imply that. Each links the individual to his social, economic and political environment in some special way, and each assumes a particular set of community relationships. With the exception of the unusual

[1] Robert J. Havinghurst, 'The Social Competence of Middle-Aged People', *Genetic Psychology Monographs*, No. 56, University of Chicago, 1957, p. 316.

Active Years of the Life Cycle

personality, most people reach the high point in most of these roles during the middle phase of the life cycle. The family-related roles, as will be seen, are the ones most likely to decline, and we are faced with the fact that the modern family also has a life cycle.

This middle phase of the life cycle has its own natural wholeness. The two decades of life preparation that went before were a looking-ahead period, and the decade or two that will come after it will be largely in retrospective of the active middle years.

FAMILY IN THE LIFE CYCLE

In pre-urban times man belonged to an extended family and this wide kinship group was his guide, his security and his government from childhood on. The primary group of parents and children was a mere unit in the extended family. The extended family tends to vanish and now the family is identified as the nuclear group. We have what Halbwachs called 'uncomplicated families of which the hard core is the married couple'.[1] Brought into being on the basis of romantic love, this one-generation family is also a contractual group. Using a military term, it may be called a 'mission-completed' family that runs its course and then disintegrates. There are different exceptions, mainly the property-holding families in which the generations are tied, often uncomfortably, together by their holdings of wealth and power.

The extended family came into existence for practical reasons, and practical reasons of another kind explain its decline. It is the nuclear group of parents and children that now, with reasonable effectiveness, performs the family role. This family in the modern community has a different type of home, but the home is not the centre of production it once was, yet it remains the principal centre of consumption. The family retains its monopoly on the bearing of children, but it shares with the community the task of rearing and educating them. Family functions tend to be timed and defined by the respective life cycles of the family members. The extended family did not have a life cycle, but the nuclear is a sensitive life-cycle group.

It is nothing new, however, for the family to be associated with social class, its status being identified generally by the

[1] Maurice Halbwachs, *The Psychology of Social Class*, 1958, pp. 13–14.

Active Years of the Life Cycle

work role of the father. As a result of this identification, as Pipping observed, children at school may be *listed* in the class of the parents and treated accordingly, that is educated to fit into the class of the parents.[1] To identify a family with social class is to identify it with a level of living and with very definite expectations regarding behaviour, social values and possessions. In addition to its one-generation character, it becomes a 'closed group', standing in sharp competition with other families, equally closed. Within the extended family the nuclear group was less exposed to economic and status competition and did not need to be in-looking and in-feeling. As it stands alone today amid competition, status and security are its major concerns. Both must be established, advanced if possible or at least maintained.

Here the family life cycle begins with the union of two adults who had previously 'weathered' family life in their parental homes as junior family members. In marriage they become legally and economically as well as sentimentally a new unit that will have its own time span. Speaking of the newly-formed family, Glick made these observations:

> ... there are many demands for household goods to equip the home and, in some cases, to start a business. Furthermore, within a short time the wife is likely to be preoccupied with child rearing and hence unable to help her husband make a living. During this period, while the husband's work experience is still limited, the family income is relatively low. Within about ten years, however, the family income generally has increased about one-third. Between the ages of 35 and 54, when the wife may have returned to the labour force and some of the older children who live with their parents may be working, the family income is at its peak, about 40 per cent above the level of newly-formed families. After the family head has passed age 65, the family has only about half the income it had at its peak.[2]

Besides being the practical enterprise, as correctly presented by Glick, the family is still a social unit with its hearth, although

---

[1] Hugo E. Pipping, *Standard of Living, the Concept and its Place in Economics*, Copenhagen, 1953, p. 104.

[2] Paul C. Glick, 'The Life Cycle of the Family', *Marriage and Family Living*, Vol. 17, No. 1, February 1955, p. 9.

Active Years of the Life Cycle

less the institution that it once was. It is less the family of heirlooms and ceremonials, and yet many families endeavour to carry on the ceremonial side of this changing institution. Dumazedier observed that in France there is a tendency among the young to either tolerate or depreciate the ceremonials.[1] Halbwachs observed that often it is some single member of the family who endeavours to keep alive family tradition, and in many cases this family loyalist is engaged in a losing struggle.

The family established by the individual and his marriage partner usually starts with romantic courtship (a practical beginning would be deemed vulgar) and courtship usually bridges the gap between uncertain youth and responsible adulthood. The beginning of the family is usually in leisure experience with all the adventures of dating, but it turns at once to work, or at least faces work obligations. The home-establishing effort is one of creating the milieu in which the family and work roles become central, and in relation to these the individual becomes oriented or re-oriented to his other roles; friend, club member, citizen, etc. While this new centre is a place where things accumulate, it is also to some degree ceremonial. The new unit acquires a collective way of thinking, of managing its money and spending, but it is a centre of some or varying degrees of intimacy. One has fun here but here he also faces the problems of life.

SOCIAL CLASS AND OCCUPATION

The individual usually enters marriage at the level of his social class, so he enters the labour market at about the same time. The problem, at least of the American family, is to hold fast to its class status and perhaps climb to a higher class. The worker family feels impelled, if the parents cannot climb higher, at least to educate the children for upward social mobility. This has been the story of immigrant families.

Class-occupation relationships are known. The manager has a fine office and a secretary. He has a liquor cabinet and flowers on his desk. He comes late to work and goes home early. A chauffeur drives his car. He also has long vacations. Clerical workers have no secretaries, but they do wear pressed suits and

[1] Joffre Dumazedier with C. Friedmann and E. Morin, 'Les loisirs dans la vie quotidienne', *Encyclopedie Francaise*, T. XIV, 56. 10.

white shirts while on the job, and they are paid salaries. Their work is light, clean and they have a month vacation. The artisan, a hand worker, handles tools and machines. His work is rarely heavy, but it is exact and respected. He has less vacation than most white-collar workers. Then as all know, the less skilled and unskilled of workers are found at the two bottom levels. The former is usually identified with routine work and he may acquire general skills, while the heavy and dirty work usually goes to the unskilled worker. Either may move up into the artisan class, but that is unusual. Such is the social class picture of the occupations as seen by most workers: the higher the occupation the more it pays. Also, the higher the occupation the more 'respect' it affords.

The individual may enter his occupation or be on the way to it even before reaching the yearned-for goal of youth, adulthood, but rarely does adulthood turn out to be a snug harbour. In a more utilitarian sense, it turns out to be more of a competitive arena than youth was. This becomes increasingly the case when the individual, besides entering adulthood and his occupation, also enters marriage. Now he is a home maker and the competitive factors become more complicated. Modern society is like that, as Bendix and Lipset observed, 'characterized by unresolved tensions', but there is order and one competes according to the rules of the game.

> Specifically, societies are characterized by status distinctions and a division of labour which involve tensions between individuals and groups who see their position as relatively advantageous and who seek to defend and increase their advantages, and other individuals and groups who see their position as 'too low' or as disadvantageous and who seek to come to terms with this experience by escape, by accommodation or by conflict.[2]

As there are different sorts of competition so there are varieties of tension and these continue through the individual's active years. They are the expected challenges he must meet if he would get ahead; that is, advance himself in both occupation and income. Social class meets occupation in one's productive activities as well as in his spending and consuming activities,

---

[1] Reinhard Bendix and Seymour M. Lipset, 'Political Sociology', *Current Sociology*, Vol. VI, No. 2, 1957, p. 87.

Active Years of the Life Cycle

his 'life style', a term used by Havinghurst and Feigenbaum. Life style relates not so much to one's work as to his leisure and social living.[1] It is, moreover, a social class identification, but life style is in the main that level of living that one can afford. The manager can afford a different life style, a more expensive style than that of the artisan, as the artisan may have a correspondingly higher life style than the unskilled worker.

Life style may reflect social class in earning and spending, things one can display. It may also be evidenced in terms of 'cultural' distinctions, what one does, how he appears and the values he holds in keeping with his social level. Whatever that level, as it is often reflected in one's education, it is also reflected in his occupation. One can be a common labourer and not feel out of place with only a common school education, but if he is occupationally of the upper-middle class he might feel and be regarded quite out of place if he had less than a high school education. Life style has quality, and as Marshall put it, 'It is quality that counts.'[2] Inasmuch as social class is competitive, these evidences of class fitness are the weapons and devices of competition. They are acceptable to the Puritan idea of success for advancing in this world and the next, although they are not always used, as Barker indicated, 'as a spiritual exercise'.[3]

Whatever the social class of the individual, and his occupation may be anywhere on the scale from common labour upward, he is identified with all the roles indicated by Havinghurst. But he may be identified at the level suited to his class, and that identity finds expression in his leisure as well as in his work. The satisfactions derived from work may differ from one level to another, but those derived from leisure are often the same, or nearly so. This is illustrated in motoring or in fishing. Just so, the satisfactions from role identities may be fairly similar, which may be seen in such roles as friend or citizen.

Whatever his class or occupation, a person may become so well adjusted in his style of life with respect to his role as a citizen or club member and he feels no need of leisure role satisfactions. Or he may be fully oriented in his leisure and social roles, but not to the role of work. Conversely, he may get

---
[1] Robert J. Havinghurst and Kenneth Feigenbaum, 'Leisure and Life Style', *American Journal of Sociology*, Vol. 64, No. 4, January 1959, p. 396.
[2] T. H. Marshall, *Citizenship and Social Class*, 1950, p. 130.
[3] Ernest Barker, *National Character*, 1940 (4th Ed.), p. 181.

all the satisfactions that concern him out of his work and family life roles. When the individual tends to neglect an essential role he will find himself under pressures to shift the emphasis a little. Even when there is a lack of balance, the individual may still be conscious of his social position and still preoccupied with ideas about getting ahead, doing just that in whatever role holds out the greatest promise.

PURSUIT OF STATUS AND HAPPINESS

During the active and productive years of his life cycle the individual is normally concerned with status and security and with realizing some enjoyment out of the effort. When he enters marriage it is not with the idea of leaving behind the lust for life with which he entered adulthood. On the contrary, marriage is looked forward to by the marriage partners as an opportunity to get some of the happiness not possible during their supervised youth or while they were still in the parental home. The vision of happiness need not obscure the firm realities of marriage; making a home and rearing a family, gaining social status. These are seen as goals for joint effort. Mead claims that modern newly-weds do have these goals, and work jointly towards them.

> The home, in which one was once allowed a limited amount of recuperation and recreation in reward for working hard, has now become the reason for existence, which in turn justifies working at all. This does not mean that many young people are not working very hard. Husband and wife often both work, combining work, children and going on getting an education. But the emphasis is different. Jobs are selected as they will bear on the home. In the familiar phrase of how a man will account to his Maker for his life on earth, having been a good husband and father heads the list.[1]

Aside from going out occasionally and having good times, the major source of enjoyment for most newly-married pairs is found in the accumulation of things, arranging things and fixing things, things that can be seen when they have visitors. There is satisfaction in owning things, but also in displaying them,

[1] Margaret Mead, 'The Pattern of Leisure in Contemporary American Society', *Annals of the American Academy of Political and Social Science*, Vol. 313, September 1957, p. 14.

Active Years of the Life Cycle

perhaps to the envy of visitors. From its point of beginning to its final dissolution, the modern home is the family showcase; ior the family collectively and for its separate members. As for any showcase, the exhibits must be changed from time to time. Nothing accumulated in the home directly bespeaks the work by which the family lives, but it must and usually does bespeak the social level of the family, much as does the family automobile, the house inhabited by the family and the quality of the neighbourhood. This showcase feature of the home relates to a whole combination of things, furniture, wall decorations, dishes and silverware, even the family clothing. All is put on display because the impressions that others get is the stuff out of which social status is built.

These showcase aspects of home life when effectively carried through comprise one of the major sources of happiness in marriage and family living. That can be said even though the effort is continuous. As the mode changes or as family fortunes change, the showcase must be redecorated again and again. The family, of course, must work for other goals, but success in other goals, or failure in other goals, are usually reflected in the showcase.

Riesman and Roseborough use the term 'domestic package', which includes what the home contains at any one time. At marriage the newly-weds assemble their initial domestic package, but it may not be the same domestic package visitors will see five years later. This initial package 'represents one's integration into the society and allows, once it is bought and paid for, further goal-directed moves in preparation for an open-ended future'.[1] The package changes bit by bit and, whether it reflects sophistication change in the family or not, at least it proclaims the social and economic position of this nuclear group.

Those who enter the homemaking and family compact for the pursuit of happiness become a separate competitive unit, a focal point for the major economic processes. To this point the earnings are brought and out of this centre the earnings are expended for consumer goods and services, including spending for leisure. It is in this relationship of getting and spending, and

[1] David Riesman and Howard Roseborough, 'Careers and Consumer Behavior', see Lincoln H. Clark, Editor, *Consumer Behavior*, New York, 1955, Vol. II, pp. 8, 17.

Active Years of the Life Cycle

with it the acquiring of things, perhaps saving a little, that the basic satisfactions of living are found. The satisfactions may result in part from leisure, but they also derive from the individual's other roles, especially those of spouse, homemaker and parent. For most people, this is the pursuit of happiness during the active middle years of the life span.

SOCIAL MOBILITY AND DISPLAY

Perhaps family living was never more responsive to the occupational status of the chief income-earner, but the phenomena of the 'showcase' and the 'domestic package' mentioned above do not depend entirely on change in the occupation of the family head. The family is an on-going unity in the midst of a network of relationships in which it has a recognized status. Whether it advances economically or remains at the same level, it must continue to maintain its 'front'. However, if the family advances economically then it is not only better able to hold its social status, but it finds itself facing the need of advancing in social status, of making certain shifts.

One may advance economically if his earnings increase although his occupation may not change. He may advance from one occupation to another but for the time being not increase his earnings. Increases may come later, but his occupational status has advanced. One may be so fortunate as to advance both in occupational status and in income. When this happens it amounts to a mandate to change his style of life.[1] The family is really the recipient of this mandate, which calls for a whole complex of changes.

Moving up the scale in occupation and income may call for change to a roomier dwelling, perhaps in a more select neighbourhood. It may call for the replacement of various house furnishings, a 'new outfitting'. But it may mean leaving behind old associates as well as old furniture. All the roles of the family members may be altered to suit the new family role; the role that the family hopes to acquire. While all members of the

[1] The pursuit of status and happiness as described here may be less evident in European than in American communities, but it is not absent there. The urge for this kind of social mobility in the United States was great among immigrants from Europe and their children. It was probably encouraged also by wealth-getting on the frontier. The idea that success must be displayed is probably common to most people if the situation permits it.

Active Years of the Life Cycle

family may not share in it to the same degree emotionally, and while it may not yield the satisfactions hoped for, this effort to move up is of the pursuit of happiness the essence. As the supporting occupation of the family head has changed, a work change, so now the family must adapt its leisure participation role to suit the new life style.

Needless to say, a downward move in occupation and earnings, meaning a possible loss in status, may stimulate a firm closing of ranks within the family to 'keep up a front', at least for a while. Normally such a change does not occur until late in the middle phase of the life cycle. What is normal for most families is that in the course of the years between marriage and the departure of the children there may be a number of such status changes which call for style-of-life adaptations. Whether these mandates for radical change come or not, there are still the day-to-day compulsions of the mode with which house furnishing, like clothes, must keep pace. Stone, in a comment on the Riesman-Roseborough domestic-package concept asks his readers to reflect on their own lives, to think of the livingrooms they have known, how these have changed through the years in response to social circumstances.

Certainly, the circumstances often represent fundamental alterations of social position. The same is true, I suspect, of most of the items of the standard package—the car, the home, the table setting, foods and furniture. I know it is true of clothing, for every major change in the social position—birth, entrance into school, graduation, marriage, parenthood, and even death—involves a change of wardrobe. I mention these things to indicate how personal mobility—changes of one's social circumstances—and the items of the package are intricably interlinked.[1]

A great many families, perhaps the majority, do not change from one social and economic level to another but they are still within the compulsion sphere of the mode. We may assume, for example, the family of an artisan who follows the same work year after year, yet with the general rise in wages through the years he and his family find themselves moving into a new style of life. The new style of life for such a family means a higher

[1] Gregory P. Stone, Comment on 'Careers and Consumer Behavior', see Lincoln H. Clark, *Consumer Behavior*, New York, 1955, Vol. II, p. 25.

level of living. The children of the artisan may attend school a few years longer and enter the labour market at a higher occupational level than his own. The home will be better furnished, with efforts to be distinctive. In such a case the family is subject to social and cultural compulsions, and urging of the children, to strive for the new life style, a style perhaps higher than that usually associated with the occupation of the artisan.[1] Who doesn't know such examples?

USING LEISURE AT HOME

While the home is the place where family members do most of their radio listening, television viewing, reading, hobby puttering and various domestic duties. It is the workplace for the mother. Here is done most of the talking with friends, some loafing and other purposeless activity, not always unproductive of friendly and neighbourly relations. We don't know how much of such easy activity is enough, but even a little is frowned upon by those who believe that all free time should be used to a purpose. We must say that such easy time-passing speaks well for the congeniality of the home. Since one is not bored with such easy time-passing, it may evidence congeniality with leisure.

This passing of leisure at home is new. Formerly the man of the house strayed away to the corner, the barber shop, the 'pub', the *Gasthaus* or café; the children came into the house only to eat and sleep, while even the mother with free time took her chair out to sit with other women on the sidewalk. The home becomes more inviting. We learn that in Holland today 62 per cent of the free time of family members is spent at home. It ranges from more than 80 per cent for older members down to 39 per cent for the age 18 to 23 group.[2]

It may be that spending time at home could be credited to radio and television, but probably even more credit should be given to the home furnishing industries and their high-pressure advertising to make the home more attractive, more a place to

---

[1] In his study of the middle-aged in Kansas City, Havinghurst found that 75 per cent of the group conformed to the life style of their class, 15 per cent were above their class and 10 per cent were below their class in thinking and life style. Robert J. Havinghurst, *Genetic Psychology Monographs*, op. cit., p. 337.

[2] *Vrije-tijdsbestreding in Nederland, 1955–56* (Free-time study in Netherlands), Den Haag, Centraal Bureau voor de Statistick, 1957, Deel 2, p. 31.

Active Years of the Life Cycle

live. The home-beautiful magazines have done their part, joining their industrial advertisers in a great educational campaign. This has been helped along through the years by the high school domestic art and science classes.[1]

When leisure was much less plentiful, a holiday was the signal to join in various community activities in such pastimes as Wish mentions as usual:

> Most of the recreations of townsfolk like dancing, group singing, cockfighting, and card games had their rural devotees on a large scale. More distinctive of the country were the lively southern barbecues centering around a stuffed porker basted with wine. Country dances, as already noted, were mostly Old World importations, though some of the jigs were attributed to African origin. At country fairs sturdy farmers wrestled for prizes, competed in footraces, or chased a greased pig while others sang ballads, danced or lost themselves in drink.[2]

The fun was not so much at home or in the house but in the community. The home was mainly used for working, eating and sleeping. City pastimes were much less varied than the rural, but few of them were open in rural style for family participation or for women. For city young people a good fortune was the invention of the bicycle which could be used by both sexes, and the first poor man's vehicle. Young folks now could get out of the city on a free day. It was not, as Stoetzel observed, until people began to have more free time that urban people began to find new ways of using it.[3] But many of these developments, like the bicycle, took members of the family in different directions for their leisure.

It is also true of most commercial amusement of the spectator type (movies, theatre, ball games), they must lure family members out of the home for enjoyment. The same holds for most organized activities for leisure; they are away-from home

---

[1] 'Leisure, Pursuit or Pleasure?' *House and Garden*, Vol. 115, No. 4, April 1959, p. 104. An editorial arguing that leisure at home means 'time for reading... time to explore the art of fine eating... time to yourself, time to appreciate what you have, to cultivate the mind and senses, to renew the spirit'.

[2] Harvey Wish. *Society and Thought in Early America*, New York, 1950, pp 80, 133.

[3] Jean Stoetzel in discussion on the family, see Georges Friedmann, Editor, *Villes et Campagnes*, Paris, 1953, p. 357.

Active Years of the Life Cycle

enjoyments, which is no complaint against them. It needs to be mentioned in contrast to the present trend in which the home seems to be gaining as a centre for using leisure, something to think about for those who fear the family is disintegrating. While this seems true, it appears also to be true that family members as individuals spend more of their leisure away from home than formerly. Father, mother and children, each goes out to meet with their peer groups. There is no contradiction; there is more leisure today, more for both home and outside activities. The family as a group participates less in community life than before, the individual participates more than formerly and in a variety of ways.

The observation just made emphasizes the rising importance of the individual in the modern society and the receding of the family for all but home-centred functions. This, some believe, is as it must be. Heckscher expressed the view:

> Uniformity is very probably increased by making the family the dominant interest. Free time comes to mean time with the family, and that too often means the domestication of the adventurous spirit. There was shrewd insight, we realize now, in those authors of Utopias who saw danger in the citizen's staying too much at home and being cut off from the liberalizing influences of society. In descriptions of the ideal society, where work is not burdensome and leisure is plentiful, the home is frequently pictured as comfortable yet so simply arrayed as not to preoccupy men unduly.[1]

But most of the homes in which most of the people lived at the time when the Utopias were written were no more than crude meeting-places for the family. By comparison the Utopian home would have been palatial. Aside from that thought, we find a trend in which family members figure increasingly in community life as individuals, including also the modern mothers. This community participation is mainly in the individual's leisure or non-work time. Even as it might be in Utopia, the family is the social unit for bearing and rearing the young. The home is the centre where life is lived and enjoyed, where personality develops. When that service has been completed, the family begins to disintegrate as far as the parents

[1] August Heckscher, 'Time, Work and Leisure', *Twentieth Century Fund Report*, New York, 1956, p. 14.

are concerned, but reappears in the homes of the children. While inhabited by the family the home is the principal centre for the enjoyment of life. This does not describe all modern homes, but most of them.

FASHION AND ZESTFUL LIVING

What has already been said about the showcase aspects of the modern home comes within the scope of fashion. But the scope of fashion extends beyond the home, and temporally it is very near a life cycle interest. We cannot speak of fashion as a leisure activity because it enters all interests and phases of life, but its principal domain, at least the arena in which it is most conspicuous is the area of leisure. When Simmel wrote on fashion at the turn of the century he was not thinking about leisure as such; he was thinking of the role of fashion in competition between social classes.

Fashion is the imitation of a given example and satisfies the demand for social adaptation; it leads the individual upon the road which all travel, it furnishes a general condition, which resolves the conduct of every individual into a mere example. At the same time it satisfies in no less degree the need for differentiation, the tendency toward dissimilarity, the desire for change and contrast, on the one hand by the constant change of contents, which gives to the fashion of today an individual stamp as opposed to that of yesterday and of tomorrow; on the other hand, because fashions differ for different classes— the fashions of the upper stratum of society are never identical with those of the lower; in fact, they are abandoned by the former as soon as the latter prepares to appropriate them.[2]

Simmel saw fashion as not a matter of dress alone, but of manners and of household furnishings; it concerned things owned and displayed and behaviour as well. In the main, it was a function of consumption, being only of indirect concern to work and the workplace. We must add the observation that the principal revolving centre of fashion is the home, although different family members may be differently under its influence. Much that it means to family members tends, in part at least,

[1] Georg Simmel, 'Fashion', *American Journal of Sociology*, Vol. 62, No. 6, May 1957, p. 543. Reprint from *International Quarterly*, October 1904.

Active Years of the Life Cycle

to be under supervision of the wife and mother. It is in this revolving centre where we find that most of the manifestations of fashion are related to leisure and social interests.

In his study of middle-class suburbs, Whyte found that the strain of keeping abreast of the mode is a continuous worry for all families, so much so that among families of the same class living in close proximity various attitudes develop frowning on the urge for display, the reverse of the urge to 'keep up with the Joneses'. The social expectations discourage the lust for outstripping the neighbours in the showcase race. 'The levelling process is just that, levelling, and those financially above the norm who let the fact be visible are risking trouble.' Under such circumstances it is apparently the fashion to nicely reflect the common denominators. 'For, the more vigorous the search for common denominators, the stronger is the pressure for alikeness.'[1] Whyte speaks of a social mandate in a one-class suburb inhabited by families engaged in occupational climbing, families hoping to move to more exclusive suburbs later. Until they can go higher it is mutually convenient to call a truce in the fashion and display race. While the truce is not a consciously organized arrangement, it serves a mutual need of a highly fashion-devoted, ambition-dedicated homogeneous suburb.

Davidson mentions how Woodrow Wilson in the early 1920s condemned the way rich people displayed their automobiles, to the envy of the lower classes, showing the 'arrogance of wealth with all its independence and carelessness'.

> But within a decade Wilson's complaint was as obsolete as the horseless carriages he had complained about. The improving car was rapidly endearing itself to the rank and file of Americans. It had the spread of the railroad trains their fathers had developed and the ranging freedom of their grandfathers' ox-carts: the country was magnificently large and inviting; and its people enjoyed increasing well-being and leisure.[2]

The rich in showing off their automobiles were doing about what the rich have always done, enjoying, in Simmel's terms, the exclusiveness of fashion, much as in the Middle Ages when

---

[1] William H. Whyte, Jr., 'The Consumer in the New Suburbia', see Lincoln H. Clark, Editor, *Consumer Behavior*, New York. 1955, Vol. I, pp. 10–11.

[2] Marshall B. Davidson, *Life in America*, Boston, 1951, Vol. II, p. 85.

Active Years of the Life Cycle

they set the fashion of eating with knives and forks. But when the automobile became a common property, they did not renounce it. Instead, they had more exclusive cars made for their own use. While they do not set all fashions, it is true that once a fashion spreads to the lower classes, becoming 'common', they must retreat from it. Similarily, the common people turn from a fashion once it becomes habitual. For most people this is not an ordeal, but an interest-absorbing preoccupation.

This zestful and costly phase of the pursuit of happiness is no mere occasional concern of the individual during the family years of his life cycle. Fashion competition in social and leisure relationships may figure prominently in the lesser goals on the way to the main goals. The fashion contest provides much of the emotional colouring in this struggle to hold what one has and to advance himself. Yet it must not frustrate, rather it must be sued to promote the serious business of family living.

DOMESTIC ACCUMULATIONS

Hansson described the modern home as a place where the prestige articles of the family accumulate, noting that most of these symbols of family pride are related to social life or leisure. They proclaim the social position of the family and they must be displayed with proper taste. 'The care of the home and its articles, as well as all clothes of wife, husband and children, so loaded with prestige values in our anonymous society, makes the wife into a kind of keeper of the material culture department.'[1]

What Hansson says of the modern Swedish home would apply to the modern home in most Western countries; it is filled with things and things continually accumulate, and they must be seen. Some things have a display value over years, others only for a short time and they must be put out of sight, whatever their sentimental value. This was rarely the case in the preindustrial home; many of the pieces accumulated at marriage or soon after were calculated to be lifetime possessions. They were treasured, usually in the parlour, which was closed except when special company came. Today the rate of accumulation has quickened. Not all things have sentimental value; many,

---

[1] Borje Hansson, 'Dimensions of Primary Group Structure in Sweden', see Nels Anderson, Editor, *Recherches sur la Familie*, Tubingen, 1956, p. 144.

even expensive ones, are acquired for mere convenience, comfort or attractiveness but, once acquired, they may gain sentimental value.

Since the modern family is ever confronted with a space problem, old things must be discarded to make room for new. The sofa may still have utility but it no longer has vogue. Some sentimental things may be put out of sight for a while but finally the family must make a decision. These decisions are easier to make if the family is prospering and trying to move up socially, and easier to make when the children begin moving away. But the problem of accumulating and discarding is there also for the married pair without children. They are under the same pressures to change the domestic package.

The pressures are in part social, but much of the stimulus comes through the mass media and their supporters, the house-furnishing and leisure-catering industries. They can survive only as they are able to unload their products and find customers for their services. Their problem is, as Soule reminds us, to dispose of goods; foods, drinks, furniture, utensils, wall furnishings, automobiles, books and so on. They fear saturated markets.[1]

People are encouraged to buy and consume above their class and when this becomes the vogue they do not resist greatly against being led up the Mount of Temptation by the advertisers. As Riesman and Bloomberg put it with respect to leisure consumption for which the family is the principal market, 'It is a commonplace that the mass consumption goods and mass media tend to blur class lines, and tend, moreover, not only to foster filtering down of leisure-class patterns from the taste leaders at the top, but also promote uniformities from below.'[2]

The family with children is not one market, but a cluster of markets. These family-centred markets change not only with the ageing or growth of the members, but for each the changing mode has a different meaning. Thus the home becomes the centre for a variety of accumulations, community things belonging to the family and private things belonging to family members. Day-to-day decisions must be made about acquiring things

---

[1] George Soule, *Time for Living*, New York, 1955, p. 62.

[1] David Riesman and Warner Bloomberg, Jr., 'Work and Leisure, Fusion or Polarity?' see Conrad M. Arensberg and Others, *Research in Human Relations*, New York, 1957, p. 78.

Active Years of the Life Cycle

and getting rid of things. A minor crisis may result if junior brings in a dog to join the family or the daughter gets interested in goldfish. It is all part of the family effort to make the limited home space a centre for living and for display.

THE SEEMING UNIMPORTANCE OF THINGS

Is 'keeping up with the Joneses' in domestic display and family striving merely an American characteristic? These behaviour

TABLE 6

Possession of, or expectations to acquire specific goods and facilities by families of French handworkers, clerical (white-collar) workers and self-employed workers

Articles and occupational groups	Already have	Expect to obtain	Do not hope for, or do not desire	Total
Radio	%	%	%	%
Handworkers	88	9	3	100
White-collar	93	5	2	100
Self-employed	97	1	2	100
Motor vehicle				
Handworkers	10	21	69	100
White-collar	30	34	36	100
Self-employed	50	24	26	100
Fur coat				
Handworkers	7	13	80	100
White-collar	21	21	58	100
Self-employed	40	19	41	100
Carpets				
Handworkers	9	12	79	100
White-collar	32	21	47	100
Self-employed	48	16	36	100
Television				
Handworkers	2	21	77	100
White-collar	5	35	60	100
Self-employed	8	41	51	100

traits are likely to be seen in any society where professional mobility (occupation to occupation) and social mobility (social class to social class), as well as residential mobility are high. This stimulates changing from one life style to another.

In France, for example, where, according to the French,

'people enjoy life', a study was made in 1955 of the conditions and aspirations of industrial urban workers, who reported on articles in the home, whether owned, about to be obtained, merely hoped for or not desired. Five of a long list of articles which seem to be leisure-related or status-related were selected. Table 6 shows the answers for handworkers, white-collar workers and the self-employed.[1] For each item ownership is higher for white-collar workers than for handworkers, but is highest for the self-employed where apparently social expectations are also highest. What is surprising, with the exception of radio, is the high percentages even of white-collar workers and the self-employed who indicate that they do not hope to have or do not desire a motor vehicle, a fur coat for the wife, a carpet for the home or a television set. But these figures descend with the rise of the occupational level; for example, while 79 per cent of the handworkers do not hope for or do not desire to own a carpet, only 36 per cent of the self-employed expressed that attitude. These answers were given in 1955. It would be interesting to see what the answers would be in 1960 or 1965. In the meanwhile the French urban worker is said to be able to enjoy his leisure.

In the same questionnaire the French workers were asked about their housing, but these answers did not betray resigned attitudes. Fifty-four per cent found their dwellings uncomfortable, 43 per cent complained of too little space and 22 per cent said the rooms were too small. Others complained that the dwellings were old and outmoded or that the rents were excessive. Complaints were fewer for white-collar workers and still lower for the self-employed, but all complained.[2]

Rosenmayr, in his study of the Viennese family, found much overcrowding; 71 per cent of the dwellings were no larger than one and a half rooms and 40 per cent did not have private toilets. Yet many of these families have no wish to move to better housing in the suburbs. For many of these the home is not the centre for leisure and social life. They meet on the street or in the cafés. This way of life goes back 'deep in Vienna history, to a centuries old shortage of space in a city that had had the function of a fortress, and to a conception that tended

---

[1] *'Conditions, attitudes et aspirations des ouvriers'*, L'Institut Francais d'Opinion Publique, *Sondages*, Vol. 18, No. 2, 1956, p. 18.

[2] Ibid., pp. 14, 15.

Active Years of the Life Cycle

to view the family as a framework which imposes duties and obligations with entertainment and pleasure to be sought *outside* of it'.[1] Such a pattern of family leisure is not inconvenienced by the crowded house.

Nonetheless, about 50 per cent of these Vienna families would like to move to better housing, and the wish is greater among families in crowded quarters. For those not wishing to move, 'The smaller the apartments are, the more often people meet their friends outside their own homes'. Moreover:

> Social life has little chance to develop at home. The driving of the family and its social contacts outside the home, which is too small and wanting, has given a familiarity to meeting places away from home. The pleasing atmosphere of a *Heuriger* (wine cellar in the hilly suburbs) is less the result of the way it is run by the people who produce the wine than of the family feelings which have migrated from the homes. The pleasant atmosphere and familiarity, the famed *Gemütlichkeit*, which the stranger feels in this kind of amusement culture is paid for by the negative home and family culture.[2]

Vienna is not greatly different from many another once-walled Old World city where home space did not permit much living in, so people spent their free time out of the home, and still do. But that tradition is wearing down and will wear down faster as the 'educational' programme of the house-furnishing industries moves along. Europeans too will be caught up in the problems of accumulations and the harassing concerns of the changing domestic package.

NONTYPICAL FAMILIES AND HOUSEHOLDS

Every self-sufficient adult, whether he enters marriage or not, whether after marriage he rears a family or not, and if he lives his allotted years, passes through the middle phase of the life cycle. Some marry but do not have children. Compared with the majority, they establish nontypical households. There are other kinds of nontypical households. Perhaps in the urban

---

[1] Materials mentioned are from an article by 'Wohnungsverhaltnisse und Nachbarschaftbeziehungen', *Wohnennin Wien, der Aufbau*, Monographie Nr. 8, Juli 1955, pp. 37–91. Also reported by Rosenmayr in a paper, 'The Mother in the Viennese Family', given as International Seminar on Family Research, Madrid, 1958, which has not yet been published.

[2] Ibid., p. 50.

Active Years of the Life Cycle

community the number is increasing both relatively and absolutely. Sons or daughters who have never married may be caring for aged parents.

In different ways these households of adults only, often because there are no children, enjoy various social and economic advantages. They may be less cramped in the fashion competition and they can give more attention to leisure and social affairs. They can be, if so inclined, the pace-setters in these matters. The childless wife may very well be, in the words of Myrdal and Klein, an 'ornament to her husband's home and a living testimony to his wealth'. They add that she fits ideally into the double model held up by the women's journals. On the one hand she is the efficient housekeeper, and on the other she is the lady with 'the lily-white hands'. The second role is social and ceremonial. The lady changes from one dress to another and is urgently active with matters of little consequence. Unlike the housewife with children, for whom she is the model, she has time to keep her face and figure under control.[1]

The socially successful childless housewife, not she who may also hold a job, who gets her picture in the women's journals, is the plague of the housekeeping mothers. So the housekeeping mother is also expected to look and be, in spite of the hundred details of her daily work. As Mead put it, no matter how hard the wife and mother works, when her husband comes home she must look like she had never done any work at all.[2]

WHEN WIVES ALSO WORK

Apparently such pace-setting childless pairs are more exceptional than is often believed, and probably more conspicuous in the movie, where the effect is greatest, than in real life. More frequently the childless pair is one in which both spouses work, even though the wife may be employed only on a part-time job. Some pairs decide to remain childless for a number of years until they can get a home established. Of the British, Brew says it is quite usual for the spouses 'to continue for at least a few years after marriage' and for the wife to be in a part-time job' 'at the very least until middle-age'.[3] What he might have added

---

[1] Alva Myrdal and Viola Klein, *Women's Two Roles*, 1956, p. 5.

[2] Margaret Mead, *Male and Female*, New York, 1949, p. 333.

[3] J. Macalister Brew, *Youth and Youth Groups*, 1957, p. 17.

is that the married pair takes more time to withdraw at once from their pre-marital leisure interests.

If the wife has been trained in an occupation at the white-collar level or higher, marriage may call for a choice. A retreat to housekeeping may mean living on a smaller budget, less money for prestige articles and leisure. Housekeeping becomes an intrusion on her career. Mead observed that it is hard enough for a woman to make a career in competition against men, but when she is married she has the second handicap of housework.[1] She has been convinced, having had about the same education as her brother and having read the women's journals, that she has the ability and the right to a career of her own, but apparently the idea haunts mainly the women who manage to get a higher education. Perhaps most women who work after marriage want their own money to buy things for the home, and a cash reserve.[2]

Since the earnings of husbands are generally higher relatively than a generation ago, families might get along as well as they did then without the wife taking outside employment, and many families do. But the pressure to have things and to use some leisure may also be relatively greater. However, since more wives do work, and partly because they do, prejudice against the idea tends to diminish. Husbands no longer need be ashamed of it, any more than they need longer be ashamed if they help with the housework. Nor is the wife any longer ashamed to admit that her husband helps in the house. It may be that having one's wife in the labour market helps to bring this change. How does this 'domestication' of the husband affect the marriage partnership?

Blood and Hamblin, after a study of working wives, concluded that the wife's employment 'tends to result in a more egalitarian ideology' between the spouses, but that the wife 'does not use her greater control over economic resources to bargain with her husband'.[3] Because she can find a place in the

[1] Margaret Mead, op. cit., pp. 320, 321.

[2] K. Ishwaren, *Family Life in the Netherlands*, The Hague, 1959, p. 81, notes that in spite of church opposition to the working of wives, the proportion rose from 5 per cent of labour force in 1920 to 10 per cent in 1947: 53 per cent of single women worked in 1920 and 56 per cent in 1947.

[3] Robert O. Blood and Robert L. Hamblin, 'The Effect of the Wife's Employment on the Family Power Structure', *Social Forces*, Vol. 36, No. 4, May 1958, p. 352.

labour market, the modern American woman, as Cohen observed, 'displays greater personal and intellectual independence. Intent upon attaining a social career of her own, she makes greater demands for leisure and means.'[1]

Nye made a study of working and non-working wives who were mothers of small children in the State of Washington. He found, to be sure, that women who combine a job and motherhood have great difficulty, but many manage it. The working wife, he concluded, is likely to neglect neighbourhood contacts, while she may establish wider social and recreational contacts with work companions, business associates and so on. He found little evidence that the solidarity of intra-family relations was negatively affected by the employment of the wife.[1]

How much the working wife has become a recognized factor in American society is seen by the existence in the United States of three magazines devoted exclusively to her problems. Each has a circulation exceeding 500,000. A study of these by Hatch revealed that they gloss over rather than penetrate the incompatible elements in rival roles of the working wife. The real problems are 'obscured by a crusading spirit'. The conclusion reads in part, 'The articles reviewed tend to assume that every problem can be disposed of by the application techniques and determination'.[2]

SPENDING AND SAVING

When the lovers enter marriage they also enter a contractual arrangement which permits them collectively to own property. The man covenants to maintain the wife and such children as may be born. If he dies, the wife is expected to assume these economic responsibilities. A divorce calls for a legal division of property. Normally the contract holds until the termination of the family cycle. Under this contract it is also assumed that the family accepts the major responsibility for its own economic security, that the family will be provident and forward-looking and that it will be prepared to meet the costs of the normal exigencies of life. At this point enters the Puritan doctrine of saving.

[1] Morris R. Cohen, *American Thought, a Critical Sketch*, Glenco, Ill. 1954, p. 31.

[2] Mary G. Hatch and David L. Hatch, 'Problems of Married Working Women as Presented by Three Popular Women's Magazines', *Social Forces*, Vol. 37, No. 2, December 1958, pp.150–1.

Active Years of the Life Cycle

The contract notwithstanding, the family is usually composed of very average people who don't mind working, but they also want to enjoy life. They may resolve again and again to save against the future, but very little saving is done, except saving today to buy something tomorrow. From figures assembled by Fisher we note that 61 per cent of American families are savers compared with 55 per cent of British families.[1] But when the accumulations of these families called savers are examined further it turns out that the majority do not have enough liquid assets to support themselves for more than a few weeks. Moreover, as already noted, much of the saving is for deferred spending; to build a garage, to buy an automobile or a television set, to send a child to college. We know that in the United States about 80 per cent of all consumer spending is done by women. Does this mean that the wife is responsible if the family fails to save? Apparently the family does not bother to ask that question.

That most modern families do not save as much as they might may indicate how much family interests are centred on family living, including leisure consumption. The family is certainly a money-getting unit but only the small percentage of families, making up the higher income section, report substantial savings. The rest are occasional savers, but they do accumulate some property and most families carry some insurance. Fortunately for most workers in most Western countries, they have been forced to save something under the various public or corporation insurance schemes, to be paid back in pensions later.

This brings us to the concluding thought that the individual who spends the middle phase of his life cycle in family living, working for the family, is party to an economic arrangement which financially in the long run only a little more than breaks even. What he gets out of the experience must be reckoned in other values; enjoyment of life, perhaps heading the list, and enjoyment of life in some measure means the enjoyment of leisure.

SUMMARY

For most people the active middle years of the life cycle are devoted mainly to family living. The roles of spouse, parent

[1] Janet S. Fisher, 'Family Life Cycle Analysis in Research on Consumer Behaviour', see Lincoln H. Clark, Editor, *Consumer Behavior*, New York, 1955, Vol. II, pp. 34-35.

and homemaker are paramount, and in the family the role of worker finds its principal goals. Less the work and production unit it once was, the family has not lost its consumer importance, rather it has become the centre of a more varied consumption often mixed with display. Moreover and increasingly the family becomes the individual as well as collective leisure centre for its members.

Normally in the middle years of the individual's life he achieves, if at all, his work goals, and the main satisfactions derived from work are in this period. These are usually shared satisfactions, since they determine family living and standing. The family may often be for the individual the chief incentive for endeavouring to advance himself occupationally and increase his income.

By whatever ideals the married pair may be motivated, there is the assumption in the culture that they will found a home and rear a family. Most of the satisfactions associated with this ideal concern joint efforts in the accumulation of things, and sharing the accumulations, including money income. This allows today for the individual accumulations of family members. In these relationships the modern family develops a unity apart from the community.

This unity of the family finds expression in social competition relative to the having and display of possessions. The pursuit of happiness becomes a pursuit of recognition. The home assumes the aspect of a showcase which reflects the economic position of the family as well as the cultural status of its members. This preoccupation with display, while it bespeaks the occupational and income standing of the family, tends to find its outlet in different areas of consumption; food, clothing, house furnishings, ornamentations, home location, as well as in social contacts and in spending for leisure. It is also reflected in the social roles of family members outside the home.

In such terms the pursuit of happiness continues throughout the family life cycle. Display must be continuous and the art of display must be continually refined, especially if the family or some members are moving socially upward. The inventory of things at any one time has been called the 'domestic package'. In the year-in, year-out effort to keep up with the mode the domestic package is continually changing. Old things are cast aside to make room for new. Among American families this

Active Years of the Life Cycle

display urge is common to all classes. It is apparently less true, at least for the present, of European families, but is not absent there. Social pressures are present but advertising pressure is less persuasive.

However, in all these countries, as in the United States, a third or more of all wives, whether part-time or full-time, whether briefly or for some years after marriage, are employed for pay outside the home. Some of this outside work is required to meet family need, some of it has the object of acquiring things for the home, but much of it is also used to meet social and leisure needs. Or conversely, without the extra earnings of the wife the family might be forced to relinquish certain social and leisure activities. Some wives, it is true, keep their employment to maintain their career interests.

The family as an economic unit is not, on the whole, a financial success. Most families come to the end of the cycle with only very minor surpluses. They have saved, but mainly for deferred spending. They may have some insurance, but increasingly pensions come to the rescue. These observations do not apply to the small percentage of higher-income families. While not a financial success, the family experience yields other satisfactions, found in the *living*. One observation must be added; apparently the modern home becomes more important as the place where leisure time is spent. Perhaps not in the old sense, but certainly in a new one, the home is the centre for passing time in the easy way.

8
WITH TIME ON THEIR HANDS

TO include a chapter on old age in a book about work and leisure is quite unorthodox. As most writers on work say very little about leisure and most writers on leisure almost nothing about work, so both groups tend to avoid looking at old age. Writers on leisure, particularly those interested in recreation programmes, usually give considerable space to that other unproductive end of the life cycle; youth, but old age is generally dismissed with a few pats on the back. Writers on work may at times give a thought to the further employability of workers forced to retire at sixty-five or sooner, but this is usually a marginal subject.

Neither in work nor leisure is old age a matter of mere sentiment. With the extending life span, it amounts to about a tenth of one's adult years, if one lives much past 70. Wolfbein notes that, whereas in 1900 one out of each twenty-five Americans was 65 or older, in 1950 one out of twelve was in that age bracket.[1] It is a consumer problem, observes Sauvy, in an analysis of population trends in western Europe where (with variations by countries) from 20 to 25 per cent of the people are 60 years or older.[2] The rejection of the old by the labour market, as Tibbitts finds, begins for some workers before they are 65, but some may continue active after that age.[3]

[1] Seymour L. Wolfbein, 'The Changing Length of Working Life', *Proceedings of the Seventh Annual Meeting of the Industrial Relations Research Association*, Detroit, December 1954, pp. 248–57.

[2] Alfred Sauvy, '*Les activites de non-travail, sont-elles des loisirs?*' *Education et Loisirs*, Bulletin du Centre Europen de la Culture, 7 annee, No. 2, mai 1959, p. 52.

[3] Of American men, 14 per cent between 45 and 64, 60 per cent of those 65 and over, and 80 per cent of those 75 and over were without employment, and for women in these age groups the percentages are higher. Clark Tibbitts, 'Ageing as as a Modern Social Achievement', see Wilma Donahue and others, *Free Time*, Ann Arbor, 1958, p. 23.

With Time on Their Hands

Rejection by the labour market today, Titmuss concludes, does not entail the hardships of the first Industrial Revolution when unemployment meant consignment to abject poverty. Most countries have social insurance today, but we are now entering a second Industrial Revolution which some call 'automation' and this may mean more disemployment before workers reach the usual retirement age of 65. The more efficient work becomes the more it demands the efficient.[1] For the old to be negatively affected in work means also to be negatively affected in leisure. For the old as for other workers, status in leisure often reflects status in work. Although they have 'earned a rest', their position with respect to leisure remains ambiguous, but this is not uniformly true in all industrial urban countries, as we shall see in this chapter.

A MAN AND HIS WORTH

At any point in his life the individual tends to be rated in terms of non-sentimental values; what he owns, his occupation, his work record, and the influence he wields. Perhaps the family name is considered. His worth from year to year may rise or fall. During his middle years it may remain for a considerable time at a given level. His worth curve begins in his youth, wavers as it rises to some high point and then wavers its way down.

Perhaps the same factors would be included in estimating a man's potential worth, projecting his worth into the future. Other factors may also be considered in potential worth; one's social class, his 'character', what he has invested in himself in the way of education and training, what he may have achieved. Such factors are considered when the young person applies to the business man for a job. They may also be considered when the business man applies to the bank for a loan for expanding his enterprise.

The first of these curves relates more to the present, while the potential worth curve concerns the individual in terms of the future. One's worth curve may not be high when he enters employment, but his potential worth curve may be fairly high. The worth curve may be higher toward the end of the individual's active years than his potential worth curve. For the

[1] R. H. Titmuss, 'The Case for Social Research as a Guide for the Formation of Policy', *The Need for Cross-national Surveys of Old Age*, Conference of the International Association of Gerontology, Copenhagen, 19-23 October 1956, pp. 3-4.

ordinary worker the potential worth curve may drop to zero long before he has reached the conventional retirement age.

Both worth and potential worth are social as well as economic ratings. They concern the rating of the individual by others, but they also condition in one way or other his rating of himself. He may put forth considerable effort to hold his ratings up or to raise them, but as he gets older he knows very well that the ratings will decline. Not only does he know this, but he knows that others are aware of it. Whether it is mentioned to him or not he knows in a hundred ways that they too watch his work utility decline. His utility is not always determined on the basis of his ability to work; his age may be a more potent factor in the downward turning of his worth curve, and then he makes his exit from the labour market, retirement. He has time but he can no longer sell it.

WHAT RETIREMENT MEANS

Charles Lamb had been employed as an accountant on the same job for many years, six days a week, nine to ten hours a day. He was allowed two holidays in a year, Christmas and Easter. He was free on Sundays, but the English Sunday of a century and a half ago was an occasion of stern and pious duty, of slow walking and subdued conversation, the heaviest day of the week for one who might want to use time more lightly. Unexpectedly to him, his firm decided to retire him with a pension, nor did he have any wish to be pensioned. In part, this is what he wrote later:

> For the first day or two I was stunned—overwhelmed, I could only apprehend my felicity; I was too confused to taste it sincerely. I wandered about thinking I was happy, and knowing that I was not. I was in the condition of a prisoner in the old Bastile, suddenly loose after forty years' confinement. I could scarcely trust myself with myself.
> It was like passing out of Time into Eternity—for it was a sort of Eternity for a man to have all his Time to himself. It seemed to me that I had more Time on my hands than I could ever manage. From a poor man, poor in Time, I was suddenly lifted up into a vast revenue; I could see no end of

my possession; I wanted some steward, or judicious bailiff, to manage my estate of Time for me.[1]

Lamb discovered that since every day had become a holiday the idea of holiday had lost its meaning. All his usual measures of time in terms of routines had been set aside; it was like taking the markings away from the roadside. Turning to amusement had lost its old meaning because now there was nothing to be diverted from. Once there had been limits to how much reading he might do and he had to manage well to get any reading done at all. Before his retirement he used his spare time ingeniously for his writing; it was a sort of recreation. Now writing was his only work. While in this dilemma, from which of course he recovered, the days of the week had lost their distinctive character. He became conscious of time mainly as he marked the goings and comings of people who had jobs, as if only their time counted.

In Lamb's day it was only rarely that a worker was retired with pay. A century had to pass before this became customary for salaried workers, and still another fifty years went by before the practice seeped down to the handworkers, who now claim pensions, like vacations, as a right. Lamb's position was unique because he had a vocation to which he could turn, as he did after the initial shock of retirement had passed. Only rarely does the retired person have such a special field open to him, and such talent ready for use. But even Lamb had to meet the problem of all retired persons. His habitual daily routines had to be changed and new ones established, the new routines being unrelated to his former world of work. He had to find ways of obligating his abundance of leisure.

Ours is perhaps the first civilization to invent retirement as a means of dealing with old age. Its function is to get the old out of the way so they won't get hurt and so the work of others will not be hindered, but social considerations are also present; we say the old have earned a rest. Moreover, this is seen as something to be looked forward to by those not yet old. They can expect to retire and live on a pension. One can see the day coming, but he works on and then there is an abrupt stop.

Commonly in pre-industrial civilizations people approached old age in a step-by-step manner, their work roles changing from

[1] Charles Lamb, 'The Superannuated Man', 1939, pp. 215–16.

year to year according to the individual's capabilities. There was no final exit from the work pattern and no sudden exit unless one became disabled, in which case he was entitled to care. He still had social stature, perhaps more in old age than in youth.

OLD-AGE STATUS AND SECURITY

In the modern community there are certain cultural mandates regarding respect for age, and on the person-to-person basis these are conformed to. The very idea of pensions for the aged reflects this attitude. But this respect, for the most part gratuitous, is not always seen as something the old are entitled to as a matter of right, as in primitive society. It does not generally ensure economic security for the old person. That is something for which he was himself responsible during the active years of his life. What he may have, once he leaves work behind, is a matter between himself and the economy. Many do not enter this phase of the life cycle with reasonable security, especially in the United States at this time; the social security system has not been long enough in operation. It is not unusual to hear of aged Americans being in need. Zalomek wrote:

> It is unthinkable that a nation which privately and publicly has assumed so much responsibility for the welfare of its citizens should say that after 60 or 65 years of age a man or woman who has worked for a good part of his life must now be content with a subsistence level of existence. That is the status of much of our older population today. Even recent surveys have shown that the income level of the oldest part of our population is very low and leaves little for recreation after necessities have been supplied.[1]

The final sentence above bears a second reading, it means when the old move out of the labour market they may have to move out of the leisure market as well. Understandably, they are not featured in leisure advertising. As for the studies mentioned, a summary of these were made by the Council of State Governments. The Council's report indicates; 1. a good share of the old people are in need, but 2. the situation is improving. And the report adds that many of the aged who have economic security, meaning above the subsistence level, are still not happy

[1] A. Wilbert Zelomek, *A Changing America*, New York, 1959, p. 87.

With Time on Their Hands

because emotional security is lacking. They are in a sense outside of society, not linked with community life.[1]

We don't know how much need there is among aged persons in our society, and one reason may be the pride of older persons, their unwillingness to make their needs known. This was illustrated by the work of Constantine Panunzio who after many years of teaching in a university ended with a pension that little more than paid his rent. He became interested and began assembling information about other professors who had retired and generally he found they were in need. One former professor was working as a nightwatchman to supplement his $93 monthly pension. Panuncio broadened his inquiry and found the same condition among retired professors in all parts of the United States. Perhaps this indicates how mollified a group professors have become; they did not go back to their former colleagues or their universities to report their need, as if their condition were shameful. And here it must be added that such need was not due to riotous living; it means only that professors generally live on a thin budget, but they must keep up appearances. Panunzio started a crusade which is still going on 'to stir up a holy discontent over this lost battalion'.[2]

The individual who has lived a self-sufficient life, even though he has not been able to acquire wealth, is likely to be one who has taken pride in his self-sufficiency. This means, generally that he held in low esteem those who were not self-sufficient. Perhaps, like many professors, he believed that a person in need more than likely was guilty of improvidence. When such a person is himself in need, especially in his old age, he knows very well the attitudes others will hold toward him. Rather than expose himself to contempt or even the pity of former acquaintances, he isolates himself.

RETIREMENT AND LONELINESS

So the old do not dominate the modern community in ways mentioned by Sumner, who had earlier societies in mind,[3] they become instead a tolerated group. This applies only to the old

---

[1] The States and their Older Citizens, Chicago, Council of State Governments, 1955, p. 9.
[2] Andrew Hamilton, 'Wanted, Help for Alma Mater's Lost Battalion', *Reader's Digest*, January 1959.
[3] William G. Sumner, *Folkways*, Boston, 1906, p. 11.

who lack wealth or power. Actually, the modern society is dominated by the old in high places. It would be unusual in an international meeting of diplomats to see any men under 60 years of age just as it would be unusual at an international meeting of experts, say in transportation, to see any over 60 years. Top church leaders are usually old men, as are top leaders in trade unions, women's organizations, co-operative societies and so on. Old men predominate among the most powerful leaders in business and industry, the same industries that dismiss workers at 65. When people in such top level posts retire it is not a retreat to isolation. For most farmers and for most self-employed urbanites retirement, not only comes late, but it involves no future of loneliness. This is mainly the problem of the great majority who sell their time for wages or salaries, often those especially who have reared families.

According to the already mentioned review of American research into old age by the Council of State Governments it was found that 27 per cent of the aged couples in the United States were living on an 'emergency budget', which allows no money for leisure or comfort. Moreover, of the aged single persons, most of them widowed, 33 per cent of the males and 51 per cent of the females were living on such an emergency budget.[1] What is pertinent there is that most of these old people complained of loneliness. Some, of course, were homebound because of physical or mental handicaps, but still more were apparently cut off socially, or had isolated themselves. Modern community life is such that one becomes automatically isolated when he ceases on his own initiative to be identified with it. It is true that various organized groups try to meet this situation by forming 'Golden Age' clubs, which help, but not enough. Therefore 'the number of isolated and lonely ageing people in every community is many times as high as the number enjoying the sociability and fellowship of these clubs'.[2]

Townsend, who made a study of the aged in Bethnal Green, a London working-class area, reported that:

> The average old person in Bethnal Green had six relatives living within five minutes walk, and thirteen within a mile. Part of the information concerned more than 600 children.

[1] *The States and their Older Citizens*, op. cit., p. 28.
[2] Ibid., p. 45.

With Time on Their Hands

50 per cent of all children and 44 per cent of married children lived with their parents or within a mile. Looked at from the point of view of the old people themselves, the availability of the children was striking. Three-quarters of those with surviving children had at least one living within five minutes walk and a further 10 per cent within a mile. Most children were seen every day or frequently in the week.[1]

According to this report, the aged in at least one poor section of London are not socially isolated. Other than in American

TABLE 7

Median ages of husband and wife at selected stages of the life cycle of the family in the United States, 1890, 1950

Stage of family life cycle	Husband		Wife	
	1950	1890	1950	1890
1. First marriage	22.8	26.1	20.1	22.1
2. Birth of last child	28.8	36.0	26.1	31.9
3. Marriage of last child	50.3	59.4	47.6	55.3
4. Death of one spouse[2]	64.1	57.4	61.4	53.3
5. Death of other spouse[3]	71.6	66.4	77.2	67.7

cities, when London children marry, they normally establish homes in the same neighbourhood. Townsend and his associates seem of the opinion that American researchers visualize more old-age isolation than actually exists. Had Townsend studied a less homogeneous section of London he might have found more age isolation than in Bethnal Green. However, he did find some *isolates* (aged with no relatives or close personal contacts) and some *desolates* (the lonely with few contacts).

Here we must call attention to some figures from Glick regarding the life cycle of the American family. Table 7 shows the age of the husband and wife at different high points in the family life span for 1890 and 1950. Less difference is seen for age at first marriage than for the other events. For both husbands and wives the last child was born about six years earlier in 1950

---

[1] Peter Townsend, 'Family Relationships', *The Needs of Cross-national Surveys of Old Age*, Conference of the International Association on Gerontology, Copenhagen, 19–23 October, 1956, p. 57. See also Townsend's *The Family Life of Old People*, 1957.

[2] Husband and wife survive jointly to specified age.

[3] Husband (wife) survives alone to specified age.

than in 1890, and in 1950 parents were about eight years younger when the last child married than in 1890. 1950 fathers had the prospect of 21.3 years of survival and mothers 29.6 years of survival after the marriage of the last child. Corresponding figures for 1890 were 7.0 years and 12.4 years.[1]

According to Table 7 a couple in 1890 could expect to have perhaps thirty-one years of married life before being parted by death of one spouse. In 1950 they could expect forty-one years or more of married life, but for the final fourteen years of their marriage they would be alone, their children married. Life would begin again at about age 48 for the wife and 50 for the husband. But this second beginning of life for the married pair is for many the entry into the grim phase of the family cycle.

Entering this phase of the life cycle, the ageing person soon learns that the industrial order has very little need for him, for it belongs to the young, the quick and the strong. But this observation is perhaps more true of the United States than of some other industrial countries. There is ample evidence to support the claim that a good share of the American aged find themselves pushed aside, gently in most cases, but still pushed aside.

FROM LONELINESS TO LONELINESS

Barker speaks of the Puritan lust for work as a sort of loneliness, One separates himself from the irrelevancies and concentrates on the task before him, the admired thing to do. Thus one ever reached success and could feel virtuous about it, he leaned on no one, the credit goes to him alone. 'He carries a lonely self-reliance to the verge of lonely selfishness.' Further:

> If he had been less lonely, he would have had more sympathy; and if he had had more sympathy, he would have been less of a stern Sabbatarian, less of an enemy to simple traditional pleasures—in a word, less set upon exercising, in the moral sphere, that tyranny of conformity to which he himself refused to bow in the sphere of religion. Loneliness serves well; but it may paralyze the imagination.[2]

This loneliness, as Barker recognizes, is of one's choosing; one

[1] Paul C. Glick, 'The Life Cycle of the Family', *Marriage and Family Living*, Vol. 17, No. 1, February 1955, p. 4.
[2] Ernest Barker, *National Character*, 1949, 4th Ed., p. 174.

With Time on Their Hands

isolates himself unduly in his work, or it might be another special interest, and he almost has no wishes outside this interest, but he might have a great bias against those who do have other interests. He is alone but does not feel lonely. Others, Barker for example, may call it loneliness. But when this individual, so devoted to his work, must finally set his work aside he suddenly finds himself without ability to make other uses of his time. Then he enters a kind of loneliness which is not of his choosing, a loneliness which he alone feels but of which others may not be aware.[1]

In such a society where the worth of a man is measured almost entirely in terms of work-related values, the individual, who may even be an indifferent worker, tends to orient himself to this complex of values. Then he must retire. 'Excessive reliance on gainful work for a sense of purposeful activity has left many individuals unprepared for the unnatural leisure brought by retirement. Dependence on the family circle for status and social relationships brings a feeling of isolation when the circle is broken.'[2]

If he did not know it before, once the individual retires he discovers that all the roles in which he figured to that point; spouse, parent, neighbour, friend, club member, citizen and so on leaned heavily upon and revolved about his role as worker. The more dominant the role of worker may have been, the more helpless he is likely to be when one day he must leave work behind. If he has not already learned there are other ways to use time enjoyably, he must learn after retirement, if possible, for leisure also has values, and we quote Michelon:

Work ways and values	Leisure ways and values
1. When a person is busy at work and faced with daily problems, he is engaged in vital living. Problem-facing and problem-solving are what make life worth liv-	1. The individual must now live for himself—to satisfy his own person rather than to worry about what a job or other people require of him

[1] Riesman observes that it may not be work itself that one misses, but the job in which one has self-definition. This comes in 'holding a job and the punctuations of life provided by regular employment'. David Riesman, 'Leisure and Work in Post-industrial Society', in Eric Larrabee and Rolf Meyersohn, Editors, *Mass Leisure*, Glencoe, Ill., 1958, p. 370.

[2] *Man and his Years*, First National Conference on Ageing, Raleigh, N. C. Health Publications Institute, 1951, p. 199.

Work ways and values	Leisure ways and values
ing. They lend to the development of personality	
2. The working person is important to others and then to himself—that is, he is a job-holder, family man, company man, etc. Work for a purpose, service to others, obligations—these are important conditioners of values	2. New friends and a new community of interests must be substituted for the break-up of his work and home relationships.
3. Leisure is particularly good at that time because the time free from business is made satisfying by the knowledge that there will be a return to work—with its corresponding meanings to the individual.	3. The individual must come to see that what he formerly considered peripheral activities are the most important and most satisfying. He must see in them basic, substitute values for the meaning of work.[1]

A European reader, having in mind the situation in his own country, might not accept Michelon's Point 2 under leisure values. The retired European tends to retain his friends and community contacts, as we shall note later. Michelon found that older persons differ greatly in their ability to adjust to retirement, and the difference seems to depend on the satisfactions they previously derived from their work.

> Married women seem to adjust more quickly to retirement than do married men, apparently because they need make no abrupt transition from everyday life. . . . Single women, particularly career women, seem to have as much difficulty in adjusting to retirement as professional men or business men. They also seem to have more difficulty than single men of the same age. Professional men and business men, on the other hand, are more reluctant to retire than the average working man. And when they retire completely they have more difficulty in making a satisfactory adjustment. . . .

[1] L. E. Michelon, 'The new Leisure Class', *American Journal of Sociology*, Vol. 59, No. 4, January 1954, pp. 372-3.

With Time on Their Hands

When the meaning of work to the individual is positive, the transition to retirement is more difficult. When the meaning of work is negative of neutral the transition to retirement is easier.[1]

Such observations serve again to remind us of the unrelatedness of most industrial work to living. One can become so attached to work during his active years that he is unable to live without it if and when he must retire, and the impersonal demands of work are such that one must leave it when his faculties or strength fail with ageing. He must get himself out of the way so that others may work. How he adjusts later to a no-work existence is largely dependent on his individual resources. He cannot expect much help. What he does will depend on the attachments that continue and the economic resources still at his command. A very usual first step for Americans at this point is to move.

WITH WHEELS TO RIDE ON

Retirement for many Americans is an invitation to escape, to get out of sight, or perhaps to venture into experiences not possible before because there were too many obligations or too little time. If the individual has never developed the art of escaping in fantasy or to what Butler calls 'imaginative participation in other kinds of lives',[2] then he may find escape in a change of scenes, following the American tradition of moving somewhere else. If the old couple has the means and their automobile it may be difficult not to move. This may mean selling the home, storing the household goods, or renting the home.

In different ways the retired ones may 'get away from it all', entering a type of retirement at present fashionable in the United States, travelling with a trailer pulled behind the automobile. Americans are a car-conscious people. On a holiday 60 million automobiles crowd the highways and by-roads, racing, it seems, to pack the most distance into the minimum of time. This love for the road, which may be a hold-over from pioneer times, is something one does not leave behind when he

---

[1] Ibid., pp. 374, 376.
[2] J. A. V. Butler, *Science and Human Life*, 1957, p. 146.

enters retirement. Hence the auto camps found outside every town and city, and the great auto camps outside urban places in the South. Florida, Mississippi, Arizona and California are among the mecca states for retired people travelling in trailers. Many, of course, go to these same areas to live in hotels, if they can afford it, or in cottages. Harlan mentioned that in some Florida cities every fourth or fifth adult is 65 years of age or older. In such cities business caters to the elderly, which is evident when one notes the health food stores, the drug stores, the hobby shops and the number of physicians specializing in the ailments of the ageing.[1]

Outside these same cities are the trailer camps, anywhere from a hundred parking places for trailers to camps of a thousand or more parking places. The voyager puts his trailer on a spot for which he pays rent. He then connects with the electric power and water supply and housekeeping can begin. In the trailer camp will be stores, recreation hall, a movie and a post office. He may stay for weeks, or move again in a few days. The fact that one can move any time he wishes lends an atmosphere of freedom to this living, something not possible in those cottage communities some propose for the aged, isolating them in a sort of ghetto out of contact and out of sight. But in trailer camps:

> Personal adjustment in retirement and old age is facilitated by the attitudes and institutional practices of mobile home communities. Social roles which are congruent with the needs and interests of the retired person are sanctioned. The primary interests centre around leisure and recreation. . . . The implementation of a central recreational programme is, of course, greatly facilitated by the nature of the trailer park.[2]

This opinion by Hoyt is based on a study he made of Florida camps, one of them intensively. Residents in this camp were welcome to remain so long as they did not seek employment in the area (migratory workers living in trailers were not wanted). Hoyt interviewed 194 'households' or couples. The average

---

[1] William H. Harlan, 'Community Adaptation to the Presence of Older Persons, Petersburg, Florida', *American Journal of Sociology*, Vol. 59, No. 4, January 1954, p. 338.

[2] G. C. Hoyt, 'The Life of the Retired in a Trailer Camp', *American Journal of Sociology*, Vol. 59, No. 4, January 1954, p. 370.

monthly income (1947) was $172. The median age, including both sexes, was 60 years. Of the men 61 per cent and of the women 52 per cent took part in camp activities; shuffleboard, card-playing, pitching horseshoes, bingo, Bible class and hobby clubs, to mention the more important. He found much visiting and conversation, and 'pot luck' group dinners were frequent.[1]

Hoyt found there was little contact between the retired in the trailer camp and the local community. The reason is that trailer people are not flush with money as tourists often are. That the local community establishes trailer camps for these people is to some extent a device for putting them to one side. They are people who are out of the labour market, not the customers that tourists are who usually come on vacation and will go back to their jobs and money-earning.

We return to the article by Michelon who, after noting that life in the trailer camp is genuinely sociable, considers the differences between retired persons to fill in their time.

Some try to duplicate the frenzy of their working lives by doing anything to use up the time; as Santayana said of fanatics, they redouble their efforts when they have forgotten their aims. For others, retirement is the beginning of a long, terminal hibernation characterized by lonely and maddening inactivity. Between these extremes is the rare individual who can look ahead to the golden years, make the needed changes in values, and substitute new, vital activities for the meaning of work.[2]

The trailer camp is one sort of escape activity for retired people, although they may find it tiresome after a while.[3] For some, it may be helpful in getting over the first shock of retirement after which the elderly pair may return to a new version of home life.

[1] Ibid., p. 365. It needs to be mentioned that in some regions of the United States there is a considerable number of migratory workers who live in trailers and who move from one short-term job to another, mostly in agriculture. Their camps may be quite separate from those of the aged.

[2] L. E. Michelon, op. cit., p. 371.

[3] A retired relative of this writer bought a trailer from a retired rich man who had wearied of trailer camp life. The mentioned relative found the excellently equipped trailer an ideal mobile home. After several satisfactory years of this life he and his wife began to find it depressing. 'One is only waiting for his time to die.'

THE OLD AND THEIR HOUSING

As we noted in the previous chapter with respect to the American family, there is a tendency for the 'domestic package' to continually change during the life cycle of the family. If the family moves up step by step economically that may mean so many moves from lesser to larger homes, with the contents of the domestic package being enriched. If there are children, their growing up and moving away is the signal to diminish the size of the home and the number of things. The shrinking process may have to move faster when the chief breadwinner must retire. For Americans this often calls for moving from a house to an apartment or to a smaller apartment, cutting expenses.

Moving to a new dwelling is not a serious challenge for Americans; they move frequently and different types of housing can be found. In European communities, however, residential mobility is much less habitual and therefore among the aged moving to another house is a major problem. People move reluctantly, especially old people. On the other side, if a family or old couple wishes to move they face a serious problem of finding a place. The search may go on for weeks or months.

Sauvy, reporting on the housing of the under-privileged in French cities, observed that most old people live in the old, outmoded houses. Of the occupants in new houses, 77 per cent were under the age of 50 years, while 67 per cent of the occupants in the very old houses were 50 years of age or older; age having reference to heads of households.[1]

Had Sauvy examined the matter closer he might have found less eagerness among the old to move to new housing. That would call for settling in other neighbourhoods and away from the scene habitually familiar and from contacts that have endured for years. Perhaps it would mean leaving behind relatives with whom they are in daily contact. To move would mean to start life over. Rosenmayr found this to be the case in Vienna. While many old Viennese complained that their housing was small, uncomfortable and out-moded, they expressed great reluctance to moving away to better housing. That might mean giving up much of their habitual day-to-day routine.

[1] Alfred Sauvy, 'Le logement des faibles; novelles donnees sur l'elimination du proletariat', *Population*, Vol. 12, No. 4 *octobre–decembre*, 1957, p. 594.

With Time on Their Hands

The American type of residential mobility is not in the culture of the Viennese,[1] but the aged Viennese is not lonely.

In contrast, Rosenmayr found that young families with children were eager to move from the old houses in the narrow streets. The willingness to move was less pronounced among families living in the same house a decade or more for they, like the old, had become habituated.[2]

In Holland where family and home have ever figured intimately in the individual's life, there is a trend now toward individual detachment, perhaps less emphasis on the idea of family control and guidance. One feels less bound by the old rule of grown children being subordinate to the direction of parents, and now that parents receive pensions the young feel less bound. Holland is becoming a highly industrial urbanized country. That old rural-rooted family-home way of life cannot carry over completely to urbanism. Yet among many there is a nostalgic clinging to the old family-home concepts. Ishwaren learned that among the Dutch this complex of attitudes is called 'family sickness', a conscience-driven attachment to kinship. The aged are not economically neglected or socially isolated, but they are losing much of their influence.[3]

While the aged Hollanders still cling to the old family home, that is no longer a concern of American old people among whom retirement is often followed by moving to a simpler dwelling. Interest in home as a display centre, a showcase, begins to wane. The aged, in fact, need a rather special type of residential simplicity. Federal funds are now available to finance housing projects for the old. Zelomek mentions that these places would have 'living, dining and community recreational facilities particularly directed toward the comfort of the aged. It is also generally recognized that "retirement colonies" should be afforded easily accessible churches, libraries and theatres.'[4] While some old folks would welcome living in such a segregated community, others would feel that

---

[1] Leopold Rosenmayr, 'Der alte Mensch in der sozialen Umwelt von heute', *Kolner Zeitschrift fur Soziologie und Sozialpsychologie*, Band 10, Heft 4, 1958, s. 650. Rosenmayr mentions that in Vienna 20 per cent of the population is 60 years of age or older, while in Paris this age group equals/13.4 per cent of the population.

[2] Ibid., p. 654.

[3] K. Ishwaren, *Family Life in the Netherlands*, The Hague, Van Keulen, 1959, pp. 55, 96.

[4] A. Wilbert Zelomek, op. cit., p. 88.

With Time on Their Hands

they had been 'deported' or put to one side, outside the larger community.

OLD AGE IN GERMANY

Old-age insurance has been the law in Germany since 1889, and only the exceptional German (usually self-employed most of his life) enters retirement without a pension. It would be

TABLE 8

How German workers and pensioners would use DM 50,000

How the money would be spent	Employed and employable	Pensioners
	%	%
Build or rebuild a house	54	36
Improve existing properties	21	5
Buy stocks or bonds	19	16
Buy furniture, clothing, etc.	19	14
Put in savings account	14	19
Divide it among relatives	14	40
Pay off indebtedness	11	8
Give money for good purposes (church, the poor, orphans)	8	18
Travel and journeys	8	14
Buy an automobile	8	1
Other purposes	2	3
Unable to decide	2	5
Total percentages	180	179

difficult for a German from his first work day on not to accumulate pension credits. Our interest here is not in the pension system as such, but in the status of the aged, how they seem to fit in the life of the community. On this subject we find pertinent indirect material on how retired people see themselves in relation to the community. These data are obtained from a study of earning, saving and spending by the Institut für Selbsthilfe at Cologne.[1] One of the questions used in the interview schedule asked respondents to imagine what they would do with an extra DM 50,000 (about $11,900) which they might receive unexpectedly. In Table 8 the answers are shown

[1] The data in Table 8 and Table 9 were prepared by Otto Blume, Director of the Institut fur Selbsthilfe. The report is mimeographed.

With Time on Their Hands

for two groups of respondents, employed and employable, and pensioners. Here we see, on the one hand, how much more the pensioners would use the money for the benefit of others; 40 per cent would give money to relatives and 18 per cent would give

TABLE 9
How German workers and pensioners would use more free time

How more free time would be used	Employed and employable	Pensioners
	%	%
Outings, walking, hiking	45	29
Working in the garden	28	21
Reading or study	20	14
Going to concerts or theatre	18	11
For once to get enough sleep	17	5
Sewing, darning, other handwork	17	20
Visit with relatives and friends	16	6
Spend more time with children	15	10
Fixing things around house	14	5
Participate in sports	11	2
Listening to radio	10	10
Viewing television	9	7
Going to the movies	9	9
Give time to education	9	2
Carry on hobby activities	8	4
Go places to meet with friends	7	3
Try to earn some more money	7	2
Shopping and window shopping	7	8
Help with the housework	6	4
Church and organization work	5	4
Fishing or hunting	5	1
Activities in the arts	3	2
Tenting and camping	3	0
Other activities	2	2
Total percentages	291	181

to charity, against 14 per cent and 8 per cent for the employed respondents. In general, Table 8 gives the impression that the pensioners are not in poverty and not isolated socially.

The first what-would-you-do-if question in the German study related to getting more money; the second related to more time;

what the respondents would do with more free time, no amount of time specified. Table 9 gives the answers, and here we see that the pensioners, supposed to have time on their hands, apparently have much to do and they could use more free time. Although not employed, they were very much occupied with obligations (perhaps some doing odd jobs for pay), with gardening, helping neighbours, working around the house that they were neglecting leisure activities. Note that 29 per cent of the pensioners, compared with 45 per cent of the employed, would give more time to outings, walking and hiking. More time, 20 per cent for pensioners and 17 per cent for the employed, would be given to sewing, darning and other handwork, which suggests that even the wives in the homes of the pensioned could use more free time. Most surprising, 5 per cent of the pensioners would use some of the additional free time 'for once to get enough sleep'.

It seems that, instead of retired Germans being bored with too much leisure, a good share of them have not enough free time. A second point of pertinence is that retirement involves no sudden break in community contacts, and a third point is that most of the activities visualized in Table 9 are home-centred. This is equally true for the employed respondents.[1]

AGE AND LIFE ENJOYMENT

In 1950 the National Conference on Ageing expressed the view that too many Americans 'reach late life completely unprepared for the leisure' that retirement may bring. Further regarding this emptiness: 'Millions have but seldom read a book, have rarely played a game, have taken little or no part in community affairs. They have concentrated their whole interests within the narrow confines of job and family, and when these pass

---

[1] A 1956 study in Holland found an average of 60 hours of free time weekly. *Vrije-tijdsbesteding in Nederland*, Den Haag, Centraal Bureau voor de Statistiek, 1957, Deel 2, s. 15. This free time was spent as follows:

12–17 Years	Duties	33%	Leisure	34%	Sleep, rest	33%
18–28 ,,	,,	37%	,,	39%	,, ,,	24%
29–59 ,,	,,	40%	,,	40%	,,	20%
60 and older	,,	29%	,,	47%	,, ,,	24%
Average	Duties	38%	Leisure	40%	Sleep, rest	22%

38% of the waking hours of the 60 year plus group was spent on duties mostly at home, and 62% on leisure activity, much of it at home.

their lives seem desolate and empty. They find it difficult to believe that they still have capacity for developing new interests and relationships.'[1]

Such observations apply especially to old age in the United States where life may be unduly mobile. The idea of community alluded to in the above comment hardly exists, even for many actively employed. If it did exist there would be no need for retired persons to develop 'new interests and new relationships'; their old interests and relationships, with minor changes, would continue. The task is, not to re-educate people already old or to set up programmes to bring cheer into their lives, it is rather one of manipulating the situation so that entering old age is more of a natural event.

But no matter how the situation is manipulated, people will go on trying to stave off the signs of age when they will be out of the commercial amusement market as well as the labour market. The leisure industries make youth so glamorous that the prospect of ageing becomes something dreadful to contemplate, so people resort to hair dye, elixirs, physical culture, take to modern dancing and so on to keep up the illusion of youth. Blakely calls it the cult of youth.

> As a people we glorify the decade, say between sixteen and twenty-six years of age. Is it more sad to see children trying to look and act older than they are, or to see grown-ups trying to look and act younger than they are? Our task is not just to restore old people to participation in our society. It is also the integration of the idea of growth, the essence of which is growing old, into our philosophy.[2]

Fighting against age and hiding the first signs of it, is fairly universal. Once the individual recognizes that he has crossed the line into the final phase of the life cycle, then there is nothing for him but to make the best of the years ahead. As we have seen, these years for many are dull and dreadful because many seem not to have learned to use time, but this might not be a serious matter if the old person is able to carry over various previously established interests and contacts. This we are told is the case among old people in Bethnal Green, London (see

[1] *Man and His Years*, op. cit., pp. 199, 181.
[2] Robert J. Blakely, 'The Way of Liberal Education', see Wilma Donahue and Others, Editors, *Free Time*, Ann Arbor, University of Michigan Press, 1958, p. 105.

quotation on page 189). This appears to be true, as seen above, for the aged in Vienna.

One explanation for the unhappy condition of many of the American aged at the working-class grade has been their economic dependence, their living at a subsistence level and looking to their children for help. Once the aged at this economic plane are able to live on their pensions not only will their relations with their children and other relatives improve, but their community contacts will develop. Living at the poverty level tends to break such contacts as the aged may have. As the Federal Security System gets more favourably established in day-to-day thinking we can expect a relaxation of those pressures which have operated so effectively to keep pensions at a subsistence level. This may not solve all the emotional problems of old people, but if they can feel sufficiently secure economically to maintain their self-respect they will go far in solving their own individual time-use problems.

Even in Germany where the pension system is generally regarded as highly effective there are occasional cases of old people being in great need, but relatively need has been a much greater problem among the American aged. All of this may not pass, but much of it will as old-age security becomes better established. The leisure programmes for the aged may still be needed, but this will be mainly for the house-contained and physically weak. Just as the self-sufficient old people are able to use their leisure in the trailer camps, so in the communities, if they are economically secure, they will find ways of keeping occupied and they may not have time for leisure, which will mean that living has become the absorbing interest.

What needs to be understood is that, even if the old are no longer needed in productive work, and that will be more true in the future, they are needed in the life of the community. In every previous society they performed what might be called a balancing function. As was already noted, they still have this function in our society, but the performance is limited to the very upper echelons of state, church, industry, the professions, labour organizations and so on. At the lesser levels they also have a function, if it is only to play with the children and sit on the sidelines while the young play the game. The old are not being utilized if they are pushed aside to find their laughter among the old. 'Laughter must be shared,' says Coser, 'it is

With Time on Their Hands

socially defined as the prime part of the interactive process of the give and take of social life.'[1] Community wholeness is not realized if the laughter of children is treasured while the old are left, if they can, to laugh alone.

SUMMARY

In this chapter we have considered old age mainly as it concerns the individual's exit from productive work into retirement and into the final phase of his life cycle. For many who reach this point, it also means an exit from the family-rearing phase of married life and its various competitive strains. Retirement comes generally at 65, although sooner for some and later for others. It comes earlier for women workers.

The idea of retirement, which hardly existed before, is a necessary creation of the Puritanism-Industrialism-Capitalism complex, also the source of our abundant leisure. In the Puritan Ethic retirement was idealized as the 'evening of life', an indefinite age when one could work no more. Modern retirement often separates the individual from his job while he is still employable, although perhaps not at a prime level of efficiency. It is the mandate of enterprise that he must move out of the way so others can work.

We cannot underestimate the challenge of old age to both work and leisure, or its importance to most of us. The pertinence of this subject increases when seen in future perspective. If the present trend in technological development continues, the young person of 20 may be asked to retire from productive work in the year 2000 when he has reached 60. On the other side, if the trend in medical science continues, when this person reaches the age of 60 in 2000 he may still be in a vigorous state of health, and his mental faculties may be at their peak. He may still have twenty years of life expectancy. Still, in the generally predicted 'automation industry' he will not be needed in productive employment, although a fourth of his life is still to be lived.

Whatever the status of old age may be in 2000, it is very much of a social isolation for many old people today, or of self-isolation because of economic insecurity. There is a growing conviction that many who enter this final phase of the life cycle

[1] Rose Laub Coser, 'Some Social Functions of Laughter', *Human Relations*, Vol. 7, No. 2, 1959, p. 171.

are anything but 'senior citizens', rather they are confronted with more leisure than they are able to use. Their lives have been dedicated to job and family and they lack the ability to develop new interests. Many lapse into a condition of loneliness.

This loneliness in old age appears, as yet, not a serious problem among the retired in European countries. They have been less pressed against by the demands of technological change and for them community living has been less disturbed by mobility than has been true of Americans. Their entry into retirement involves much less shock and much more continuity of established social relationships than for the American aged.

However, the situation in the United States, where the way of retirement has been rough and insecure for so many, is now in transition. The idea that old age is the individual's own problem is stubbornly yielding to a more socialized viewpoint. The fallacy of holding old people to subsistence pensions is being recognized. There is good reason to believe that a greater measure of economic security will inspire in old people feelings of self-respect which many cannot enjoy now. In that event, most of them will find the resources within themselves to meet their own leisure-time problems. There will be some in need of help, and programmes for the aged may still be needed for those who are physically weak and house-confined.

If we look at the high levels of power and leadership in our society we find that the well-situated aged ones are able to render service. They are no less needed to serve a balance function in other levels of society where life is also lived in many relations other than those identified by productive work. Apparently we are entering a phase of our social evolution when leadership is also needed in consumption, when work not for pay will gain importance. In such developments we already see emerging a new type of community life and to the balance of that life the old can make a contribution.

9

HOW MEN MANAGE THEIR BEHAVIOUR

TO see the crowd passing a busy street corner is something to stir the imagination. This mixture of individuals, each ignoring the rest in his eagerness to get somewhere, is less chaotic than may seem. One characteristic of this crowd is that, while its tempo may remain the same, its composition tends to change from hour to hour through the day. Better said, the goals of the on-goers change. They are not the same of an evening as during the day, on a Saturday afternoon as of Saturday forenoon. The streets are used differently under the white lights than in daylight, and differently again from midnight to dawn, the red-light hours. Different corners may have a different hour-to-hour character; the banking area, the wholesale district, the shopping centre.

What is pertinent to this chapter is that all sorts of people with all sorts of interests use these streets during the day. Or the same people use the streets at different times in pursuit of a different interest, wearing each time a different non-committal mask. Directly or indirectly every individual in the entire agglomerate is affected by this going and coming through which he serves and is served. The lines of contact criss-cross in a confusing mat, yet there is a striking lack of confusion. All this movement expressive of every work and leisure interest, is also expressive of unseen order. It is neither planned nor directed, nor could it be.

This is one way among others that the behaviour of modern industrial urban man is regulated. The different ways by which he manages himself in his work, leisure and other interests cannot all be examined in this chapter, but we may be able to cover enough of the subject to indicate the complexity of that subject known among sociologists as social control. Unwittingly, most of us much of our time, when not preoccupied with our own behaviour, are engaged in managing the behaviour of others by all manner of direct and indirect devices, not excluding gossip.

CONFORMITY AND SOCIALITY

One works or plays, but how he works or plays is everybody's business, or might become so. People are naturally that way, just as most people by nature are given to gossip, even those who 'mind their own business'. People may have all sorts of practical reasons for being concerned in the behaviour of others. There is no escape from it except into loneliness, but even loneliness evidences a feeling that one finds himself stranded at the periphery of social contact. Sociality, or social living, is hardly possible if one really minds his own business. The individual minds his own business mainly by trying as he can to meet the expectations of society, which means conformity.

In modern society most people live in great agglomerations. Very few live all their waking hours within vision of the 'all-seeing eye' of the community. We are told that one can live in the anonymous crowd unnoticed, so long as his behaviour and appearance do not attract attention. We are told that the individual in the crowd is dangerously free; he can do evil and none will find it out. He is outside the realm of gossip and institutional guidance. This anonymity of urban living, as others see it, is a redeeming privacy into which one gains a moment of respite, a brief escape between appointments. One can walk in the crowd and be alone, but he is seldom isolated. One may treasure a degree of isolation as privacy but, as Gutkind put it, 'privacy is not all. Man needs and wants company'.[1]

In this way of community living, says Bednarik, man is 'freed to himself', free to work and play, but not freed from society, since society alone can give meaning to his work and play.[2] This meaning enables the individual to share the life and values

---

[1] E. A. Gutkind, Editor, *Creative Demobilization*, 1944, Vol. I, p. 29.
[2] Karl Bednarik, *An der Konsumfront*, Stuttgart, 1957, pp. 70-71.

How Men Manage Their Behaviour

of society, a purpose he does not shake off when he walks in the crowd. Sharing the life of society calls for some conformity to it, and one shares it through various group associations. Halbwachs, the French sociologist, saw the individual in the urban civilization succeeding only as he is able to join with others in associations, fitting into groups. 'Men are well aware of this; hence the passionate interest now taken in every form of association and every institution inspired by community feeling.'[1] In this seemingly chaotic agglomerate each individual finds his kind, his own little areas of intimacy. Sociality as found here is a kind that belongs naturally in this type of society which we have described as secondary and contractual.

The individual in this society belongs to different types of primary groups, which may be more transient than those in the village, but they serve the social needs of the individual and extract conformity from him much as primary groups have always done. He belongs to larger formal groups to which he gives loyalty and these, too, extract conformity of another kind from him. In this modern community he is a citizen living under law. He enjoys the rights and performs the duties of a citizen, and again in still another sense conformity is extracted from him. In all of these associations; the intimate ones in primary groups, the special interests in the secondary groups and his civic interests in relation to the law, modern man is anything but a person loose in the crowd.

THE ORDERING INFLUENCE OF WORK

Modern man is not the servile worker pictured by the Hammonds in their description of the industrial English community of a century ago. He was oppressed by toil and not supposed to have any higher interest. 'Standards of taste and culture were in the keeping of a small class which had inherited with leisure the aesthetic and literary sensibilities that had been developed by generations accustomed to the atmosphere of ease and elegance.'[2] The worker not only lacked the refinements called culture and leisure, and many viewing his lot from the outside wondered whether he could use leisure if he had it. Altick cites how the workers did use such leisure as they had at a time when they could not read.

[1] Maurice Halbwachs, *The Psychology of Social Class*, 1958, p. 137.
[2] J. L. and Barbara Hammond, *The Bleak Age*, 1934, p. 5.

How Men Manage Their Behaviour

During the decades which witnessed the worst oppression of the wage-earning masses, the townsman with time to kill on Saturday night and Sunday had little choice of diversion. He could get drunk at a public house, or, to the accompaniment of song, at a concert room or a dancing saloon; he could visit a brothel, he could get into a fist fight or attend a bear-baiting, he could loaf in the streets—and not much else. The teeming cities had virtually no provision for decent public recreation; few theatres or music halls, no parks for strolling and picnicking, no museums or art galleries, no free libraries.[1]

Primitive to be sure, but the work world then was an orderly one. Mills wrote, 'It was God's will that everyone must work, but it was not God's will that one should lust after the fruits even of his own labour; they must be reinvested to allow and spur still more labour.'[2] For most men then there was no problem of how they managed their behaviour, their behaviour was managed for them. It is far, indeed, from that type of industrial urban life to the free-moving agglomerate of the present. But the discipline of work is still with us, although less the oppressor it was then. Poverty is still with us but, by comparison, it is hardly poverty at all.[3]

Work as a disciplinary force in our society is not limited to the time it takes out of the heart of the individual's day or to the hours he may give to work problems when not on the job. The work a man does and the position his occupation has in the hierarchy of occupations affords him a very definite social status which in turn confronts him with certain social expectations. His status as a worker determines largely the companions he will have, the organizations he will belong to, the leisure-time activities he will engage in, and even the style of his home life.

[1] Richard Altick, *The English Reader, a Social History of the Mass Reading Public, 1800–1900*, Chicago, 1957.

[2] C. Wright Mills, *White Collar, the American Middle Classes*, New York, 1951, p. 216.

[3] George A. Lundberg, Mirra Komarovsky and Mary A. McInerny, *Leisure, a Suburban Study*, New York, 1934, p. 12. 'Now poverty is properly defined not in absolute terms of goods and services consumed, but in terms of the gap between wants and "necessities" of all kinds and the capacity to satisfy them. In short, poverty in the modern society is fundamentally a state of mind rather than a state of the stomach'.

How Men Manage Their Behaviour

One's manner and dress may also be a reflection of his occupation. Even if he does not talk about his work when away from the workplace, the free time conversation of those of the manager group will not be like that of the artisans, or self-employed professional workers. The discipline of one's work may figure in his voting and his choice of political party. It may decide which newspaper he will read and even the sections of the paper he will read first. The permeating influence of one's work may be operating even while one is preparing to enter an occupation, while he is in training, visualizing his role.

Also work may be a discipline in terms of itself, when it holds the interest of the worker to the exclusion of other interests. He becomes the craftsman who lives with his craft. Veblen spoke of the instinct of workmanship. 'It concentrates on devices and contrivances of efficiency and economy, proficiency, creative work and technological mastery of facts.'[1] But only the occasional modern worker becomes so absorbed and disciplined. This does not suggest by any means that work is dull for those without this attitude for their work. Job dullness, as Oakley claims, is very relative,[2] and even the dull job may figure as an ordering force in the individual's life.

The conformity-impelling quality of work becomes especially evident in the absence of work. The morale of the individual falls if he cannot find work and must join the unemployed. The morale of the community falls if great numbers of workers are unemployed. The absence of work is also seen in those who avoid it and try to live by other means, as when they resort to begging or to crime. Whether they live precariously or well by these means, they find themselves de-classed by the rest of society and outside the approved relationships.

CULTURE OF THE WORKPLACE

It must be mentioned that the conformity-impelling nature of work is very different from that in urban communities two centuries ago when one's work and his class were more closely related. Each skilled craft was organized into a guild which was both social and economic. Each guild in each city was a closed group with its trade secrets, its code of ethics, its status

---

[1] Thorstein Veblen, *The Instinct of Workmanship*, New York, 1914, p. 33.
[2] C. A. Oakley, *Men at Work*, 1946, p. 160.

hierarchy, and no phase of the individual's life was outside the jurisdiction of guild leaders. The guild was its own relief organization, burial and insurance society. It even presumed to instruct its members in their choice of marriage partners. Each guild in its community had a recognized monopoly of all work in its field. Any guild craft had community respect.

Obviously the guild system could not continue in the face of rising powered factory industry, but vestiges of the guild culture carried over to industrial work in most European countries; the long out-moded apprentice system, the training of the foreman which is still oriented to handwork traditions, and the authority structure within the trade union. But the tradition of the guild is equally evident in community attitudes toward the old occupations. One difficulty is that one is so accepted in terms of his occupation and class that his wife and children bear the same identification. Thus the European, more than the American, is embraced within the conformity-impelling influence of his work most of his waking hours. But that compulsion is apparently weakening.

Under the guilds, craftsmanship was a dominant worker interest, and it still survives, the natural discipline of work and a passion for the task, but it does not apply to most modern jobs. On craftsmanship Mills wrote:

1. In craftsmanship it is necessary 'that the tie between the product and the producer be psychologically possible....'
2. Self-development is not the craftsman's goal, only such development 'is the cumulative result obtained by devotion to and practice of his skills'.
3. The worker must be free to plan his work, also 'free to modify its form and the manner of its creation'.
4. Where the craftsman pattern is found 'there is no split of work and play, of work and leisure....'
5. 'The craftsman's work is the mainspring of the only life he knows; he does not flee from work into a separate sphere of leisure; he brings to his non-working hours the values and qualities developed and employed in his working hours.'[1]

Some are of the opinion that that spirit of craftsmanship, which has departed from much of modern work, can be restored

[1] C. Wright Mills, op. cit., pp. 220–3.

How Men Manage Their Behaviour

if we make up our minds to get interested in our jobs. We submit that it is present in most jobs to some degree most of the time. But it seems true also that work can be a discipline and workers attached to their jobs, although very little under the influence of craftsmanship. On the job the worker can feel a member of the work force in a plant and still not know more than a few of his fellow workers, as he can function effectively as a worker and yet not identify himself with the work process. He may still be rated a good worker, as he may also be rated a good husband, father, friend, etc. He still has status in relation to his work. He finds at the workplace a code of ethics and he conforms to it, but this code may not extend outside the plant. Thus in connection with work there are common well-recognized rules which may be strictly conformed to, although not talked about. Jaques speaks of the workplace as having a culture, a solidarity which at times becomes articulate.[1]

One learns at work how to adapt himself to his fellow workers. Some of the attitudes and tolerance acquired there may carry over to non-work activities; the 'game of work' joins in different ways the 'game of living'. Sometimes brave efforts are made in the factory to utilize the social behaviour of men at work, or to foster it. When seen critically, most of these efforts cannot put more of the 'social' or the 'human' into work than the situation itself naturally permits or demands.

THE DISCIPLINE OR LEISURE

In almost every great city there are groups of men who gather on holidays at the small water bodies in the parks to sail their little boats. They include persons from different occupations, but in relation to this hobby they are a classless group. They are as one regarding the rules of the game. Each model ship must meet certain recognized specifications, and there are rules for sailing the boats. Most of these hobbyists made their own boats, which means they have joined their craftsmanship, as Larrabee would say, not to work but to leisure.[2]

These hobbyists not only build their boats according to specifications, they race their boats according to widely-accepted rules. The game goes on only if the rules are kept and

---
[1] Elliot Jacques, *The Changing Culture of a Factory*, 1951.
[2] Eric Larrabee, 'What's Happening to Hobbies?' *The New York Times Magazine*, 27 December, 1953.

is fully enjoyed only when the rules are enforced. To keep the rules is moral and the moral is made and enforced by those who play the game. Stone wrote, 'Participation in the game carries with it an inherent morality merely because it requires an adherence to rules.'[1]

Such rules are essentially social and are rarely written, except for certain forms of sport or sharply competitive games. In outdoor activities such as fishing, hunting, boating or camping there are right and wrong ways of doing things and of behaving, just as in conversation there are the usually recognized rules about how and when to talk. The violator of the rules may be quickly, even roughly, made aware of his failure. Knowing the rules and keeping them becomes a source of satisfaction, if not pride, to those who play the game, an observation that seems to hold as well for adults as children. This is seen in the game of mountain-climbing which has given rise to such a fraternal organization that they tend to disregard nationality in their associations.

We may wonder, perhaps, with Lundberg if some forms of play may not have become so tightly confined by rules that they 'lose their unique and primary value as recreation and so become merely another department of activity devoted to the advancement of prestige or status'.[2] It is possible that certain leisure activities, social dancing for example, can become institutionalized to such a degree that it becomes a painful duty. For some persons attending opera might be so classed. Such a development is more likely in socially-oriented leisure than in most sports, games or individually selected pastimes.

As is often observed, the discipline of work in various ways carries over into leisure and other non-work activities. On the other hand, it is believed by many that the discipline of leisure carries over into work activities. Some are prone to judge a person on 'the way he plays the game'. So often this is the argument for inducing participation in sports. On the basis of this belief many an American star athlete on leaving college walks into a good job. But another college graduate who was perhaps a better student may have to stand in the waiting line. Of the two perhaps the athlete is the better choice, at least he

[1] Gregory P. Stone, Comments on 'Careers and Consumer Behavior', see Lincoln H. Clark, Editor, *Consumer Behavior*, New York, 1955, Vol. II, pp. 26.

[2] Lundberg, Komarovsky and McInerny, op. cit., p. 17.

begins with the advantage, but the student may be the better choice in the long run.

One point of pertinence regarding the rules of play, which holds for work rules and social rules as well, is that generally there is a zone of tolerance or courtesy allowed for careless conduct or wilful violation. This zone of courtesy serves a warning function and gives the rule-breaker the opportunity to mend his ways. It is also face-saving for both breakers and enforcers of the rules, which will ultimately be upheld.

CONFORMITY AND THE SOCIAL GAME

As was noted in Chapter 7, social competition cuts across most human interests including work and leisure, affecting all social classes. Much of the money that women spend on themselves is devoted to their social and leisure interests and much of their conversation revolves about these interests. Much of the money that men spend entertaining women and sharing leisure with them is expended in social prestige efforts. One must conform and yet be distinctive; conform sufficiently not to be stared at and be sufficiently distinctive to be admired, or envied.

These observations about social conformity hold for rural as well as urban society. Reporting on their study of Nouville, a French village, Berdot and Blancard observed the importance of the dance. Here the country girls deck themselves out as on parade, a challenge for the boys to learn dancing, to put aside gawky ways and to acquire the necessary graces. This is the introduction to what may be called society in the village. Here is also where sex compeition comes into action on the way to adulthood.[1]

Warner, who studied life, work and leisure in Jonesville, a small urban community, found that practically all approved leisure activity was influenced by social-class values. Jonesville society is divided into recognized levels and leisure as well as social club activities conform to these levels. The criteria of class worth in Jonesville are, first of all, wealth, but there are others equally sacred, such as one's religion and national origin. According to such criteria the family is selected for membership in the various social clubs and other associations.[2]

[1] Lucien Berdot et Rene Blancard, *Nouville, un village francais*, Paris, 1953, p. 192.
[2] W. Lloyd Warner, editor, *Democracy in Jonesville*, New York, 1949, pp. 133-4.

How Men Manage Their Behaviour

Be it Nouville or Jonesville, the community has its competitive class structure, and almost every family or individual from high level to low level is included in whatever forms of display and whatever kinds of activity that serves to give him recognition. To be socially identified with the right groups calls for the *right* behaviour, but the discipline even carries over to *right* thinking. One also helps to guard the status of these groups. He might try to qualify for membership in a higher-class group but he would hesitate long before joining a lower-class group.

If one is a Hollander, Gadourek tells us, he must have a church identification to gain social status in the community; the Catholic church in the all-Catholic, the Reformed church in an all-Protestant community. 'These social barriers are especially strong whenever the sport association or the club offers an opportunity for social contacts between young persons of different sex. Tennis and dancing parties are strictly denominational affairs.' If the 'liberals' try to organize neutral sport groups or clubs, they will be set upon.[1] The chief difference between the Dutch village and Jonesville is that in Jonesville, since religious discrimination is unAmerican, the practice is furtively indulged in.[2]

Mills finds that in the great cities there is a tendency for the social and other élite groups to mingle in what he calls café society, a thing the socialite can do without losing caste. In the café or night club, social leaders, prize fighters, movie stars, politicians and others may sit at the same table and share the same spotlight of publicity. And there may even be such mixings in the exclusive parties of the socialites.

> Café society's publicity has replaced the 400's family line, printer's ink has replaced blue blood, and a sort of talent in which the energy of hoped-for success, rather than the assurance of background or the manners of inherited wealth, is the key to the big entrance. In the world of the celebrity, the hierarchy of publicity has replaced the hierarchy of descent and even of great wealth. Not the gentlemen's club,

[1] Ivan Gadourek, *A Dutch Village*, Leyden, N.V., 1956, p. 95.

[2] Ibid., p. 112. Of 404 persons interviewed in the village studied by Gadourek (in Holland's tulip district), 331 opposed interdenominational marriages, 164 opposed interdenominational friendships, 62 had no objection to any form of interdenominational relationship, 45 would not work with other religionists.

How Men Manage Their Behaviour

but the night club, not Newport in the afternoon but Manhattan at night; not the old family but the celebrity. . . .[1]

This does not mean that social class is less an object for striving, only that the striving is done in other ways more productive of recognition. Social class lines may at times seem loosely drawn, but social position is still the big prize. It is no less important in Jonesville than in Manhattan or anywhere else. Here we are dealing with a wide area of human behaviour in which conformity is demanded by social mandate. There is no book of rules as in baseball or in football telling all the striver should know. There are books of etiquette which spell out the conventional forms, and these we are told are read mainly by the conformers on the way up.

The social game is much more than merely a way of enjoying leisure in approved style. It is often an important adjunct of one's practical interests. At the same social party where many are merely having fun, others may be using the occasion to meet someone in connection with promoting business. Still others may use the occasion for promoting political schemes. The hostess, on the other hand, may have practical purposes of her own. Thus, while conforming to the social game the individual may play other sorts of games.

KEEPING THE HANDS BUSY

There is an idea shared alike by many recreationists, educators and parents that the young person can best be kept out of evil ways by giving him something to do. Since he may not work, except at chores around home, unless there are lessons to prepare, the popular thing is to persuade him to adopt a hobby, preferably a hobby with some 'instructive value'. Many of these efforts fail because of their made-work character (so evident to the child), but the occasional hobby may become a standing interest, at which recreationists, teachers and parents fear the child is giving too much time to it.

The merit of the hobby, apparently, extends beyond its use to keep children out of mischief, just as keeping the hands busy has wider implications than merely thwarting Satan. Many individuals who are 'hand-minded' for whom time drags when

---

[1] C. Wright Mills, *The Power Elite*, New York, 1956, p. 73.

they have leisure, who are not interested in most of the conventional pastimes, must pass the time with doing things. They work around the house or in the garden. If they have more time, a hobby serves them well. But the hobby has other uses, some of these were noted nearly a century ago by Stephen:

> The happy man who has selected his hobby always excites my admiration; whether it is sporting, or art, or artistic pursuits, or antiquarianism, or what not, he is at least able to boast of a genuine enjoyment. To be perfect, it should be happily contrasted with the regular pursuits of his life, so as to give a proper relaxation to his faculties. We are all more or less in the position of those artisans whose physical frames are distorted by one special kind of labour, and like them, are in want of something to call a special set of muscles, physical or mental into play.[1]

The hobby was seen by Steven as a psychological and physiological antidote for work, a sort of balancing activity, a way of managing one's free time to take the dullness out of life. To Greenberg it is a reaction from the purposefulness of work, taking the form of work while being something else.

> One works at a hobby for the sake of pleasure in work, and is able to take pleasure in it because its end is not serious or necessary enough to subject its means to the rule of efficiency (though one can make a hobby of efficiency too). The hobby asserts the value of one's time and energy in terms of immediate rather than ultimate satisfactions, and relates the end of work directly to the particular person who performs it.[2]

Perhaps the most ardent hobbyists are those who have turned to their solitary activities accidentally, at least without guidance. We don't know relatively how numerous they are. Clarke found that of people in upper-level occupations 20 per cent give much of their leisure to craftsmanlike activities, which would include handwork hobbies. But at the lower-level occupations 30 per cent gave much of their time to craftsmanlike

---

[1] 'A Cynic' (Leslie Stephen), 'Vacations', *Cornhill Magazine*, Vol. 20, No. 116, August 1869.

[2] Clement Greenberg, 'Work and Leisure under Industrialism', *Commentary*, Vol. 16, No. 1, July 1953, p. 60.

leisure activities. He found that generally the number of persons engaged in craftsmanlike activities is greater than the number patronizing commercialized leisure activities.[1]

The hobby is a form of preoccupation that can go on for years. Most sports and games tend to be left behind with one's youth. There is a tendency to regard the hobby as a solitary pastime. This is only partially true. Certain kinds of hobbies lead into various kind of social contacts. This is true of miniature sail boats mentioned earlier in this chapter. One enters a peer group which may have but a single interest, but that interest is mutually enjoyed. One's interest goes with him even when not at his hobby. Myrdal and Klein see in the hobby something like a return to the pre-industrial work and leisure linkage. Then the two were not separated, and they imply that one needs some activity where the two are again joined. If one can no longer do that in his work, the hobby is a good substitute which is such a mixture of work and leisure that ' it would be impossible to say where the one begins and the other ends'.[2] They make it clear that this applies to working women as well.

Hobby people, Nash claims, are a happy people. They have high emotional stability, great curiosity and creativeness, civic-mindedness, and they enjoy home life. Moreover, and this seems pleasing to Nash, they are little interested in spectator amusements.[3] Any special interest such as a hobby may be helpful for the individual in keeping him occupied at times, but too much must not be expected. It is not a way to life and salvation. Bednarik tends to be suspicious of the hobby craze. Other Europeans also seem of the opinion that it is over-promoted by industrialists and recreationists. Bednarik would have the individual try to find a consumption interest that develops talents other than those excessively used in his production activities.[4]

The idea of avoiding temptation when one is alone by keeping the hands busy is good Protestant doctrine, and is of course not shared by Pieper. He feels that much of time-passing, pleasure-seeking leisure activity is 'without rhyme or reason, and, morally speaking, unseemly; another word for idleness,

---

[1] Alfred C. Clarke, 'The Use of Leisure and its Relation to Levels of Occupational Prestige', *American Sociological Review*, Vol. 21, No. 3, June 1956, p. 306.
[2] Alva Myrdal and Viola Klein, *Women's Two Roles*, 1956, p. 30.
[3] Jay B. Nash, *Philosophy of Recreation and Leisure*, St. Louis, 1953, p. 15.
[4] Karl Bednarik, op. cit., pp. 145–6.

laziness and sloth'.[1] This is not a criticism of hobbies as such, but of the keep-the-hands-busy idea. For him it is good for man in his leisure to be alone, that he might contemplate and draw near to the Divine. Pieper holds that true leisure 'is an attitude of the mind, a condition of the soul' without which leisure is pointless. 'Compared with the exclusive ideal of work as activity, leisure implies an attitude of non-activity, of inward calm, of silence; it means not being *busy*, but letting things happen.'[2] This Catholic ideal of leisure use, which antedates Protestantism, assumes that if the individual can acquire 'inward calm' the entire problem of social control is solved.

UNREST, LEISURE AND IDLENESS

Pieper's idea of sitting it out when one has leisure, of acquiring 'an attitude of non-activity' would probably be wholesome for Western industrial urban man, if he were able to expose himself to this treatment for brief periods. On the whole, it is not in keeping with the Western idea of leisure. Few people, Western or others, are capable of silent contemplation, and many an Easterner who can sit motionless for hours is not contemplating at all. He lapses into a half-sleep. But this way of behaving among some peoples is very old, much older than Pieper's doctrine. It is traditional in some cultures. Say Larrabee and Meyersohn: 'Where tradition rules, time empty of obligations is empty of everything else; there is literally nothing to do with it, and the peon sleeping in the sun is the perfect image of the man with free time but no leisure. And in the Orient, where men have always made a virtue of transcending the human lot through inactivity, there least of all does leisure in our sense exist. . . .'[3]

In Western thinking Pieper's 'attitude of non-activity' practised beyond the needs for rest would be idleness. One is expected to be active at work or leisure and the idea becomes so much a part of his consciousness that his normal reaction to inactivity is unrest. He loses self-respect if he is unemployed and, while this joblessness may not be his fault, others may call

---

[1] Josef Pieper, *Leisure, the Base of Culture*, New York, 1952, translated from German by A. Dru, p. 48.

[2] Ibid., p. 52.

[3] Eric Larrabee and Rolf Meyersohn, Editors, *Mass Leisure*, Glencoe, Ill., 1958, p. ix.

How Men Manage Their Behaviour

him an idler. Soule calls this concept of respect and self-respect a great force in our lives.[1] It is only the occasional Westerner who does not mind being the 'village loafer'.

In asking how men manage their behaviour, we must not underestimate the compelling force of that something in Western conscience which pricks the individual into unrest when he has time on his hands. The most unnatural thing for him to do would be to sit it out in contemplation. If he has no other activity when he sits then he turns to reading, to talking, to listening to the radio.

It may be said that Western man is dedicated to work because he knows that is the expected thing. For this reason he may have guilt feelings when at leisure, he is unable to 'let himself go'. Even while having a good time, his mind may be on what he should be doing. For the work-dedicated man to have fun is like 'playing hookey' from school. Thus for many, as Barker notes, one makes use of leisure in an atmosphere of nervousness.[2] This attitude of unrest may be largely a response to social expectations, but it is not that alone. Even the liberal novelist and journalist Daniel Defoe planted this unrest in the soul of Robinson Crusoe. Instead of basking in the shade, as well he might have, Robinson went to work, and he taught his good man, Friday, to work.

Precisely because of this unrest when one ceases, if only briefly, to be active, and because this is so universally a Western trait, it comes natural to be curious or suspicious about one who does not drive himself, who in a state of idleness is not restless. In cultures where one may sit as long as he wishes, whether contemplating or lapsed into a state of emptiness, such behaviour is hardly reason for wonder or suspicion. But such behaviour in Western society is reason for concern. First, one's inertness may be a bad example for others; and second, the idler is one who has lost command of himself. In a society that leaves the management of behaviour so much to the individual conscience, the idler is a misfit. The behaviour of the peon lying in the sun can be predicted, but not the behaviour of this idler.

Understandably there was real concern about the moral consequences of the millions of unemployed during the Great

[1] George Soule, *What Automation Does to Human Beings*, 1956, p. 93.
[2] Ernest Barker, *National Character*, 1949, 4th edition, pp. 101–2.

Depression. It was not all mere intolerance.[1] Many people honestly believed that the spirit had gone out of the American people. The revival later was a denial of all these fears. Out of that great economic crisis, as many believe, came the beginning of a new attitude toward unemployment but, more important still, a more mellow attitude toward leisure. At least, as observed by Soule, Americans began to understand the difference between leisure and unemployment.[2] Mitchell and Mason are even more positive about this changing trend in thinking. They believe that because of the depression experience people are beginning to recognize 'that leisure is an inevitable part of the new social and economic order, a permanent part of our lives'.[3]

This learning to accept leisure and not to feel guilt while at play, which seems to be in process, does not mean any sudden change over. Western man is no less prone to unrest when not active. His tempo of activity is not slackening. Even while becoming less uncomfortable with leisure he is not less the individual taking pride in being in command of himself.

SMALL-GROUP VITALITY

Boys in the Boston Italian slum area studied by Whyte were almost all members of tightly-knit groups that met regularly on street corners or in adjacent cafés. One did not leave this group to join that and it was hardly likely that he would belong to more than one corner group. Each boy was known by his group and each group by its usual meeting-place. The group rarely had a purpose other than that of coming together. Members shared their good fortunes or received friendly sympathy if bad luck came.[4] Whyte tells us nothing that has not already been said by others; what he does do is to demonstrate that such firm primary groups are also found in areas that appear to be socially disorganized.

This intimate type of personal contact group which rarely exceeds a dozen or so members is found in almost every type

[1] Dixon Wecter, *The Age of the Great Depression, 1929–41*, New York, 1948, pp. 219–20.
[2] George Soule, 'The Economics of Leisure', *Annals of the American Academy of Political and Social Science*, Vol. 313. September 1957, p. 20.
[3] Elmer D. Mitchell and Bernard S. Mason, *The Theory of Play*, New York, 1948, p. 33.
[4] William Foote Whyte, *Street Corner Society*, Chicago, 1943, p. 141.

of human situation because it meets the need for intimacy and confidence. People have that need whether male or female, young or old and regardless of social class. Whyte's street-corner groups tend to monopolize the members when at home and at leisure. The same youths may belong to other groups, perhaps less tightly-knit, at their workplaces. The street-corner group might convert itself into a predatory gang, and that sometimes happens, and not in the slum districts only. This likelihood of a primary group becoming predatory is not limited to youth groups.

Efforts are being made continually by the organized community to transfer these naturally-formed primary youth groups into conventional clubs or troops or perhaps brigades, to bring them, as it were, into captivity. For this purpose settlement houses, community centres, boys' clubs and the like may be established, particularly in the poor districts. The purpose is to provide the informal group, held together by friendship and acquaintance, with a socially approved meeting place and a linkage with the community. Efforts may be made to inspire the captured group with a purpose. Whether this can be done depends largely on the skill of the adult leader. But even while it is being done the same group will continue its associations quite independent of the centre, much the same as informal adult groups do. This does not mean that the boys' club or other centre has failed, quite the contrary. Even though we cannot measure the effectiveness of settlement houses, centres and clubs, they must not be undervalued.

FORMAL ASSOCIATIONS AND GROUPS

One reason, perhaps, for concern about the informal groups of youth is that they seem so intangible and elusive, if not evasive when approached by non-members. Adult informal groups behave about the same, but adults feel they must be responsible for the youth, which helps put the youth group on the defensive. We associate with adults other types of groupings; the organized group with a purpose and it is mainly through such groups that adults participate in the life of the community.[1] The community, in fact, is a network of organized groups linked in terms

[1] Mary Morris, 'Adult Groups', see Peter Kuenstler (Ed.), *Social Group Work in Great Britain*, 1954, p. 129.

How Men Manage Their Behaviour

of interest and, as Hill found in a rural town, stratified according to social class, and each individual tends to have his niche.[1] These relationships tend to be more firm in the small town and more fluid in the large cosmopolitan place. In the city these organizations may be much larger and more complex in their structure. Boulding remarks on man's ability to build such organizations, they bespeak 'his capacity for abstract communication and language and his ability to enter in imagination into the lifes of others.... An organization might almost be defined as a structure of roles tied together with lines of communication.'[2]

The organizations with which the individual in the industrial urban life becomes identified may differ greatly in size, in structure and purpose, but not all individuals may be members of organized groups although they may behave much as if they were. The wage bargaining of the trade unions, for example, tends to set the wage level for non-members as well as members of the trade union. Wright and Hyman found that among urban families 58 per cent have members who belong to formal organizations, while the figure for rural families was 33 per cent. They found that organization membership is most frequent among persons of highest income as well as those of higher education and of higher occupational status, also higher among home-owning than among non-home-owning families.[3]

Reigrotzki found that among German adults 37 per cent of the females and 73 per cent of the males belonged to formal organizations. Again, as with Americans, membership was higher among the better educated and those with higher occupations and income.[4] Cauter and Downham found that of English adults 68 per cent upper-class, 57 per cent middle-class and 40 per cent working-class person hold formal organization

---

[1] Reuben Hill and Associates, *Eddyville's Families*, Chapel Hill, Institute for Research in Social Science, 1953, p. 55, Mimeographed. Hill defined three classes of whites: the Social Set holding much economic power, the Sober Set in the middle layer, and the Poor Whites at the bottom. Negroes were outside. Of 47 leaders in the town, 21 were of the Social Set and 7 of the Sober Set. The 47 leaders represented 35 families.

[2] Kenneth E. Boulding, *The Image*, Ann Arbor, 1956, p. 27.

[3] Charles R. Wright and Herbert H. Hyman, 'Voluntary Association Memberships of American Adults', *American Sociological Review*, Vol. 23, No. 3, June 1958, 284–94.

[4] Eric Reigrotzki, *Soziale Verflechtungen in den Bundesrepublik*, Tubingen, 1956, p. 169.

memberships, and of these classes respectively 25, 12, and 4 per cent hold three or more memberships.[1] Such figures tend to confirm the thesis of Homans, that 'The higher a man's social rank, the more frequently he interacts with persons outside of his own group.'[2] This thesis was tested in a youth study by a Finnish group which concluded that 'Young people belonging to formal groups and associations are more likely to participate in informal groups than do those who do not belong to any associations.' About 40 per cent of the Finnish youth interviewed belonged to no formal organizations, and of these 72 per cent reported no informal peer group memberships. It was found that youth who were leaders in the formal groups (elected leaders) were more likely than rank and file members to hold membership in other groups, formal and informal, and also more likely to hold leadership positions in other organizations.[3]

In Demark, according to a study reported by Svalastoga, 69 per cent of the adults belong to organizations; that is 85 per cent of the males and 53 per cent of the females. Of the joiners, a higher percentage of the men belong to more than one organization, up to five or more. But of the women who join organizations the rate of attending meetings is higher than for the men.[4]

These organizations, chambers of commerce, trade unions, political parties, professional associations, patriotic societies, social clubs, co-operatives and many others, represent the different interests of the people. To a high degree they guide and control their members. Without them the agglomerate society could scarcely function. They are the contact between their members and government. Each to some degree is a kind of government. These are an important part of any answer we might give to questions about how people in the modern society manage their behaviour. And we would need also to look to the

[1] T. Cauter and J. S. Downham, *The Communication of Ideas*, 1954, pp. 64–66.
[2] George C. Homans, *The Human Group*, 1950, pp. 185–6.
[3] Eric Allardt, Pentti Jartti, Feina Jyrkila and Yrjo Littunen, 'On the Cumulative Nature of Leisure Activities', *Acta Sociologica*, Col. 3, No. 4, 1958, p. 166. In a study of Glasgow youth Ferguson and Cunnison found that boys who were steady in work had most group memberships, while boys who moved frequently from job to job had the fewest. Boys who were steady in work were most numerous among those attending evening classes, and their attendance was most regular. T. Ferguson and J. Cunnison, *The Young Wage-earner*, 1951, pp. 88–89.
[4] Kaare Svalastoga, *Prestige, Class and Mobility*, Copenhagen, 1959, pp. 253, 254.

leaders of these groups who form part of the controlling élite of the community.

ASSOCIATIONS FOR THE COMMON GOOD

Practically all private organizations to which the previous section applies stand four-square for law and order and all the conventional virtues. The trade union when it goes on strike, the medical association when it resists proposals for a public medical service, the chamber of commerce when it tries to prevent using 'taxpayers' money' to provide public recreation facilities, the association of sportsmen when it opposes the removal of a swamp known to be detrimental to health, because it is also important as a wildlife area; all of these have in fact an interest in community welfare. Not only do they profess to have, but they do have a social conscience, and they usually believe that in promoting their own interests they are promoting the common good. They usually give financial as well as moral support to a great variety of special service agencies and organizations that are active in the community.

These private associations, whether they give relief to families, help to the aged, medical care for the sick, guidance to the wayward or engage in promoting recreation services, have ever been an influence in community life. In the past they were in the forefront demanding better housing for the poor, playgrounds for the children, playfields, parks and beaches for youth and adults, and they took the lead in demanding that the school expand its services to include adult education, concern itself about child health and give more attention to the play interests of children.

Some of these associations have been and still are active in safeguarding public morals. They have concerned themselves with getting books and plays banned, in observing and complaining about conduct in public dance halls, in waging war against race tracks and gambling, in keeping children off the stage, and some of the more ardent ones still are against the stage entirely. Most forms of popular entertainment today, including books, had to cope with the resistance of these reform groups. All of this can be recognized, but still much credit must be given to reformers in general for the role they play in representing the community conscience. It may be said that they represent the community conscience much as the trade unions represent labour or as the employers' association represents industry.

On the American scene the private agencies interested in children, a major reform interest, had much to do with securing much that exists in the way of public facilities and services for recreation. In developing these programmes, they had much to do with turning recreation work into a professional service for which one studies and prepares as for other professions. Today the recreationist is far removed from the reformers of the 1890s who campaigned for public playgrounds against the wall of public and official indifference. The recreationist today is not met with indifference but he is confronted often with the ideas about the use of playgrounds that reformers advocated in the 1890s; that playgrounds are for little children only, or poor children only, or their main function is to keep the young off the streets.[1]

Much of this activity of private associations as it relates to leisure and recreation started in the cities and most of it is still confined to urban areas. Saville, in his book about rural England, complains that by comparison rural life is dull. With the advent of new leisure interests, the old folk pastimes are losing interest. Nothing is done in the country to develop the recreational guidance and facilities found in town. The needed leadership is not developing in the rural areas.[2]

Still keeping our attention on the private associations occupied with the problems of leisure, it can be said that they still represent the public conscience. They perform the useful service of establishing goals and standards. They are the chief contact in these matters between the community and the public bodies. Says Fitzgerald, 'Such an understanding is particularly necessary in communities where private and voluntary agencies have preceded the establishment of a publicly supported programme.'[3] He adds the thought that the private services need also to recognize the importance of the public programmes.

[1] On this thought see Howard G. Danford, *Recreation in the American Community*, New York, 1953, pp. 123-5.

[2] John Saville, *Rural Depopulation in England and Wales, 1851-1951*, 1957, pp. 35-36.

[3] Gerald B. Fitzgerald, *Community Organization for Recreation*, New York, 1948, pp. 14, 18.

How Men Manage Their Behaviour

PUBLIC SERVICE IN WORK AND LEISURE

Anderson and Weidner speak of government as a 'process for doing things', or an instrumentality standing at the service of the people when individuals or groups try to get things done.[1] Muller, observing how the many sport groups, trade unions, church groups and others in Germany try to get public money or try to get the government to do things to help them, concluded that this is a poor example for the individual.[2] This view, which is frequently met, fails to recognize that the individual in modern society is most effective as he belongs to and functions through organizations (assuming that as a member he helps control the organizations). The viewpoint taken here is that government exists for service and that with respect to the work and leisure interests of people it renders a great variety of services. These are too numerous for more than a partial examination.[3]

1. *Public Services for Work*. Under its police power government has always regulated markets: weights and measures, money, trade practices and contracts, making it possible for people to work in security and fair dealing. Government provides facilities such as roads and bridges and assumes responsibility for safety in transport and at the workplace. It may establish measures for the security of workers against unemployment and penniless old age. Now that government becomes a principal employer of labour, it shares in the task of setting standards for a fair day's work and fair pay.

Because of the increasing global interdependence of work and the now recognized inability of private enterprise to insure full employment or free markets, national governments must assume greater leadership in overall work planning and in promoting global relationships favourable to trade.

2. *Public Services for Leisure*. Since much of leisure activity is consumption and relates to private enterprise, it can look to

[1] William Anderson and Edward W. Weidner, *American City Government*, New York, 1950, pp. 247-8.

[2] Eberhard Muller, 'Freiheit als Frage des Ethos', *Gewerkschaftliche Monatshefte*, 8 Jahr, August 1957, pp. 480-1.

[3] For a further examination of the role of government in work and leisure, see Nels Anderson, *The Urban Community*, 1959, Chap. 12. 'How Communities Get Things Done', Chap. 13, 'Work and its Place under Urbanism', and Chap. 14, 'Leisure, By-product of Urbanism'.

government for the services extended to other work insofar as these enterprises produce the goods and services consumed in leisure. But in the consumption phases of leisure other public services are needed, for leisure concerns the cultural interests of people and their social values.

(*a*) *Regulation and Protection.* While communities may differ widely in this matter, every community has certain commonly-accepted moral standards against which leisure activities are evaluated. These, of course, may change from year to year, but whatever they are at any time, demands accordingly will be made on public authorities for their enforcement. When we look closer we find that the moral and decency standards demanded by one section of the community may be much more strict than those expected by the more liberal sections. Public authority is in a difficult position, and it usually follows a sensible middle course, but the right of regulation is firmly retained.

The demand for public protection against what is deemed unwholesome in leisure activity appears to concern commercial amusements and leisure services more than any other. Seldes speaks of these as the 'public arts', and he observes that, although they are in a sense outside the law, 'the public has sovereign rights over them, since these arts, no less than the institutions of government, belong to the people'.[1] Without suppressing the art in radio, television and the cinema, the people have the obligation to prevent these institutions from undermining accepted social values. Seldes would surely agree that before that delicate problem is faced certain widely-accepted standards need to be established. This idea of regulation extends to a great variety of leisure interests and activities, behaviour in dance halls and other public places, dress, and it may extend to the reading of books.

(*b*) *Public Initiative and Leadership.* We are told there are more than 25,000 professional recreation leaders in the United States, and a good share of these are in public employment.[2] They work on playgrounds, in summer camps, on the beaches, in

[1] Gilbert Seldes, *The Public Arts*, New York, 1956, p. 331. The federal investigation of 'rigged' television quiz shows may illustrate how government may step forward when a moral issue in commercial entertainment is involved, touching the idea of Seldes.

[2] Norman P. Miller, 'Professional Education', *Annals of the American Academy of Political and Social Science*, Vol. 313, September 1957, pp. 38–39.

recreation centres and so on. This is one kind of public leadership in recreation. Public agencies may also conduct athletic meets, carnivals and even give dancing instruction. What is done is usually what seems to be needed or what the community may demand.

(c) *Public Facilities for Leisure.* In many European cities the opera, theatre and concert hall are public institutions. In most large cities everywhere may be found public sport arenas, parks, promenades, dancing pavilions and a great variety of facilities for leisure. Again, it depends on what is needed or what is demanded. American cities until recently have been hesitant about providing even parks. The first parks in some American cities, in fact, were private gifts to the people, Swope Park in Kansas City, for example. Danford mentions that in many cities and towns the public attitude toward services for leisure is still negative.[1] The resistance against providing public facilities for leisure is that there will follow continuing cost for their maintenance.

In his study of a southern rural town, Hill found the same attitudes. 'To a considerable degree, the widespread general concern over the lack of recreational facilities and the desultory and spasmodic efforts of townspeople to meet this need indicate how the established system of political patronage renders the community nearly impotent for self-government. Recreational facilities and programmes *cost money*; public recreation *costs tax money.*'[2]

Thus, as far as people managing their behaviour is concerned, government functions mainly as it provides certain facilities and services which are auxiliary to what the people do for themselves and among themselves. Perhaps the most important function of government is that it is the final authority.

WHAT GOES ON THE RECORD

If the amateur athlete would engage in sport for hire, even though he goes to another town and changes his name, he finds himself in a delicate position. Somewhere on paper there will be a record of his action, just as every action of his legitimate participation is entered into the record. The same holds for the man who works. When he enters his first job he can present his

---
[1] Howard G. Danford, op. cit., pp. 50–52.
[2] Reuben Hill and Associates, op. cit., p. 53.

How Men Manage Their Behaviour

employer with his entire school record. As he moves from job to job his record often follows him, as it follows if he moves from place to place. The individual's contacts with organizations, his activities in these groups, all of it enters the record, or into the press which is also a record. Whatever contact he has with government; taxes paid or fines paid or money and services received, that is also written down. Often his consumer expenditures come to him in bills at the end of the month. Payments are made by check. So through the years the individual leaves a trail behind on paper. He may have to be clever at times to keep some of his actions 'off the record'. The record is a source of security for the honest man.

In the complex anonymous society the record takes over a task too great for memory. In it is found the mainstay of the contractual society. In simpler societies where life was lived in the full view of all, the written word was hardly needed. Witnesses did not move away, thus agreements could be trusted to the spoken word in the hearing of others.

Here, then, is another factor to be considered among others when we ask how people in modern society manage their behaviour. The record is supplementary to various other factors. Without this supplement to the spoken word modern life could hardly function at all.

SUMMARY

When we ask how society maintains order and how people manage their behaviour we find a cluster of related answers. Some degree of control inheres in all social behaviour and everyone is a party to social order even while resisting some phase of it. While our interest here is in work and leisure, behaviour in these areas is interwoven with all other behaviour. In work or leisure as in other phases of living the individual is normally socially oriented and in various ways under compulsion to conform to the expectations of his social milieu.

The individual's need for sociality, his desire for approval and good standing, and the resulting feelings of security coax or impel him into social conformity. Even in the anonymous crowd the individual is conscious of these compulsions. In the modern changing complex society the social expectations vary from one segment of the community to another, as from time to time. Conformity also varies with individuals. On the whole, social conformity is realized mainly through the social pressures attending human intercourse in the various social situations, and is very little the result of naked force. Rarely is force resorted to even under law.

Regarding work, the individual is confronted with the fact that work is expected, one who does not work is likely to be suspected. For many, work itself holds attractions and we speak of the instinct of workmanship or the ideal of cratfsmanship. But this affinity develops only on special types of work and can hardly develop on most jobs. Thus for most workers the compelling control is the status reward; one is among those who work, and this status will decline if he is unemployed overly long. The opposite social attitude is the negative social status assigned to the idler.

In social and leisure activities, which tend to take more time out of the individual's day than work does, the social expectations are usually morally defined but, since social values are ever changing, the moral mandates may be differently defined from one section of society to another. These differences notwithstanding, those who play the social game find it necessary to know and conform to the minimum rules. The reward is social acceptance, but that is not all of it. Besides the feelings of virtue that come to him, the socially accepted individual through his conforming, consciously or not, helps enforce the mandates. This holds also for sport and group games; the rules become the control code for the players who, in obeying the rules, help enforce them. This may be said also of the intimate primary groups to which most individuals belong; they establish rules when and as needed. If the rules are ignored the group is likely to disintegrate.

Life for the individual in the industrial urban agglomerate would be difficult were it not for the large special-interest formal organizations in which he may have membership. These organizations bring order in the mass society. In different ways they ensure security to the individual. Because they exist and function, each promoting its own kind of interest, government of the mass society is possible. The primary intimate groups may function within the framework of the large formal organizations and their secondary controls.

How Men Manage Their Behaviour

In the mass society government functions in numerous intermediary service roles. It renders services to facilitate both work and leisure activity. It is the final arbiter in conflicts between groups and interests, and the final enforcer of community standards for proper conduct. While much of the regulating of individual and group conduct is the result of social pressures and law is relatively seldom resorted to, this does not lessen the prestige role of government, so long as it stands firmly ready in the background.

One of the most potent forces for the control of individual conduct in mass society is the written record. Modern man can scarcely have any contact with institutions, with corporations, with organizations or with the agencies of government without some record resulting. He needs the records for his security in the contractual society. He knows the ever-ready-witness value of the records written on paper and this knowledge figures in all of his work and non-work associations with others. It adds to the observation that people today manage their behaviour through a great variety of means, most of which they hold in their hands.

10

TIME-USE TRENDS AND PROSPECTS

IN the foregoing chapters we considered work and leisure in terms of time use, and we saw how both tend to change in response to technological, economic and other change. We saw how work and leisure tend to be separated and how leisure as such tends to be in competition less with work than with non-work obligations. We recognized that leisure has come among us without our being prepared for it and is still regarded with suspicion by many who remain dedicated to previously established forms and values which seem to be challenged as Western man finds more time for play. Just the same, leisure is here and is changing our views about time. Davidson wrote:

> Time once saved in the name of Christian virtue has come to be saved in the name of simple efficiency, but the urgency to save it has hardly diminished. That efficiency, in turn, has piled up more leisure for more people than has ever been known elsewhere in history. It happened quickly, within a few short generations, and to a nation with a recent pioneer tradition of unmitigated hard work—a nation trained to believe that killing time was a crime. What to do with leisure now that we had it became a major problem of our civilization.[1]

Davidson might have added that this first civilization to learn to live better with less work is now faced with the problem of learning to live. We have some evidence that Western society,

[1] Marshall B. Davidson, *Life in America*, Boston, 1951, Vol. II, p. 78.

Time-Use Trends and Prospects

in a random, trial and error fashion, is learning to live better, is not settling into the rut of passivity or losing its sanity. This is not wishful optimism.

What we need now to do is to consider the trends, recognizing that what seem to be trends are subject to different interpretations. Moreover, as Dumazedier cautions, trends are complex, clearly evident to some but not to others. They are not the same for different segments of society, and yet they are interrelated. Those that relate to work also relate to leisure and those relating to leisure also relate to culture.[1] Were it otherwise the examining of trends would be far less intriguing.

Whoever dares to examine trends can hardly avoid coming to certain conclusions about prospects, and this involves risk. We need only recall how often the demographers fail in their estimates of population change, and their materials are more concrete than ours. The changing scene is largely one of man's own creation and he himself is the most dynamic element in it. It is not so much his inventions at which we should marvel, it is, as Whitehead said, that man has invented the 'method of invention'[2] and tends himself to be the source of unpredictable behaviour. This uncertainty about the future applies to both work and leisure.

WHAT THE FUTURE MAY HOLD

Our society, Wax believes, has so concentrated on practical things that the art of living has been neglected. But we are beginning to discover the art of living through our leisure, that is through our learning to play, a great liberating force.

> For while we are trying to associate the former (work) with most of the virtue and moral qualities of our society, we have unwittingly defined play as an activity in which these virtues receive their ultimate and ideal expression. By this paradoxical statement I mean that while we may think that we are free and democratic in our workaday lives, most of us are capable of being genuinely free and democratic only when we play.[3]

---

[1] Joffre Dumazedier, 'Realites du loisir et ideologies'. *Esprit*, 27 année, No. 274, juin 1959, pp. 871–2.

[2] Alfred North Whitehead, *Science and the Modern World*, 1925, p. 141.

[3] Rosalie H. Wax, 'Free Time in Other Cultures', see Wilma Donahue and Others, Editors, *Free Time*, Ann Arbor, 1958, p. 14.

Time-Use Trends and Prospects

The thought expressed here is that modern man is coming to grips with his work and leisure problems, not so much through planned programmes as through unplanned and unguided situational influences. As the gift of leisure was itself unexpected and not planned for, so the use of leisure may bring results not planned for, which may also effect work changes. This optimism is expressed in other words by Russell in his Utopian view of the future:

> The work expected will be enough to make leisure delightful, but not enough to produce exhaustion. Since men will not be tired in their spare time, they will not demand only such amusements as are passive and vapid. At least one per cent will probably devote the time not spent on professional work to pursuits of some public importance and, since they will not depend upon these pursuits for their livelihood, their originality will not be hampered, and there will be no need to conform to standards set by elderly pundits. But it is not only in these exceptional cases that the advantages of leisure will appear.[1]

Russell assumes that when people become more accustomed to leisure there will be less suspicion and more of good nature among them, less moral supervision needed and less concern about it. One wonders about the idea of more people as a leisure pursuit engaging in public service and ignoring the 'elderly pundits'. We must remember that many who will have the leisure will themselves be elderly. Perhaps people will be more good natured, but social change resulting from changing ways of leisure may itself be controversial. Russell's idea of the future is still this side of Heaven.

Bendiner, looking at the possible relation of leisure to our future pursuit of happiness, concludes that the great need will be for more people to learn more, that is, more about living as an art. He finds that educators are not sure, at least are not agreed on what education is needed and the ends to be attained. He mentions that the trade unions are becoming aware of the problem and are promoting educational programmes. Business leaders are encouraging junior executives to take further courses in the humanities.

[1] Bertrand Russell, *In Praise of Idleness and Other Essays*, 1948, 4th edition, p. 28.

Time-Use Trends and Prospects

But far outbalancing these haphazard approaches is the constant commercial drumfire urging the public to spend its money on ways to spend its time. Right now it is business that is selling the life of leisure, and the life of leisure that business can sell is necessarily a life of aqua-lungs, outboard motors, Skotch Koolers, and house paint—all good in their way, no doubt, but none of them suggesting for a moment that there was more to Greece than marathons and more to Rome than baths.[1]

Soule ventures the opinion that as more people get accustomed to leisure there will be a more general turning to the arts. Once secure in their jobs, opportunity will come for 'scholars to pursue their research, writers to write, painters to paint, and thinkers to think'.[2]

But the future offers practical problems which must be faced even though in the pursuit of fun they may be ignored. If they are not faced and in part resolved, leisure becomes less secure. The first of these practical obstacles is employment. The individual cannot assure himself continuous employment, that calls for wider organization and planning. Mass society must be equally organized to guard against the maldistribution of population, especially in the urban agglomerations. There must be the assurance that mass society enjoys reasonable health and is not exposed to health hazards. The environment must be safe. If people are to enjoy leisure there must be the necessary public and other facilities.

These practical considerations must have place in any effort to see the future possibilities of work and leisure. Thus Meadows remarks for cogent reasons that the 'future in industrial urbanism has become very uncertain'.

As the community counterpart of big enterprise, the big city finds itself meshed in endless inefficiencies and wastes of human resources. The massive patterns of the city—e.g., its mammoth recreations, supermarkets, crowded tenements—grind the personal relations of industrial man exceedingly

---

[1] Robert Bendiner, 'Could You Stand a Four-day Week?' *The Reporter*, Vol. 17, No. 2, 8 August, 1957, p. 14.

[2] George Soule, *What Automation does to Human Beings*, 1956, p. 174.

Time-Use Trends and Prospects

fine and thin, and they create, as two critics have recently said, 'a fast-rippling' but 'shallow volume of life'.[1]

SPEAKING OF AUTOMATION

Many who look ahead, trying to visualize man and society four decades or so hence, in the year 2000, find it convenient to speak of 'automation', a very handy word for filling the empty spaces. It has reference to the workerless or nearly workerless factories of the future. That opens the way for speculation about what man will do with all his leisure. Diebold, who first made the term popular, apparently does not see as much automation in the future as do other writers, but he sees much partial automation.[2] And while automation will abolish some jobs many other jobs will develop. There will be more paper work, more repair work, but also less unskilled work.

The trend toward automation under various other names has been going on in most industries for a long time. It began with the stop-watch experts more than a generation ago. Its first grand step was the assembly line. The function of the assembly line was to mechanize the flow of work by all sorts of machines making all sorts of parts, which came together in the moving assembly process. In this process, quoting Arensberg, the man had become 'an *interchangeable hand* tending an *interchangeable machine* making *interchangeable parts* against the stop-watch and the moving line of the co-ordinating manager-engineer'.[3] Automation assumes that in the future there will be fewer men and more machines which will be operated by remote control. One man, sitting in the control room, will be able to operate many machines. Groups of machines will be co-ordinated as if into a single mechanism.

The more we know about work the less we are fooled about automation. As Macmillan observes, where it can be used, it ensures greater efficiency and precision, more economy when man's hands are out of the process.[4] It calls for a high level of

[1] Paul Meadows, 'The Industrial Way of Life', *Technological Review*, Vol. 48, No. 5, March 1946. The two critics are F. L. Wright and Baker Brownell, *Architecture and Modern Life*, New York, 1937, p. 80.

[2] John Diebold, *Automation, the Advent of the Automatic Factory*, New York, 1952, Preface and p. 143.

[3] Conrad M. Arensberg, 'Work and the Changing Scene', see Conrad M. Arensberg and others, *Research in Industrial Relations*, New York, 1957, p. 61.

[4] R. H. Macmillan, *Automation, Friend or Foe?* 1956, p. 51.

Time-Use Trends and Prospects

scientific and technical capability for those who 'supervise' the mechanisms; they must spend more years in school. Macmillan reminds us that automation has its limits.

Nevertheless, in spite of the risks involved, the economic advantages to be gained from automation are so great that there will surely be a vast extension of its use. As we have seen, the first industries in which it has been applied are those making relatively long runs of a product that changes little and for which there is an assured and even expanding market—canned goods, motor cars and plastics, for instance. Other articles which may well be made and assembled automatically in the near future are ball bearings, typewriters, cameras, radio and television sets, clocks, ovens and refrigerators, bricks, fertilizers, soaps and textiles.[1]

If we would have some idea about what automation may do to us over the next three or four decades, we can get part of the answer by asking what it is doing to us now and what it has been doing over the past three or four decades. It has little room for expansion in making our chairs, tables, bedding, clothing and shoes, in printing our books or building our houses. Certainly, as much as there can be of automation, will give us more leisure time, and more money will be spent on leisure consumption. But since leisure consumption is so responsive to the modes, production in these areas is not likely to be profitable for more than marginal automation.

That much of industrial work will come under automatic controls and only a few workers will be needed, this idea is a little unrealistic. Diebold reminds us there is much more to automation than pulling levers. 'Although automatic control mechanisms are *necessary* for the achievement of fully automatic factories, they are not *sufficient* in themselves.'[2]

ON KNOWING WHAT TO FEAR

Apparently automation attracts more attention among Americans than, for example, among the British and Germans, which is to be expected, since developments have been faster in the United States. Except for short periods, the hindering influence of under-employment has been a minor factor in the United

[1] Ibid., p. 85.
[2] John Diebold, op. cit., p. 2.

States. There was the rich frontier and ever-increasing stimulation to create wealth and to increase production. There was, as Soule notes, the absence of an aristocracy and fixed class lines, and people were stimulated by the presence of people of different origins.

My suspicion, however, is that the reason runs much deeper than this. The nation was dedicated to a new civilization unhampered by European inhibitions. What could be freer than the discoveries of science and their application in technology —a continuous stream in tangible and immediate form? Every new gadget is a symbol, however unworthy, of the original dedication.[1]

All developments leading up to what is now called automation have all along been taken for granted. It is only the occasional observer who asks where is it leading us. One view is that we are heading into ultimate mass disemployment. Those allowed to work will be more carefully selected and even if allowed to work the cycle of employment will be more brief. Retirement will come at an earlier age. Macmillan answers that other kinds of work will be found, a very commonsense observation.[2] For every individual taken away from the machines at least one must be added 'behind the lines' routing raw materials, disposing of products, storing, testing, and doing the greater amount of paper work. The difference will be that the productivity for the entire plant will increase.

Dubin ventures the opinion that automation will negatively affect the labour market for women. More workers with technical and scientific capacity will be needed, and for such jobs men qualify easier. Women will have to return to housekeeping if they cannot find other work This opinion[3] will bear closer examination. It is not unlike the view of a generation ago that women cannot be trained to operate mechanisms such as the large cranes in an aeroplane industry, for example. Women are doing such work today. One could find grounds for coming to an opposite conclusion, that more automatic factory jobs will be available to women.

[1] George Soule, *What Automation does to Human Beings*, op. cit., p. 11.
[2] R. H. Macmillan, op. cit., pp. 22–23.
[3] Robert Dubin, *The World of Work*, New York, 1958, p. 202.

Time-Use Trends and Prospects

Pollock calls attention to another possible consequence of the trend toward automation, and to this many agree; it is that unskilled labour will virtually disappear. Even skilled labour will need to have more technical or scientific education than at present.[1] This trend is already under way. It will mean that more young people will have to spend more of their early years in school. Harking back to the previous chapter, there will be more institutional control over their time in youth.

When we ask again how much of all work will come under the sway of automation, we find that it is not likely to be great. Even today no more than 20 to 25 per cent of all work in the industrial urban community is really industrial. Perhaps not more than half of that will submit to full automation. The various jobs in the public service, and the number increases, would hardly be included. The same holds for most private services, which also become numerous; places for eating, drinking, sleeping, and places where people go for entertainment. Stores and service shops are outside the realm of automation (with minor exceptions), so also the different professions, so also most forms of transport. The automatic factory would block off only a small part of the entire labour market.

Fears that man may be debased or regimented by his own creations are not new, although new versions of these fears appear with each creative advance. Here we present a thought from ten Have:

> Indeed, when some people complain that mankind is on the way to replacing himself with robots, and will thus make himself a superfluous kind of creature in the world, they apparently forget two things. First of all, that man does not lose any of his powers—neither his bodily nor his mental powers—when he endows other things or creatures with them; he does *not* impoverish himself, but multiplies his original forces by providing other things with them. Secondly, that in the last resort the living man is the creator of the automatic machine or, if you like, of the automatic man; and that he may remain as creative as before even if he were to succeed in endowing things with creative powers. Thus we may conclude that endowment in the above sense does not

[1] Friedrich Pollock, *Automation, Materialen zur Beurteilung der oeconomischen und sozialen Folgen*, Frankfurt-Main, 4956, pp. 13–14, 103–4.

necessarily mean delegation nor projection nor impoverishment nor alienation.[1]

As Soule sees it, the problem is not one of machines regimenting man, but of man learning to regiment his machines. He gives examples to show that we are learning. For example, with rapid transit, urban populations are escaping their slums, so native to cities in former times. We are raising our standards of living and we know better than ever before how to make and distribute things.[2]

It is not regimentation via the machine that needs to be feared. A considerable amount of such regimentation is imperative, even the automatic factory may be needed, if man will live better and better use his time. What needs to be feared is the time lag between the point when man is given more free time and the point when he learns effectively to use this free time. Nor do we need to fear the mass production industries entering the leisure field. In a mass society they are needed. We can even agree with Mills that much of the offerings of commercial amusement serve only to 'astonish, excite and distract but they do not enlarge reason or feeling, or allow spontaneous dispositions to unfold creatively'.[3]

It is too much to hope that all of us can learn effectively to live as balanced beings in their non-work time, or that all of us can be made into creative beings. Still we do not need to fear that automation will take over our leisure time as it may take command of a good part of our work time. It is unlikely that we will be regimented into so many laughing or weeping, but unthinking, viewers, hearers and readers. The creativity that is bringing automation into use will not be less creative when confronted with making use of the time we have been freed from work.

We may say that for a people to learn how to live fully and to use time is the work for educators. Doubtless educators will have a part in this learning process, but the learning process is now under way and people of all sorts are having a part in it.

---

[1] T. T. ten Have, 'Automation, Work and Leisure', *Range*, No. 15, Philips' Telecommunicatie Industrie, Hilversum, 1960, p. 5.

[2] George Soule, *Time for Living*, New York, 1955, p. 175.

[3] C. Wright Mills, *White Collar, the American Middle Classes*, New York, 1951, p. 236.

Time-Use Trends and Prospects

USES OF ATOMIC ENERGY

It is not unlikely that future uses of radioactive materials will influence man's use of time for both work and leisure, but we can only guess at this time how these influences will operate. As these materials afford a compact, long-lasting fuel, it was possible to make submarine explorations under the ice cap at the North Pole. This suggests other possibilities, exploring the ocean floor, for example. With such compact fuels man may one day be better fortified in his efforts to explore space.

From one point of view it is unfortunate that most of the effort expended in developing atomic energy is focused on national defence in the East-West cold war. On the other side, it must be recognized that without this global contest for security it is unlikely that governments would have provided the billions of dollars needed for atomic research. The cost is so great that it could not, and probably would not have been undertaken by private enterprise, at least for a long time to come. The ever-pending threat of aggression in the cold war forced governments to assume the leadership in these developments and, once assumed, this leadership becomes a continuing public responsibility. This illustrates the function of a crisis in getting things done. The same was true for airplane development in the two world wars.

Much that is learned in this atomic research for defence will be used in peaceful applications of atomic energy, which is coming to be a great international interest.[1] These materials and technics can in different ways be put to the service of man, after more is learned about the hazards and after international controls have been established. These uses will relate not only to promoting health, in various ways now being visualized, they may serve to increase food supplies, perhaps new sources of food supply and yield new materials for clothing, housing and other necessities. Living standards may be affected and to some extent new types of work will develop.

[1] The four international bodies for the peaceful use of atomic energy are: European Organization for Nuclear Research, Geneva, founded 1954; International Atomic Energy Agency of the United Nations, Vienna, 1956; Euratom, Brussels (for the Europe of the Six), 1958; European Nuclear Energy Agency, Paris, 1958, organ of the Organization for European Economic Co-operation, an advisory and co-ordinating agency. The other three are for research and development.

Time-Use Trends and Prospects

In several countries atomic energy plants are now in operation. They serve as pilot projects where experience is gained. In the main, they provide a substitute for the conventional fuels such as coal and oil. Such a new fuel might have a revolutionary influence in developing industries in areas where other resources exist, but conventional fuels are lacking. It would speed the industrial and urban trend in certain underdeveloped countries. Urbanism as a way of life will be extended to remote regious. The advanced countries will benefit indirectly as they will have access to additional raw materials and finished goods. It is not unlikely that in the remote future, as nuclear materials become more abundant, they may influence the relocation of many industries and even bring about a redistribution of population. How this will affect man in his work and leisure can only be guessed at this time.

OF MAN'S WORK AND SECURITY

Whatever else may be said of leisure, man can neither have it nor enjoy it if he does not have work security during the active years of his life. If he has work during the active years, this is good only if he can store up security for his later inactive years. Outside this frame of reference leisure has very little meaning; it is surplus time when man enjoys the surplus gained from his work. But work security is a matter over which the individual has almost no control. Nor can the enterprise that employs him give any assurance of continuous employment, for its own security depends on the markets, the availability of raw materials and production costs. Some security for the enterprise may result from the fact that industries are linked in global networks, steel, rubber, petroleum, motors, and so on.

The individual getting his work in areas dominated by big organizations does have reasonable assurance of continuous employment, but the labour market is one of complex and far-reaching relationships in which he alone is fairly impotent. He joins a trade union and the trade union becomes a provider of a sense of security, at least against discrimination. With this measure of assurance he is certain of a voice to speak for him. But even the trade union cannot merely by making demands ensure continuous job security. Besides big business and the big union there is need of a common authority; government must

Time-Use Trends and Prospects

also be a party if work is to be planned and controls established. Local government can be helpful, but the major responsibility belongs to national government. It is only with such wide assurances that the individual can move toward old age without fear.[1]

That ideal of tri-partite co-operation in full-employment planning is still far from being realized. However, and few will dispute this, the individual is much more secure than when the Great Depression began in 1929. During that period there were millions who had no leisure because they had no work, only free time which, without money and self-respect, could not be used. The situation stimulated Lundberg at the time to write, 'When the full history of human stupidity is written, there will surely be no chapter to equal that which recounts unemployment, poverty and starvation among millions in the midst of abundant natural resources and adequate means of converting them into all the satisfactions of life.' And Lundberg added:

> If the social malorganization which today prevents the masses from realizing the fruits of technology is ever to be corrected, men will have to work at these problems as seriously as they ever worked at the problems of physical production. . . . This means work of a kind hitherto quite unfamiliar to the masses of men. Citizenship under these conditions would be more than an occasional residual interest. Diligent citizenship, rather than material production, may become the chief job by which man, in a broad sense, makes a living. It may be, too, that this job will, for some time to come, absorb much of the leisure which the machine has won.[2]

To some extent the Great Depression helped to awaken that sort of citizenship interest. Apparently the war which followed also helped. At any rate, even though hard times may come, another deep depression is not likely.

WIDER CITIZENSHIP PERSPECTIVES

However old the idea of citizenship may be, its popular implications are relatively recent. Prior to the Industrial Revolution

[1] R. M. Titmuss, 'The Case for Social Research as a Guide to the Formation of Policy', International Association of Gerontology Conference on *The Need of Cross-national Surveys of Old Age*, Copenhagen, 19–23 October, 1956, pp. 3–4.

[2] George A. Lundberg, Mirra Komarovsky and Mary A. McInerny, *Leisure, a Suburban Study*, New York, 1934, p. 348.

citizenship had little meaning to the masses of people, but as the masses in the industrial centres grew larger the struggle began for a sharing of the authority of government. Ideas about the participation of the previously excluded classes in the work of government gained ground. Accordingly, the base of citizenship widened. In the widening process citizenship tended to be identified almost exclusively with political matters; the obligation to vote, one's duties under law and his rights as a citizen participant with reference to government.

Today there is evolving a wider and still more pervasive conception of citizenship. It concerns more than public rights and duties, embracing other forms of community participation than the merely political. Political interests are seen as a phase of other interests which may be social or political. Action in politics is expressive of these other interests, a means to practical ends. One's citizenship finds expression in his group relationships, in his work relationships as well as in a great variety of community contacts.

Citizenship in this wider sense functions to facilitate living in the mass society. One's leisure as one's work may be citizenship concerns, but the activities of citizenship can hardly be identified as either work or leisure; they stand between work or leisure activity. They must be identified with the non-work and non-leisure activities. In his capacity as a citizen, the individual today may join with neighbourhood groups to establish a playground for children or a swimming beach for the old and young. Tomorrow he may exert his influence with others to improve the transportation system that workers may travel to and from their jobs with less discomfort and greater speed. Citizenship in one case may lead to demands for more or better public service, but in another case it may involve more and better co-operation between private organizations.

We find that many persons who protest that they have no leisure, and seem not concerned about it, are really using most of their free time in different forms of community-related activities. Since having little or no leisure seems to give them little or no concern, we may assume that these citizenship efforts afford abundant life satisfactions. It may mean, too, that they do not need to seek these satisfactions in leisure. It is no less a citizenship matter if one spends much of his free time promoting public concerts or if a woman spends her free time

Time-Use Trends and Prospects

improving welfare services (public and private) in the community, or one may organize and instruct youth groups. Some have argued that citizenship participation is the ideal activity to which old people should turn. Some Utopias have depicted the old as having graduated into the role of full citizenship for which their active work years had been a sort of maturing and learning period. In this connection Tibbitts observed that in old age is when 'opportunity for new adventures in personal growth arises and the exploration of new interests become possible'.[1]

That kind of citizenship seems to be developing, but one must move into it and become naturally a part of it long before old age. One must be rooted into such a community participation before leaving his active years, as in the Scandinavian countries, the so-called 'welfare-state' countries where all sorts of services, public and private, are interwoven. In these countries the new idea of citizenship finds outlet in a great variety of interests; trade unions, co-operatives, sport associations, housing and planning schemes, even temperance movements, and each area or activity is political in its own way. Each activity and interest area in its own way concerns itself with both work and leisure. There is controversy, to be sure, but this only adds zest to this type of all-around citizenship participation in community life.

A RATIONALE OF EXISTENCE

We have seen that many who sell their labour have no interest in their work, but this is hardly a problem so long as they perform their work well. Much of the work many people do, does not challenge their interest, or require it. For workers to have a lively interest in their work might interfere with their efficiency. Thinking about the work is the job of management. Thus it is said that workers do not focus special interest on the job and they put the job out of mind at quitting time. This does not evidence a lack of interest in holding one's job or the lack of pride in workmanship or feelings of pride in one's occupation. It means only that one keeps his job isolated from his main interests in life; so long as the job is there and his status as a worker is good, it requires no off-the-job worry.

---

[1] Clark Tibbitts, 'Aging as a Modern Social Achievement', see Wilma Donahue and others (Eds.), *Free Time*, Ann Arbor, 1958, p. 27.

On the other hand, we know that many of these workers who keep the job out of mind may be energetically occupied much of the time in their pursuits of leisure, often looking for satisfactions they rarely find. Hence the pursuit of leisure may seem purposeless. Quoting Durant:

> Thus work completely fails to supply to the workman the rationale of his existence. To the religion which formerly interpreted his world he remains indifferent; even if he responds he no longer hears a message justifying man's ways to man. The spontaneous relationships once assured to him by his family and the community in which he dwelt have all disappeared. He stands a lonely figure surrounded by his fellows, lacking contact with the world of things and the world of men. What must now suffice to link him with society?[1]

This viewpoint, that many people have no life rationale, has been expressed many times before and many times during the intervening two decades since Durant wrote the above. Sombart about the same time also expressed concern that modern industrial man seems to be drifting. No longer able to get a deep satisfaction out of his work, he turns to pleasures, but he gets nothing out of leisure that may be called a life interest.[2] As Sombart saw it, the pursuit of thrills and excitement turns out to be pointless, like drinking ice water in the tropics, one's thirst is not quenched. People seem in flight from boredom, but all their efforts end in restlessness and more boredom. We are told that the simple values of former leisure pursuits are absent.

This thirst that is never satisfied and the restlessness that keeps returning may, after all, be assets. People move this way and that, trying this and that; and why not, that has been the history of work over the past two centuries. The search for an interest in leisure could hardly be more wasteful than the search for success where for each who found a golden apple hundreds came out of the contest with empty hands.

That so many people seem unable or appear unconcerned about finding life meanings either in work or leisure is not a condition peculiar to this generation. Mann speaks of a potential for leisure (*Potenz zur Musse*), and he speaks of many people

[1] W. H. Durant, *The Problem of Leisure*, 1938, p. 17.
[2] Werner Sombart, *Vom Menschen*, Berlin, 1938, pp. 56–57.

as having an *Impotenz zur Musse*. They seem not able to use leisure for any purpose.[1] Yet these same people, Mann would admit, manage to have fun, often with fewer inhibitions than many who have the *Potenz zur Musse*. It depends on who does the judging.

A rationale of existence does not need to be exhibited with philosophical pondering. It should be enough if one is able to live in his milieu in some integrated, orderly and satisfying fashion; if he can work when he must and not feel frustrated, or play when play is in order, without losing social balance. He can behave in a rational way without rationalizing the whys and wherefores of his conduct.[2] The farmer is generally one who has achieved such a rationale of existence, for his life is adjusted to various routines. He is able to use his time without conflict between work and leisure needs, but for him the rationale is perhaps more in the situation than in himself.

Rationalization in this sense is not so easy in the industrial urban situation. The urban man-made environment is not stable like the rural environment where man times his movements by the sun and the seasons. The urban man has no firm community habit structure with which he can co-ordinate his activities through the days and years of his life cycle. In that kind of situation one can be very well adjusted and still not be especially bright. In the urban situation the matter of becoming adapted (rationalized) is very much left to the individual. Out of the many who make fair or good adjustments many others, certainly not the majority, are frustrated. Martin feels they need help in learning to use leisure.

Mental health services now cost $1\frac{1}{2}$ billions yearly and the costs are rising 100 millions annually. There are 700,000 patients in mental hospitals, and out-patient clinics have three to six months' waiting lists. Sleeplessness, inability to relax, fear of leisure are the first signs of mental illness. Millions of dollars are spent for sleeping pills. New 'tranquillizing' drugs are being widely used by psychiatrists to cut

[1] Adolf Mann, *Arbeit und Musse*, Baden–Baden, Frankfurt/Main, 1957, pp. 27–28.

[2] Theodore Caplow, *The Sociology of Work*, Minneapolis, 1954, p. 24, speaks of the rationalization of industrial work. It substitutes order for 'the informal, personal and spontaneous devices which regulate human activity in unplanned social situations.... Rationalization is effective in that it allows for greater predictability of work results and, consequently, for more efficient allocation of resources'.

off compulsive drives. Another symptom of mental illness is the auto death rate—30,000 annually, and an injury rate over 1 million. Last year (1956) 38,000 were killed, 1½ million injured. This is the result of our demand to keep going, to be wide awake, to be first, to avoid relaxation.[1]

Many, if not most of the people pointed to by Martin do have a rationale of existence, but the pace is fast and the strain excessive. He might have also included the millions who have ulcers, many of them successful individuals, but under excessive pressure, and there are the many who have 'manager sickness'. If we say there is a lack of rationale, it is in the high places as well as the low. There is lacking the balance described by Gutkind which is realized only when recreation has its proper place among other basic life interests.[2]

Whether industrial urban man in the future will find the kind of rationale of existence that will enable him to enjoy interests in his leisure while shielding him from the excessive demands of work, remains to be seen. It is possible that the wage worker who forgets his work when he leaves the plant is closer to such a rationale than is the manager. But worker and manager alike still have much to learn about using time as the farmer does.

YET, PEOPLE ARE LIVING LONGER

We do not know what physiological and neurological effects may be expected from the tempo and tension of modern living. Statistical items, such as the one quoted above, give us reason to pause. We must ask how these look against the background of 175 million Americans. Moreover, we need to see them in time perspective against health hazards of earlier days, which were thought to be such a menace that some believed we were on the way to becoming a population of weaklings. Today we hear predictions that we are on the way to becoming a population of nervous wrecks.

Of one thing we are certain, that man's expectation of life is being extended. But here we must ask if this is due to better health, or due to the lower death rate among children. Neither

---

[1] Alexander Reid Martin, 'Live—In the All', *American Recreation Society Bulletin*, Vol. 9, No. 3, May 1957, p. 8.

[2] E. A. Gutkind (Ed.), *Creative Demobilization*, 1944, Vol. I, p. 66.

factor can be excluded. It is true that fewer babies die and a higher percentage of those born enter adulthood. It is also true that birth is less of a hazard for mothers, which means that more mothers may now expect to be grandmothers.

A point of interest is that these advances in health security have moved faster and gone farther in urban than in rural communities, which really means that life security in the cities had been very low.

One measure of improved health is mentioned often by educators. School children today tend to gain in height and weight faster than did children of the same age groups a generation ago. This means mainly that we are better informed about diet than we were a generation ago. But it also means that, especially in cities, the levels of living have risen.

Perhaps a higher percentage of young people, and especially women, are active in sport than previously. This in itself may prove nothing, but some conclusions about physical and nervous co-ordination may be gleaned from the fact that in all sports records are continually being broken. Even nonsensical records of endurance in marathon dancing, singing, talking and even flagpole sitting are being broken. It evidences capacity for something. When the health of the people is looked at in such wide terms, it is hard to come to a pessimistic conclusion.

LEISURE CHOICES AND PRESSURES

If the individual tries to be individual in his choice of leisure activity he will very soon find that whatever forces helped in arriving at a choice have already influenced others. The boy who would make a model aeroplane, as Larrabee noted, would find himself among 500,000 others and a customer of the model-parts industry which did a $30 million business in 1953.[1] This need not diminish the enjoyment one may get out of making and flying his own model aeroplane. If we speak of this boy as a hobbyist, he would be merely one among millions. He would be among millions again if water sports and boating turned out to be his special interest, and the customer of several leisure industries which, if they did not help him in making a choice, are doing their best to get him to widen his activities in this area.

[1] Eric Larrabee, 'What's Happening to Hobbies?' *The New York Times Magazine*, 27 December 1953.

Time-Use Trends and Prospects

On the matter of leisure choices Soule wrote:

It would be a calamity if choices were determined by social pressures, however subtle or disguised; but there can only be gain from a more general use of genuine and intellectual critical faculties in evaluating the relative worth of various ways of spending time. If, as seems probable, our society becomes one characterized even more by leisure than by work, the sharpening of such critical awareness by many individuals might even be a condition of its survival. Certainly, it would aid any possible flowering into a society comparable with the golden ages of the past.[1]

We can only judge the golden ages of the past on the basis of fragmentary records left by the few individuals, each of whom was one among hundreds, common people who had no part in that particular age. Even for the limited élite of the golden ages engaged in leisures which were the choices of most of their associates, much as every man of feudal times learned swordsmanship, provided he was high and well-born. There are many more areas of choice today, and it is hard to think of any choice in which pressures do not figure. This goes not only for the books we read, the songs we sing, the jokes we tell, the evening at home, but for practically every artifact needed in leisure.

The Federal Reserve Bank of Philadelphia, recognizing frankly that leisure is now big business, assembled figures on the number of participants and the money spent on twenty different outdoor sports in the United States during 1958. The estimates showed that there had been during the year no less than 286 million participants in these activities, and the financial outlay amounted to $8.3 billion. It was also estimated that there had been another $10 billion of indirect spending; erecting facilities, public services, travel and so on. Some of the high points in these estimates were:

1. 37 million persons were active in boating during 1958, double the number for 1954, and more than $2 billion was spent.
2. 30 million fishermen and 20 million hunters took fishing or hunting licences in 1958 and spent about $3.6 billion

---

[1] George Soule, 'The Economics of Leisure', *Annals of the American Academy of Political and Social Science*, Vol. 313, September 1957, p. 24.

3. Bowlers increased from 12 million in 1946 to 20 million in 1958, and that game cost $400 million.

4. 4 million golfers in 1958 was ten times the number in the 1920s, and their financial outlay was about $750 million.[1]

Similar trends in participation and in expenditures might have been recorded for such non-sport activities as camping, hiking, touring, etc. No matter what outdoor activity, even though one's likings may move in that direction, there are pressures urging him on. Perhaps in no phase of leisure is the pressure more pervading than with respect to vacations. Commercial pressures are so reinforced by social pressures that if one spends his vacation at home he exposes himself to pity. Some educators feel that not only can one gain skills and knowledge in education, but he can also be helped in his choice of leisure activities and interests. We quote Hutchinson:

> Lastly, the life of the child, youth or adult includes much leisure—free time which is put to some use. The early and continuous development of leisure attitudes, habits, skills, and knowledges leads toward developing an educated judgment about recreation. With this type of recommended approach, education for the full life—leisure and vocational—become a real possibility.[2]

What Hutchinson proposes is more than wishful thinking. The modern school, plus the load it must deliver, is utilizing recreation and play to some extent when they facilitate the learning process. Youth and leisure meet in the school, but the meeting is mainly extra-curricular activity. Here the school is the meeting place where values are acquired and it is none the less worthful if they are not entirely acquired in the formal teaching. Before the teacher as teacher can be helpful he needs to learn something about work and leisure in terms other than the old shibboleths. He must see leisure, to quote Riesman, as the problem of the "bountiful future" and less in terms of "remedies which did not work in the less bountiful past, such as individualism, thrift, hard work, and enterprise on the one

[1] 'Much ado about Doing', *Business Review*, Federal Reserve Bank of Philadelphia, July 1959, pp. 11-13.

[2] John L. Hutchinson, 'Recreation in the Education Process', *Annals of the American Academy of Political and Social Science*, Vol. 313, September 1957, pp. 52-53.

hand, or harmony, togetherness, and friendliness on the other."[1]

Guidance in leisure choices from the school or any other institution would also be pressure. Pressures, social or commercial, will continue, however much they may change their form, and leisure choices will continue to be influenced by pressures. The final test of the choices must find expression in activities which facilitate the integration of the individual into family and community life.

MIXING LEISURE AND CULTURE

Whatever the faults of the old leisure class, Russell declares that it was creative and gave us civilization. "It cultivated the arts and discovered the sciences; it wrote the books, invented the philosophies, and refined social relations. Even the liberation of the oppressed has usually been inaugurated from above."[2] We must add, however, that it was only the occasional member of the leisure class who was creative and he was rarely typical of his class.

Many people believe that leisure is opportunity for cultural development; one should turn to the arts, attend the theatre and opera, read classics and so on. Anything less than this is to waste time. Culture in this sense may have more devotees than is sometimes recognized. We are told by Ernst that in 1955 Americans spent more for classical music records than on baseball. He mentioned the sewing machine, once a mere implement for work, but now it finds wide use for artistic sewing, a leisure facility.

> We have eight million bird watchers, sixteen per cent of all the vegetables eaten in our country are grown by the homeowners themselves. There is an entire new industry for making do-it-yourself clothes—not sport clothes and now work clothes. Two hundred thousand people tonight in our Republic are building boats in their cellars and garages. Twenty per cent of all the homes in our country, ten million homes, have power tools, a saw, a lathe. All this goes to show

[1] David Riesman, 'Leisure and Work in Post-industrial Society', see Eric Larrabee and Rolf Meyersohn, Editors, *Mass Leisure*, Glencoe, Ill., 1958, p. 381.

[2] Bertrand Russell, op. cit., p. 36.

in a sketchy way what we are doing with our leisure time. You will see a renaissance.[1]

Not all of this would be called culture by those who feel we are lacking, but it does indicate how people tend to venture into new (for them) activities. It is not, of course, at the level of opera and landscape painting, but apparently people get no less satisfaction.

Some who may not be opera-minded think of culture in terms of good manners. Veblen six decades ago mentioned that many gentlemen of the old school regretted the 'under-bred manners and bearing of even the better classes'.[2] This is not surprising for a country then still under the influence of the frontier. This complaint about Americans is seldom heard today, a fact that the culture advocates should note. Much of the credit must be given to the school, especially the high school, and we must not withhold credit from the movies and radio, or the greater amount of reading people do now compared with the time cited by Veblen.

Lynes thinks the time has come in our society for reviving the cult of the dilettante. The original dilettanti was a lover of the fine arts, but the idea and the term were unpopular with the Puritans, and that disdain for the term carried over to the United States. We accepted and still hold the Puritan idea that the dilettante is a trifler, parasite, gadfly, something to look down our noses at. A Dilettante Society, founded by learned and artistic Englishmen in 1733, still exists. The dilletanti may not be an artist or a scientist, but he is informed. He is a consumer, but a discriminating consumer. He may be an authority in some special field, but his interests are essentially cosmopolitan.

He is a man who takes the pursuit of happiness seriously, not frivolously, and he works at it. He is part sensualist, part intellectual, and part enthusiast. He is also likely to be a proselyter for these causes in which his interests are involved, and to be rather scornful of those people who do not take

[1] Morris L. Ernst, 'New Sources of Energy, Leisure and World Culture', *Proceedings of the International Recreation Congress,* New York, National Recreation Association, 1956, p. 7.

[2] Thorstein Veblen, *The Theory of the Leisure Class,* 1899, p. 46.

their pleasures seriously and who are passive instead of active in the cultivation of them.[1]

Many people of that sort are among us but they are known by other names. The least tolerant of them are among the complainers about the lack of cultural interests in the leisure pursuits of most ordinary people. The most tolerant of these are likely to hold with the view that the cultural level of the common people is rising.[2]

LEISURE AND OBLIGATED TIME

Lundberg found that many wealthy housewives in a suburb of New York declared they had no leisure, yet they had almost no work to do, being in the servant-employing class. They were giving their time to welfare, church work, political party work or their social obligations. Nor did the husbands of these socialite wives have leisure; their time was taken up with other obligations in behalf of organizations or the community. Business men, most of them, they could hardly avoid these obligations.

By Veblin's definition, the wealthy people in the New York suburb would be of the leisure class, and yet a good share of them had little leisure. Their time was allocated to all sorts of social and other responsibilities to organizations and the community, doing what was expected and getting satisfaction from it. In this respect many upper-class and even middle-class American circles perform much as the British nobility by whom they may have been influenced. Durant observed how in a few

[1] Russell Lynes, 'Time on our Hands', *Harpers Magazine*, Vol. 217, No. 1298, July 1958, p. 37.

[2] It must be mentioned that we have been speaking of culture as it is associated with refinement and good manners in the upper social-level sense. This popular use of the term will not meet with the approval of those who think of culture as a whole way of life, including things associated with that way of life. That meaning is seen in the way of life of Oriental Jews in Israel. They live easily. The way of life in Israel is more Western. One must work all the time. Israel must build strong and fast. Leisure is for rest or self-development to make work more efficient. Leisure can come when security has been achieved. Israelites are the modern Puritans. The Oriental Jews will have none of this. They cannot change their traditional pattern of time use. All other values would have to change. But their children accept the Western idea of work tempo. The result is some degree of cultural conflict in the family. See Carl Frankenstein, Editor, 'The Problem of Ethnic Differences in the Absorption of Immigrants', *Between Past and Future*, Jerusalem, Henrietta Szold Foundation, 1953, p. 27.

decades the nobility of Britain moved from prideful isolation into many community service roles.

The aristocracy, having lost some of their former spheres of action, were soon invited from many quarters to contribute their prestige, their influence and their abilities. They provided business, as we have seen, with titles; administration and philanthropy with a never-failing supply of unpaid servants, to the envy of the world. Hence the tradition that those who have time at their disposal undertake 'good work' of some kind has become firmly rooted in English social life, and has assisted till today in maintaining popular sympathy for the aristocracy.[1]

One does not need to look into the upper social ranks for people who have free time but little leisure. Western man at all social levels is faced with like demands on his non-work time. If he gladly accepts responsibility in organizations, the neighbourhood and the wider community he will find himself with very little leisure. Even if he limits his activities to being a good neighbour and a willing worker at home, most of his free time will be pre-empted. In relation to this thought, de Grazia concludes that, notwithstanding all that is said about the abundance of leisure today, few of us have no more leisure than had our grandfathers. In coming to this thought he lumps together both work and non-work obligations, weighing them as work against leisure. He asks whether we are really moving in the direction of the good life.

There is no doubt that Americans have reached a new level of life, but whether or not it is the good life is another matter. This much is clear: it is a life without leisure. For leisure is not hours free from work, or even week-ends or months of vacation or years in retirement. It has no relation to time, if time is conceived of as a flow of evenly paced equal units of which some are free and some are not. Leisure is a state of being free of everyday necessity, and the activities of leisure are those one would engage in for their own sake. As fact or as ideal it is rarely approached in the industrial world.[2]

---

[1] H. W. Durant, op. cit., p. 35.
[2] Sabastian de Grazia, 'Tomorrow's Good Life', *Teachers College Record*, Vol. 61, No. 7, April, 1960, p. 385.

Time-Use Trends and Prospects

De Grazia holds we cannot achieve that conception of leisure until and as we achieve an education for leisure. Such a new education would divert attention in leisure from the things that cost money, from the lust to have and display leisure things that cost money, since getting the money imposes more demand on our time. He concedes that such an education is not now in sight. He might have added that before such an ideal is realized, education for work (which much of modern education is) must also change.

Work and non-work obligations cannot be lumped together as work, since in the latter one has choices somewhat as in leisure. Non-work obligations contain a quasi-leisure quality, as does the work of the craftsman whose job is creative and challenging. For many, and the number increases, non-work obligations afford satisfactions equal to those we are supposed to gain from leisure. These activities are much more individually defined than most recognized leisure activities. They may contribute as much or more to integrating the individual into family, group and community life. We have no method yet of measuring the satisfactions afforded by leisure, but if we ever learn to evaluate the satisfactions derived from leisure perhaps then we can also weigh and evaluate the satisfactions coming from these quasi-leisure time uses which we call non-work obligations.

SUMMARY

In this study of work and leisure we have frequently looked at the past. We look back again to get perspective on what may be ahead. The outlook seems favourable, but some will disagree. There may be more agreement about work than about leisure. This must be expected.

The prospect is more leisure and less work in the future, There will be more technological advance. As in the recent past workways will change and consumer behaviour will change, which means continued social change. There will be continuing social disintegration, which for too many is hard to understand. But there will also be, as heretofore, social integration, but many will refuse to recognize it as such.

We are reminded that automation will revolutionize productive work, and atomic energy will not only revolutionize

Time-Use Trends and Prospects

mechanical power, it will in many ways facilitate to the good life. It is too early to foresee what the social effects of atomic energy will be, but there have been dire predictions about the influence of automation, that it will produce unemployment as well as leisure. If these problems arise, they are man-made and the mass society is capable of meeting them. We need first to know what we are fearing, and why.

While the future offers more leisure and time for living, we are told man must first learn to use leisure. We are reminded how people turn from one activity to another but cannot escape boredom. The restless spirit may be an asset, driving one until he finds an interest, something not provided by the traditional goals of life. Each generation coming on the changing scene must begin the search anew.

Culture (using the term in the popular sense, meaning taste, manners and learning) at any social class level changes slowly, but it changes at all levels. Most critics of the culture level expressed in the leisure of the masses identify themselves with the culture level of the upper-classes. They make comparisons as of the moment. If we make comparisons in long-term perspective we find that culture at the lowest level is changing faster than at the self-satisfied higher level. The gap between high and low continues to narrow. Some of the credit goes to the schools but possibly more of it to the mass media.

We are told that people stranded without interest goals, who seem to have no rationale of existence often become frustrated and lapse into physical or mental illness. This is more likely in the tense, tempo-conscious industrial urban than in the rural way of life. We don't know the inroads being made on personality equilibrium or what the casualties are. We do know that the health of the total population seems good and the span of life lengthens, and this becomes more true of the city than the country.

Those who regret that modern man is not permitted to make individual choices, especially in leisure, because he is so much under commercial pressure, have good reason for complaint. But the individual may be fortunate because he stands between rival pressures; different kinds of social and different kinds of commercial pressures. In the good old days the individual was subject to the social pressures entirely, and he had almost no possibility for choice. He did not have to concern himself then

Time-Use Trends and Prospects

about a rationale of life; it was given to him. Today he must make at least some choices and find his own rationale of existence. If stereotype choices are made, that has ever been so, but there is greater variety in choices made today, and more originality. This is not declining.

The opposite may be true of youth, but adults today tend to be less under lesiure-time pressure than they are with respect to non-work obligations. It seems that the better-adjusted and the more socially-integrated the individual becomes the less his central, life-satisfying interests are identified with leisure. He may spend more time on his family, social, community and other obligations than on his work. Some leisure may afford diversion, but it does not constitute a central life interest. It probably does not for most people, for which reason many who do not have these obligations turn to hobbies.

INDEX

'Accidie', 47
Accumulation, 61-2, 91, 162-3, 171-2; and life span, 72; and·security, 9-10
Activity and duty, 104
Adaptation and conformity, 151 ff.
Administration, mass, 15-16
Adult, being an, 160; goals for youth, 139; guidance, 146, 152
Adults and play, 132
Age and family cycle, 195-6; and leadership, 188; and life enjoyment, 200 ff.
Alcohol and leisure, 124-5
Alexander, Franz, 134, 148
Allardt, Eric, 126, 223
Altick, Richard, 208
Ambiguities of leisure, 90 ff.
Ambition in leisure, 30; in work, 31
American individualism, 19; school, 138
Amusement, commercial, 117 ff.; defined, 45
Amusements, spectator, 87
Anderson, Helga, 148
Anderson, Nels, 9, 171, 226
Anderson, William, 226
Anonymity, fear of, 206-7; utility of, 8
Apprenticeship standards, 142
Arensberg, Conrad M., 61, 172, 236
Aristocracy, changing, 254
Art of living, 233
Associations, 16; formal, 221 ff.; social, 213-14
Atomic energy and population, 241-2; uses of, 241
Attitudes, work, 209
Authority and individual, 18-19; and youth, 151 ff.
Auto camps. 193-4
Automatic factory, 236, 239
Automation, fear of, 236 ff.; and jobs, 237; limits, 237

Bancroft, Gertrude, 40
Barker, Ernest, 137, 161, 190, 219
Baxter, Richard, 77
Beaglehole, Ernst, 31, 131
Bednarik, Karl, 206, 217
Behaviour, predictable, 233
Bell, Clive, 21
Bell, Howard M., 145, 151
Bendiner, Robert, 235
Bendix, Reinhard, 160
Berdot, Lucian, 213
Beveridge, William H., 47, 112
Blakelock, Edwin, 67, 68
Blakely, Robert J., 201
Blancard, René, 213
Blood, Robert O., 177
Bloomberg, Warner, Jr., 172
Blücher, Viggo Graf, 145
Blum, Fred H., 29, 59, 64
Blume, Orro, 198
Bond, Robert J., 105
Books on leisure, 182
Boredom and leisure, 246-7
Boulding, Kenneth E., 222
Brew, J. Macalister, 95, 105, 142, 150, 176
Brownell, Baker, 17, 236
Butler, George D., 43
Butler, J. A. V., 193

Café society, 214
Calvin, Jean, 52
Camping and youth, 109
Caplow, Theodore, 249
Cardiff, Ira D., 18, 27, 131
Carlson, Raymond E., 149
Carnival tradition, 123
Cauter, T., 125, 223
Child, Marquis, 136
Children, absence of, 176; in family cycle, 158; and growth, 134; and play, 131-2

Index

Choice in leisure, 34–5, 114, 116, 250–1
Church and community, 214
Citizenship, social, 135–6, 243–4
City, dynamism of, 7
Clark, Lincoln H., 163, 165, 170, 177, 212
Clarke Alfred C., 114, 120, 217
Class and idleness, 77; and life style, 161
Clawson, Marion, 109
Cleeton, Glenn U., 78
Clément, Pierre, 21
Clock control, 14
Clocks, evolution of, 55 ff.
Cohen, Morris, R., 13, 94, 178
Comic books, 125–6
Commager, Henry Steele, 19
Commercial amusement, 44, 83–4, 117 ff., 167–8
Community and child, 136; and family, 168; and festivals, 92–3; group work, 221; and guilds, 210; and leisure, 227; living, 206; participation, 244
Competition and fashion, 169–70; social, 213
Competitive play, 148–9
Concepts of recreation, 43
Conformity and social game, 151 ff., 213 ff.; and sociality, 206–7; and work, 209–10
Consumer expectations, 164; spending, 179
Consuming and leisure, 91, 98 ff., 163
Consumption and fashion, 169–70; mass, 16
Contract society, 17
Control and records, 228–9
Conventional vacation, 109 ff.
Coser, Rose Laub, 203
Cost of Leisure, 99 ff., 250–1
Craftsmanship and hobbies, 216–17; spirit of, 210
Creative minority, 88; work, 29
Creativity and automaton, 239
Crozier, Michel, 85
Cult of recreation, 81
Cultural values, 60
Culture, industrial, 3, 5; and leisure, 208, 252–3; levels of, 253; and mediocrity, 84 ff.; work, 209 ff.
Cunnison, J., 144, 223
Cutten, George B., 76

Danford, Howard G., 225, 228

Dangers of leisure, 76
Daric, Jean, 57
Davidson, Marshall B., 170, 232
Daylight-saving time, 58, 67
Definition of leisure, 33, 36; of recreation, 42
Defoe, Daniel, 219
Dehmel, Richard, 61
Democracy and class, 89
Denney, Reuel, 20, 42, 83
Dewey, John, 45, 46
Diebold, John, 236, 237
Dilemma, work-leisure, xiv.
Dilittanti, need for, 253
Discipline of leisure, 211 ff.; of machines, 4; of work, 208–9
Display, familial 164 ff.
Diversion, 36
Division of labour, 53–4
Do-it-yourself kits, 105
Domenach, Jean Marie, 1, 85
Domestic accumulation, 171–2
'Domestic package', 163, 165, 196
Donahue, Wilma, 182, 201, 245
Donald, Marjorie N., 35
Do-something complex, 80–1, 86–7
Downham, J. S., 125, 223
Dru, Alexander, 79, 218
Dubin, Robert, 67, 238
Dulles, Foster Rhea, 95
Dumazedier, 26, 36, 70, 104, 109, 159, 233
Durant, W. H., 28, 47, 118, 246, 255
Durkheim, Emile, 57

Earned leisure, 79
Earning in youth, 144
Economic level and modes, 165
Education as investment, 62; for leisure, 233–4, 251; and life span, 72; and life style, 161; and play, 45–6, 132; for work, 138
Educational functions, 134 ff.
Elites, 21, 94, 256; and work, 32
Employment and age, 182–3; and morale, 209; steady, 235–42; of wives, 106 ff., 177–8; of youth, 141–2
Empty time and leisure, 59, 92
Entertainment industries, 65–6; spending, 63–4
Environment, man-made, 3–4, 247–8
Erikson, Erik H., 45, 132
Ernst, Morris L., 253
Escape into leisure, 143; and tempo, 14; in travel, 193 ff.

260

Index

Ethics in work, 211
Expectations and leisure, 114 ff.
Extra jobs, 40, 104

Facilities for recreation, 43, 82
Factory system, 53
Family, conflict in, 254; home activity, 166–7; home space, 172; life cycle, 157 ff., 179, 189–90; and mobility, 164–5; nuclear, 157
Family status and youth, 146
Family vacations, 111–12
Fashion, competitive, 171; and leisure, 169–70
Fearing, Kenneth, 58
Fear of automation, 237–8
Feigelbaum, Kenneth, 161
Ferguson, T., 144, 223
Festivals and fiesta, 92, 122
Fisher, Janet S., 179
Fitzgerald, Gerald P., 32, 38, 43, 82, 225
Flugel, J. C., 19, 45, 134
Folk culture and alcohol, 124
Foote, Nelson N., 123
Ford, Clellan S., 72, 133
Formal associations, 221 ff.
Frankenstein, Carl, 254
Free time and leisure, 41, 199; and old age, 188 ff.
Freizeitsuchtikeit, 86
French, Thomas M., 45
Friedmann, Georges, 26, 36, 57, 109, 159, 167
Frontier and individual, 19; and manners, 253
'Fun morality', 90
Function of associations, 222–3; of family, 157 ff.; of leisure, 36 ff.; of play, 134 ff.; of records, 228–9
Future of leisure, 233; visions of, 234–5

Gadourek, Ivan, 214
Galloway, George B.,
'Game of life', 138
Gift of leisure, 2, 234
Girard, Alain, 106
Girls and employment, 141—2, 145
Glazier, Nathan, 20, 83
Glick, Paul C., 158, 190
Globality of urbanism, 5 ff.
Goals of the family, 163; of youth, 139–40
'Golden-age' clubs, 188
Gossip and privacy, 206

Government and associations, 223
de Grazia, Sabastian, 255
Great Depression, 243
Greenberg, Clement, 33, 216
Groos, Karl, 45
Group vitality, 220–1
Growth and play, 133–4
Guidance of youth, 131, 252
Guild organizations, 209–10
Gutkind, E. A., 206, 248

Habit and time use, 67–8
Halbwachs, Maurice, 157, 207
Hall, G. Stanley, 45
Hamblin, Robert L., 177
Hamilton, Andrew, 187
Hammond, Barbara, 54, 207
Hammond, J. L., 54, 207
Hansen, N. Elkaer, 148
Hansson, Borje, 171
Happiness, pursuit of, 234
Harlan, William, H., 194
Hatch, David L., 178
Hatch, Mary G., 178
ten Have, T. T., 146, 240
Havinghurst, Robert J., 35, 156, 161, 166
Hawley, Amos H., 61
Health security, 248–9
Heckscher, August, 168
Herskovits, Frances S., 122
Herskovits, Melville, J., 122
'Highest human nature', 119
Hill, Reuben, 222, 228
Hobbies, cost of, 249–50; objections to, 217; value of, 211 ff., 215 ff.
Holidays for mothers, 112; old style, 184, 185; and vacations, 102, 107 ff.
Hollingshead, August B., 144, 146, 153
Homans, George C., 223
Home, a leisure centre, 166 ff.; making a, 162; space and family, 172; work, 105, 116
Homes on wheels, 194 ff.; without children, 176
Hours for leisure, 102–3; for work, 54, 145
Households, non-typical, 175–6; and retirement, 196–7
Housework, hours of, 106
Housing for the aged, 196
Hoyt, G. C., 194
Huisinga, Johan, 37, 131
Hutchinson, John L., 251
Hyman, Herbert H., 222

261

Index

Ideal of work, 217-18
Idle hands and temptation, 215 ff.
Idleness and leisure, 46-7, 119; views on, 218-19
Income and occupation, 164
Individual and life span, 72; and social game, 215; and urban life, 6, 207; worth of, 183-4
Individualism and authority, 18-19
Industrial culture, 3, 5; Revolution, 53; work, 28-9
Industry, adaptability, of 65-6; and clocks, 55 ff.; housefurnishing, 166-7, 172; and leisure, 66, 117 ff.
Insecurity and youth, 145
Institutions for recreation, 43
Integration and mobility, 10-11
Intellectuals and leisure, 93 ff.
Interdependence, urban, 8
Interests, cultural, 85
Ishwaren, K., 177, 197

Jacks, Lawrence P., 62, 87
Jaques, Elliott, 28, 211
Jartti, Pentti, 126, 223
Jelden, Helmut, 112
Jensen, Aage Bo, 148
Jobs and automation, 236 ff.; and youth, 144-5
Jyrkila, Feina, 126, 223

Kieslich, G., 111, 115
Klein, Viola, 176, 217
Komarovsky, Mirra, 33, 99, 103, 104, 208, 212
Kuenstler, Peter H. K., 143, 151, 221

Labour market and age, 187
Lafitte, Paul, 29, 40
Lamb, Charles, 185
Larrabee, Eric, 139, 191, 211, 218, 249, 252
Larrue, Janice, 39, 117
Laughter and age, 202
Leadership and age, 188; in associations, 222-3; public, 227-8
Learning as a process, 130, 153
Leisure and alcohol, 124-5; ambiguity of, 3, 90 ff.; class, 21, 89, 208; consumption, 63, 163; costs, 99 ff.; creativity, 85, 117; and culture, 252-3; defined, 33, 36; and discipline, 20, 211 ff.; and empty time, 59; in family cycle, 159; fashion, 169-70; fear of, 90; functions of, 36 ff.; a gift, 79; and guilt feelings, 220; at home, 166-7; hours for, 102; and idleness, 46-7; and industry, 117 ff., 250-1; and life style, 165-6; and living, 233; mass, 84; in mass society, 17; and mobility, 11-12; for pensioners, 198-9; planning, 113-14; preparation for, 201; public cost of, 100; as a pursuit, 64; and reading, 126; and recreation, 42 ff.; and reform, 80-1; and religion, 51-2; rules of, 212; satisfactions in, 35, 161; and the sexes, 121 ff.; and small groups, 220-1; and social change, 95; and social life, 171-2; spending for, 98 ff.; and success, 30; tempo of, 59; those without it, 254-5; and tradition, 69-70; trends in, 95, 232-3, uninvited, 76-7; unreadiness for, 78; and unrest, 218 ff.; and welfare, 224; for wives, 107 ff.; and work, 25-6, 34, 205-6; and youth, 138

Level of leisure interest, 85
Levy, Herman, 124
Lewis, Oscar, 39, 93
Lewis, Roy, 51
Liebermann, Ernst, 150
Life employment and age, 200 ff.
Life rationale, 246-7
Life style and class, 161; compulsions of, 165
Life cycle, 70-1; of family, 168; phases of, 130-1, 156
Lindeman, Eduard C., 79
Lipset, Seymour M., 160
Littunen, Yrjo, 23, 126
Living as an art, 193, 233-4
Loneliness and age, 187 ff.; and insecurity, 206
Lundberg, George A., 11, 33, 99, 103, 104, 208, 212, 243
Lunt, Paul S., 147
Luther, Martin, 52
Lynes, Russell, 254

Machines and regimentation, 239-40; and work, 236
McInerny, Mary A., 99, 103, 104, 208, 212, 243
MacIver, Robert M., 59
Macmillan, R. H., 236, 238
Man and automaton, 239-40; worth of, 183-4
Man-made environment, 34

Index

Man's total time, 70-1
Management of behaviour, 205, 219
Mann, Adolf, 247
Mannheim, Karl, 136
Markets, leisure, 66
Marriage goals, 162
Marshall, T. H., 18, 20, 161
Martin, Alexander Reid, 248
Mason, Bernard S., 44, 76, 78, 202
Mass disemployment, 237-8; leisure, 84, 89; media, 101, 172; organization 15; production, 240
Maude, Angus, 51
Mayntz, Renate, 21
Mead, Margaret, 42, 107, 162, 176, 177
Meadows, Paul, 3, 5, 82, 236
Meanings of leisure, 35
Measuring work and leisure, 34, 98
Mechanisms, 3; and clocks, 55
Mediocrity in leisure, 85-6
Meerloo, Joost A. M., 15, 76, 137
Memberships in associations, 222
Meyersohn, Rolf, 41, 69, 139, 191, 218, 252
Michelon, L. E., 192, 195
Miller, Norman P., 227
Mills, C. Wright, 65, 92, 100, 208, 210, 215, 240
Mitchell, Elmer D., 44, 76, 78, 220
Mobility and aging, 193 ff.; and integration, 10-11; tradition of, 193-4; utility of, 11
Modern home a showcase, 162-3
Money, rules of, 51; spending plans, 198; and time, 54
Money values and time, 61-2
'Moonlighting', 40, 104
Morals and leisure, 77
Morin, E., 26, 36, 70, 159
Morris, Mary, 221
Motives for work, 27 ff.
Müller, Eberhard, 226
Mumford, Lewis, 14, 55, 56
Myrdal, Alva, 176, 217

Nash, Jay B., 43, 81, 87, 119, 217
Neumeyer, Esther S., 41, 43, 87, 119
Neumeyer, Martin H., 41, 43, 87, 119
Non-activity, attitude of, 218
Non-work obligations, 39 ff., 65, 254-5
Non-work time, 103 ff., 168

Oakley, C. A., 113, 209
Obligated time, 103 ff., 254

Obligations and leisure, 39 ff.
Occupation and fashion, 170; love of, 27-8; and social class, 21, 154 ff., 208 ff.
Old age in Germany, 198-9; and professors, 187; research, 182, 189; and security, 185
Old-fashioned leisure, 118, 167
One-generation family, 157-8
Order in mass society, 205, 247; and in work, 207 ff.
'Organization man', 15, 90
Organizations for youth, 147
Other-directedness, 83
Outdoor recreation, 250-1
Owen, Wilfred, 11, 17

Panunzio, Constantine, 187
Parents and youth, 141-2
Parker, Sanford S., 99, 103, 108, 115
Participation in leisure, 87
Passivity and commercialism, 118; and leisure, 15, 82
Patrick, Clarence H., 124
Patterns of leisure, 33
Peasants and time use, 69-70
Peer-group influence, 152
Pensions as a right, 185
Personality and leisure, 37
Pieper, Josef, 79, 218
Pipping, Hugo E., 16, 104, 158
Pizzorno, Alessandro, 10, 99
Play and amusement, 44 ff.; and childhood, 77; defined, 45; and democracy, 233; discipline of, 133; functions of, 37; Toleration for, 131-2
Planned vacations, 113-14
Planning employment, 242
Pollock, Friedrich, 239
Population and age, 182
Potential for leisure, 246
Potential worth curve, 183-4
Pre-industrial leisure, 30
Prestige articles, 171
Primary groups, nature, 207
Privacy and company, 206
Production, mass, 16
Professional recreationist, 81-2
Protest against passivity, 82
Protestant ethic, 25
Protestantism, 50-1
Public and leisure cost, 100
Public service and leisure, 82, 226-7; and work, 226

263

Index

Puritan ideology, 29, 91
Puritanism, 51–2, 77; and the unemployed, 46–7
Puritans, a new type, 254 n.

Radio and time precision, 64
Rationale of existence, 245 ff.
Reading, 115, 125; and class, 85; levels of, 126
Records and control, 228–9; personal, 18
Recreation, 80–1, 249; in auto camps, 195; and education, 137, 251–2; guided, 149; and hobbies, 216; and leisure, 42 ff.; organized, 224–5; public and private, 225; rules of, 212; rural and urban, 225
Reform and leisure, 80–1, 93 ff.
Reformers, utility of, 224–5
Reigrotzki, Eric, 222
Relaxation, 36
Religion and leisure, 121–2; and life span, 71; and work, 208
Residential mobility, 174–5, 196–7
Restlessness and leisure, 246
Retirement colonies, 197
Retirement and loneliness, 187 ff.; meaning of, 184–5; shock of, 184; transition to, 191–2
Retrait culturel, 84
Richards, Edward A., 136, 143
Riesman, David, 20, 42, 69, 83, 139, 163, 173, 191, 252
Robbins, Florence G., 76, 126
Roles of life, 156; and retirement, 191, of women, 177
Roseborough, Howard, 163
Rosenmayr, Leopold, 175, 197
Ross, Edward A., 118
Rules for leisure, 212; of play, 123, 211–12
Rural security, 9
Rural and urban health, 249
Russell, Bertrand, 234, 252

Sage, Robert, 110
Salz, Beate R., 4, 39
Santayana, George, 18, 27, 131, 195
Sariola, Sakari, 125
Satisfactions, leisure, 161
Saunders, Dero A., 99, 103, 108, 115
Sauvy, Alfred, 182, 196
Saville, John, 225
Saving and spending, 178–9
Schelsky, Helmut, 86

School, leaving, 144–5; limitations of, 138–9; and social change, 135–6
Secondary groups, 207
Security and accumulation, 9–10; emotional, 186–7; and old age, 185–6; and work, 242–3
Seldes, Gilbert, 227
Self-image of youth, 131
Self-improvement, 36, 71, 79
Seniority rule, 30
Services for recreation, 44, 224
Sex as play, 123
Shils, Edward, 4
'Should be' and leisure, 75
Siepmann, C. A., 138
Simmel, Georg, 169
Small-group control, 221
Smiles, Eileen, 46
Smiles, Samuel, 46, 52, 81
Social change and education, 135
Social citizenship, 244, 256
Social class and associations, 222–3; and buying, 173–4; and family, 158; in leisure, 34, 88–9, 114, 213; and occupation, 159 ff.; as a system, 20 ff.
Social discipline and play, 33
Social integration, 256
Social mobility and display, 164 ff.; of families, 173–4
Social reformers, 93 ff.
Social security, 10
Social status and fashion, 169
Social striving, 215
Sociality and conformity, 206–7
Sociology and leisure, 80
Sombart, Werner, 56, 60, 246
Sonne, A., 148
Sophistication and urbanism, 7
Soule, George, 26, 33, 63, 89, 172, 219, 220, 235, 238, 240
Space and time, 12
Spectacles and leisure, 87
'Spectatoritis', 86–7
Spending for leisure, 65–6, 97 ff., 101; and saving, 178–9; by youth, 144
Sport and education, 138; and gymnastics, 145; increase of, 249; outdoor, 110–11; rules of, 212
Staley, Eugene, 42
Standardization, 4
Status and happiness, 162; and security 186–7
Steiner, Jesse F., 81, 99
Stephen, Leslie, 89, 113, 216

264

Index

Stereotypes, American, 83; in leisure, 94; vacations, 112
Stoetzel, Jean, 167
Stone, Gregory P., 165, 212
Street-corner groups, 220–1
Streets and functions, 205
Success and leisure, 30
Sumner, William G., 62, 187
Sussman, Marion B., 80
Svalastoga, Kaare, 148, 223
Swados, Harvey, 40
Swain, Joseph W., 57

Taboo and leisure, 38
Tax, Sol, 122
Teachers and leisure, 251–2; and youth, 140
Technology and films, 120
Teenage at leisure, 150; in romance, 150
Tempo, modern, 58–9; and time, 14
Temptation and leisure, 217–18
Thomas, W. I., 133
Three-holiday weekend, 68
Tibbitts, Clark, 182, 245
Time and commercial amusement, 120; consciousness of, 12–13; and emptiness, 59; investment cult, 50 ff.; and leisure, 38; measurement of, 56; pre-industrial, 57; in retirement, 184; saving of, 232; sold, 100; and tempo, 58–9; use-traditions, 69, 103; and work, 26, 63; worth of, 52
Titmuss, R. H., 183, 243
Tolerance of play, 131–2
Touraine, Alain, 84, 93
Tourism and vacations, 109
Townsend, Peter, 189
Toynbee, Arnold, J., 2, 88, 119
Tradition-directed, 20
Tradition, familial, 158; and time use, 69; and urbanism, 6
Trailer camps, 194–5
Training for automation, 236, 239; for work, 140 ff.
Transport and leisure, 17
Trends in leisure, 233
Tropp, Asher, 80, 137
Turner, Ralph, 7

Unemployment and leisure, 46–7, 220
Unrest and leisure, 218 ff.
Urban heterogeneity, 9
Urban life, order in, 205
Urban man and time, 56–7

Urbanism and age, 196–7; and associations, 221 ff.; and atomic energy, 241; citizenship of, 244–5; future of, 235; globality of, 106; and vacations, 108
Uses of leisure, 114 ff., 199
Utility of associations, 222–3; of hobbies, 216; of play, 132
Utopias, homes in, 168

Vacations and holidays, 11, 107 ff.
Vacations, conventional, 109 ff.; cost of, 99; and tourists, 193
Values in leisure, work, 65
Vausson, Claude, 110
Veblen, Thorstein, 22, 60, 209, 253, 254
Viewing with alarm, 88 ff.
Vito, Francesco, 69
Volkart, Edmund H., 133, 135
Vontovel, Clara, 25, 33, 46, 51, 78

Walker, Patrick G., 57
Warner, W. Lloyd, 147, 213
Wax, Rosalie H., 233
Wealth and time investment, 62
Webb, Beatrice, 54
Web, Sidney, 54
Weber, Max, 51
Wecter, Dixon, 220
Weidner, Edward W., 226
Welfare and recreation, 224–5
Welfare state issue, 245
Wesley, John, 51, 52
Western man, character, 17; and clocks, 50; and life span, 71–2; as time-user, 232; as worker, 20–1
'Westernizing society', 2
Whitehead, Alfred North, 57, 233
Whyte, William F., 152, 220
Whyte, William H., Jr., 91, 170
Wilensky, Harold L., 33
Wilson, Woodrow, 170
Wirth, Louis, 4, 5
Wish, Harvey, 167
Wives who work, 176–7
Wolfbein, Seymour L., 182
Wolfenstein, Martha, 90
Women and automation, 238; and family spending, 179; journals for, 178; leisure for, 106 ff.; and vacations, 111–12; and work, 27
Work, competition in, 31 ff.; dedication to, 89, 117; entry into, 140 ff.; and good works, 51; and hobbies,

Work—(continued)
216–17; and learning, 142–3; and leisure, 3, 32, 100, 205; in life span, 70–1; and machines, 236; and mobility, 11; motives for, 27 ff.; and non-work, 39 ff.; occupation, 159 ff.; order in, 207 ff.; and play, 78, 133; and Puritanism, 46–7; and religion, 25; roles in family, 158; and security, 242–3; social status in, 208; and time, 12–13, 26, 38, 52; time investment for, 62; tempo in, 58–9; trends in, 232–3; utility of, 184; values in, 191; and youth, 137–8, 143 ff.
Worker attitudes, 64
Workers, vacations for, 108
Working wives, 176–7
Workmanship, instinct of, 60; pride in, 245
Worth of a man, 183–4
Wright, Charles R., 222
Wright, Frank L., 236
Wurzbacher, Gerhard, 145

Xydias, Nelly, 21

Youth, and authority, 151 ff.; clubs for, 221; illusions of, 201; and life cycle, 131; and old age, 131; organizations of, 147; vacations for, 109; and work, 137–8
Youth work, quality of, 143

Zelomek, A. Wilbert, 186, 197